EVOLVING DIGITAL LEADERSHIP

HOW TO BE A DIGITAL LEADER IN TOMORROW'S DISRUPTIVE WORLD

James Brett

Apress®

Evolving Digital Leadership: How to Be a Digital Leader in Tomorrow's Disruptive World

James Brett
Forest Lodge, New South Wales, Australia

ISBN-13 (pbk): 978-1-4842-3605-5   ISBN-13 (electronic): 978-1-4842-3606-2
https://doi.org/10.1007/978-1-4842-3606-2

Library of Congress Control Number: 2018945614

Managing Director, Apress Media LLC: Welmoed Spahr
Acquisitions Editor: Shivangi Ramachandran
Development Editor: Laura Berendson
Coordinating Editor: Rita Fernando

Cover designed by eStudioCalamar

Distributed to the book trade worldwide by Springer Science+Business Media New York, 233 Spring Street, 6th Floor, New York, NY 10013. Phone 1-800-SPRINGER, fax (201) 348-4505, e-mail orders-ny@springer-sbm.com, or visit www.springeronline.com. Apress Media, LLC is a California LLC and the sole member (owner) is Springer Science + Business Media Finance Inc (SSBM Finance Inc). SSBM Finance Inc is a **Delaware** corporation.

For information on translations, please e-mail rights@apress.com, or visit http://www.apress.com/rights-permissions.

Apress titles may be purchased in bulk for academic, corporate, or promotional use. eBook versions and licenses are also available for most titles. For more information, reference our Print and eBook Bulk Sales web page at http://www.apress.com/bulk-sales.

Any source code or other supplementary material referenced by the author in this book is available to readers on GitHub via the book's product page, located at www.apress.com/9781484236055. For more detailed information, please visit http://www.apress.com/source-code.

Printed on acid-free paper

In memory of my grandfather
Walter (Wally) Hinchliffe

I miss you every day

Contents

About the Author

James Brett describes himself as a digital leader who is passionate about developing people and organizations to create a positive future for humanity.

Ultimately, he is a geek at heart. At the age of 11, he learned to code, and at 18, he had replaced the engine in his first car. James's curiosity about how things work and his knack for fixing things continued into his adult work life.

James studied micro-electronics and computing at university, spent the next 10 years in software development, and more recently, has focused over 10 years on leadership and coaching.

As a technology expert, James leads strategic thinking from the board level through to team implementations, covering digital strategy, organizational transformation, and product development. He holds a global perspective on digital, having lived in the United States, UK, China, and Australia, and this allows him to understand the complex cultural and market dynamics that impact technology and product delivery across continents.

He is well-respected in the tech industry and has presented at several Agile/digital conferences globally. As the ThoughtWorks Transformation Practice Lead, James had the privilege of working alongside his mentor, Agile Thought Leader Jim Highsmith, on the global rollout of Adaptive Leadership. This started James down a path of "finding a better way" for teams and organizations. James is a certified Leadership Agility Coach, Integrative Enneagram Coach, NLP Master Practitioner, and Holacracy Practitioner. He leverages this unique combination of psychology and digital skills to grow high-performance teams, leaders, and organizations.

Ultimately, James wants to leave the world a better place for his children and our future generations, so it's no surprise that he donates his time to charities and not-for-profit organizations such as Redkite and Burn Bright.

Outside of the office, you'll find James enjoying time with his family, capturing photos at http://jamesbrett.4ormat.com/, building and flying drones, or in his workshed constructing cubby houses.

James can be reached by email at: james@evolvingdigitalleadership.com

Foreword

We have all heard the mantra multiple times and in multiple ways. The world is changing—fast. Technology is driving change—even faster. People need to adapt to these changes—rapidly. People need to adapt again and again—don't slow down yet. In order to adapt to our rapidly changing, technology-driven digital businesses, we need a new leadership culture, leaders with new skills, new behaviors, new talents, new outlooks, and new ideas. The core question for many organizations is "how do we grow the kinds of leaders we need in the future?". For many individuals, the question is "how do I transform myself from a technical specialist to a technical leader?".

Evolving Digital Leadership, by my colleague and friend James Brett, seeks to answer these questions by drawing on years of personal experience and extensive interviews with leaders from organizations, large and small. Growing yourself into a leader and helping others to grow into leaders is more complex these days. But it isn't an either/or situation, it's a both/and situation. Technical experts need to be leaders at times. Business leaders need to be technically competent at times (actually at most times). As technology, specifically digital technology, increasingly moves from a business support role to being an integral part of your businesses products and services, we need a better model for growing leaders—one that James provides.

Is there anyone who thinks the pace of technology-driven change will lessen? Where will we be in 5 years, or in 10? If your crystal ball is working well, let the rest of us know. Otherwise we are probably safe in saying that advances in technology will continue at a fever pace; those technologies will lead to more complexity; and the importance of integrating technologies and business practices will increase. We need a roadmap to address these issues.

Why *Unnatural Selection?* Is this just a play on words or do the ideas behind *natural selection,* the biology of survival of the fittest, provide insight into our leadership development dilemma? A rebel group of biologists contend that even billions of years is not enough time to generate the diversity of life we see on our earth. They contend that there is another force at work they call *arrival of the fittest.* While survival forces create small increments of change that eventually add up to big changes, arrival forces, grounded in collaboration and cooperation, create big jumps in adaptability. Today's pace of change demands more than survival and slow adaptations to change. Today we need arrival of the fittest driving Unnatural Selection as a way to adapt to continuous change. We need to grow a cadre of unnatural, survival-skilled leaders.

So, how do we do this?

James defines the Unnatural Selection framework, at the heart of which is the evolution helix.

The evolution helix is a four-step process designed to evolve a digital leader's awareness in order to constantly create and respond to change. The four steps of the evolution helix are Awareness, Intention, Attention, and Reflection. These may sound like traditional skills, but in this book they go beyond tradition. For example, tomorrow's leaders need to be as aware of what they are not measuring as what they are. Most measurements reflect what we considered to be successful *yesterday*. Digital leaders need to answer the question, "What are we not measuring today that we need to measure tomorrow?"

For example, over the past 5-10 years one of the major transitions for technology (and business) leaders has been to move from a cost-driven to a value-driven view of technology. Measurement systems tend to get locked in. When to unlock and move on to new measures of success is one way in which digital leaders need to be aware.

In his Unnatural Selection framework, James leverages his experience in coaching and psychology to help us understand the nuances of how and why people do what they do. Building on this advanced psychology, James presents several digital specific models that help us understand and "do" digital leadership in a more effective way.

The Digital Situational Leadership model is one such tool that identifies two axes of leadership that are essential to success: Tactical/Strategic and Delivery/ Culture. In the quadrants formed by these axes, he then describes four modes of leadership—Get Stuff Done, Friend of the Team, Utopian, and Futurist. He goes on to say, "All four modes are essential to success, and all are dangerous if we spend too much time locked in one. Digital Situational Leadership is a leader's ability to understand the current situation and maintain their agility to move around the four modes as required."

In closing, I'll just say that the Unnatural Selection framework provides a path to answering the two key questions from the first paragraph: "How do we grow the leaders we need now and in the future?" and "How do I transform myself from a technical specialist to a technical leader?" Adaptability is key to surviving and thriving in tomorrow's world. You only achieve adaptability by growing adaptive leaders. *Evolving Digital Leadership* provides a path to do just this.

Jim Highsmith
Lafayette, Colorado
June 2017

Acknowledgments

I've always loved fast cars and motorsport. As a boy, I would spend Sunday afternoons watching Formula One Grand Prix on TV. I loved the speed and excitement of the racing as I cheered for my favorite British drivers. Back then, I thought winning races was all down to the superhuman skill of the drivers and about who could drive faster and more consistently than anyone else. Only over time did I fully comprehend the relatively small role the driver plays in getting the car over the finish line first, race after race, season after season.

Until I wrote this book, I viewed authors the same way. Now I realize that being an author is much like being a racing car driver—there is a huge team of people that supports and contributes to producing a great book. I am truly grateful to all those on my team who made this dream possible. This book is as much theirs as it is mine.

I would like to specifically thank a number of individuals:

My partner, Marina Chiovetti, for always believing in me and supporting me. She's juggled our two children and a day job and even found time to edit my writing. This book is the latest chapter of our journey together, and it simply wouldn't exist without your support. Thank you love x.

My mum, Jackie Brett, for being there for me through rain and shine. The world would be a better place if every son knew that his mother would always love him no matter what, and that she will always be there for him. You have given this gift to me. Love you mum x.

Jim Highsmith, for mentoring me through this process of sharing my vision for the world. Thank you for opening your house and your family to me over the years. Jim, you are a genuine inspiration to me, thank you.

Karina Woolmer, for connecting me to Dave Thompson and the crew at the Inspirational Book Writers Retreat[1]: A.J. McCoy, Georgia Lee, and Runn Wild. They helped me create the first outline of this book.

"Mikey" Princz, for the years of great friendship!

The friends, reviewers, and connectors that were of tremendous assistance during all stages of the process: Anthony Sochan, Craig Rees, Darren Cotterill, Jody Podbury, Jonathan Jefferies, Jody Weir, and Stephen James.

---

[1]http://www.inspirationalbookwritersretreat.com.au/

Maria Delfino,[2] for creating the great visuals in this book.

The digital leaders, technologists, and gurus who contributed their experiences, insights, and heartbeats to the interview process:

Alister Bell, Aneta Beocanin, Cam Swords, Caoilte Dunne, Charlie Simson, Chris Iona, Craig Edwards, Craig Penfold, Craig Rees, Craige Pendleton-Browne, Dan Sandiford, Darren Cotterill, Dave Coombes, David Bolton, David Vitek, Deon Luddick, Hubert Truong, James Turnbull, James Wilson, Jason Stirk, Jeff Paton, Jon Tirsen, Josh Price, Leah Rankin, Leonardo Borges, Liz Douglas, Luke Stubbles, Mark Cohen, Nick Drew, Nick Randolph, Nick Wong, Rebecca Parsons, Richard Webby, Rick Grundy, Sandy Mamoli, Sean Geoghegan, Simon Geraghty, Stephen James, Stewart Gleadow, Sujeet Rana, and Victor Kovalev.

The editorial team at Apress: Rita Fernando Kim, Shivangi Ramachandran, and Laura Berendson—it was a pleasure!

Thank you all!

---

[2]https://www.behance.net/galaxiemaria

Digital Leadership

Before you are a leader, success is all about growing yourself. When you become a leader, success is all about growing others.

—Jack Welch[1]

Digital technology is responsible for the exponential pace of change we are experiencing in industry and society today. Incredible computing power that's always on, in the form of high bandwidth Internet access, mobile devices, wearables, bio-tech, artificial intelligence, and virtual reality is everywhere. These are but a few of the key technologies that are changing the world we live and work in.

Digital is disruption.

Leaders that lead the digital world, lead the world.

In Part I of the book, we look at what it means to be a successful digital leader and the transitions that are required to grow from a hands-on technical specialist to a leader of people and technology.

The chapters in Part I are grounded in my own personal experience and those of the 40 digital leaders I interviewed as part of the research for this book.

Once we have established a shared view of what digital leadership is and how we might get there, I share with you (in Chapter 4) the career success pyramid, which combines over 400 years of digital leadership experience into five concise recommendations for you to follow in order to achieve success.

---

[1]*Winning* (New York: HarperCollins, 2005).

I then discuss the changing landscape and the challenges we face as digital leaders by comparing the shifts in the last 10 years with those that are likely to happen in the next 10 years. I present the Unnatural Selection framework as a potential solution.

Start Here

The breaking of a wave cannot explain the whole sea.

—Vladimir Nabokov[1]

Disruption, innovation, turbulence, change, and competition are words that define our world today. If you aren't aware of this already, you're in trouble! If you are, then you have likely been looking at how best to respond to these changes. Maybe you are a leading edge innovator creating your own waves of disruption and watching your competition struggle to stay afloat. Congratulations if you are, but you're not safe either. The ocean endlessly sends wave after wave, and at some point, your ride is going to be over. You then need to paddle hard, back out through the swell to catch your next wave. All too often, leaders and innovators achieve success and then stagnate. They fail to paddle back out into the swell, to adapt, change, and learn new skills. Their wave ends, washing them up high on the beach and then it's too late for them to go back out again. Equally, new leaders often crash out of the wave early and can't pick themselves back up to try again! Digital Leadership is a game of survival of the fittest.

Darwin's theory of Natural Selection prunes out the weakest individuals, who are least suited to the changing environment. Our human evolution occurs slowly, over millions of years, adapting as needed to the earth's climate and food supply. In the digital ocean, waves come a lot faster and more often than this, sometimes accompanied by hurricane force winds and rain.

---

[1] *The Real Life of Sebastian Knight*, by Vladimir Nabokov (1941)

© James Brett 2019
J. Brett, *Evolving Digital Leadership*, https://doi.org/10.1007/978-1-4842-3606-2_1

One such storm is the combination of Artificial Intelligence (AI) and Virtual Reality (VR)—these are dramatically changing society and the way we work. Artificial intelligence will commoditize a significant number of jobs, including software development. It began with the basic automation of mundane tasks and is progressing to more advanced jobs such as X.ai's, Amy, the artificially intelligent personal assistant. Eventually, AI and (Ro)bots will perform fully automated product development in a conversational manner with humans. Virtual reality will change the way we work, and more specifically, where we work. We are only a few years away from the end of the office block, as the majority of the knowledge-based workforce will connect remotely into virtual offices. These two tsunami waves are creating immense change, right now!

As digital leaders, we need to evolve faster than this pace of change; we need to hone our skills and capabilities to constantly ride on top of the waves. Unnatural Selection is a framework for how to become a leader who does this. It isn't a framework that shifts you once; it's a framework that drives your constant evolution, keeping you sharp and ready for each new wave of change. It gets you paddling back out there faster and easier, and even helps you select your wave. Grab your board and let's go find the waves!

Our Journey

On an evolutionary scale, an individual human life is short. The average life expectancy is mere pinprick of 70 years in a universe that is thought to have been in existence for 14 billion! During our lifetime, our hearts will beat an average of 2.5 billion times, and so I want to start by deeply thanking you for choosing to share some of those heartbeats with me as we go on this journey.

However, this is more than a journey, this is the start of a relationship. A relationship that I hope will continue past the life of this book, where we form a community of like-minded people creating the best future for our fellow humans, future generations, and our planet.

I want our relationship to be a two-way conversation, not a one-way download of what I have to say to you. We have the technology to connect, share, and talk almost anywhere in the world and even meet physically when the opportunity presents itself. I am in constant evolution, just as you are, and you have as much to offer me as I do you.

■ **Note** For more information about the community, visit `http://evolvingdigital` `leadership.com`.

Yes, But…

"Yes, but…" This is one of the more common ways technologists begin a response. It's how we have learned to test a concept to see if it makes sense. We find the edges of it—the faults and issues—and we challenge them. It's a learning strategy and it serves us really well. The problem is, we "yes, but" so much that we don't even know we are doing it. This is a real issue in conversations when a team member or stakeholder shares an idea or suggestion and the first thing we respond with is "yes, but,…". It subconsciously tells the other party that you have negated what they said. (Unless of course the other party is an experienced coach, in which case they understand immediately your mental filters.)

So in service of any "yes, buts…" you may have about this book: *Evolving Digital Leadership is my offer to you.* My hope is that, in reading this book, you will find at least one key concept that resonates, and it will change the way you think and operate in the world for the better. You may have a strong aversion to some aspects of what I am offering, and that's okay too. Take what you want; reject what you don't. You will get exactly what you are meant to get from this book, exactly when you are meant to get it.

This Book Isn't an Agile Book

I love Agile. I have over 14 years of experience in Agile product development and large-scale, enterprise transformations in the UK, United States, Australia, and China. I've presented at numerous Agile conferences globally and have achieved various Agile certifications, including becoming one of the first Certified Scrum Coaches (in 2008). I cut my teeth early on Agile and it's provided an amazing foundation in product, people, and process understanding. If you don't have at least a basic grasp of Agile, I urge you to develop one first and then return to this book once you have those skills dialed in. This book is an evolutionary step beyond the mechanics of Agile and implicitly includes its values and principles.

It Isn't a Generic Leadership Book Either

There are a plethora of great leadership books available and, therefore, I don't believe the world needs yet another leadership book. What it does need is a book by a digital leader, for digital leaders. A book that approaches the subject of leading technical teams and organizations, founded on years of technical experience within those teams.

With the right complement of skills, technologists are the best people to lead other technologists. We think and operate differently than others; we are wired for cognition and problem solving and for building things, sometimes even invisible things. Our work is complicated, complex, and chaotic. Our products and services are pervasive. What we create and build will be utilized in almost every aspect of society. Digital is the future; we are the future. We need to be ready to lead better, to create better products, better teams, better organizations, and a better society. Are you up for the challenge? If so, read on...

How to Use This Book

I've designed this book so that the content is valuable, digestible, and actionable. The high-level structure is such that you can choose how you digest the material.

The main body of the book contains digital leadership content and the Unnatural Selection framework. At the front and back of the book are two productivity hacks—the "Too Long; Didn't Read (TL;DR)" chapter (Chapter 2) and the "It's Not Cheating" chapter (Chapter 21), respectively.

The "TL;DR" chapter summarizes the whole book in one chapter. That way, in about an hour, you can get an overview of the concepts, principles, and frameworks presented. The "It's Not Cheating" chapter contains links to full color, downloadable versions of the visuals used throughout the book you may freely use as appropriate. You can, if you like, read the "TL;DR" chapter and then cherry pick the content you want from the main body and the visuals. If you have the time, you will get most value from reading the book sequentially. If you don't have the time, ask yourself: What's more important than developing your digital leadership capability?

The main body of the book consists of five parts, as discussed next.

Part I: Digital Leadership

This section sets the groundwork for the journey by outlining the path to digital leadership, recommendations for a successful career, the evolution of digital leadership over time, and the introduction to the Unnatural Selection framework. Once you have a basic understanding of the framework, Parts II-V break down each step of the framework, guide you through the concepts, and explain how to execute it.

Part II: Awareness

The first step in the Unnatural Selection framework is awareness. This part of the book provides three highly valuable awareness downloads, which bootstrap your **understanding of people**. You can read this part in isolation if you are solely interested in understanding how people work, their stages of development, and their personalities and preferences. These are presented through the analogy of the human as a full technology stack.

Part III: Intention

The power of intentionality—choosing and becoming focused on what you want—is critical to success. In this section, we look at how to set and hold intentions, and we explore three intents for digital leadership success, focusing on self, team, and stakeholders.

Part IV: Attention

With our intentions set, Part IV looks at our attention and how to execute Unnatural Leadership on a daily basis. We explore tools and techniques that enable our personal evolution, empower the growth of our teams, and build long-lasting stakeholder relationships.

Part V: Reflection

Evolution is raising our awareness through reflection and learning. This part of the book looks at ways to evolve effectively through journaling, reflecting, and feedback loops. We also look at concepts such as judgment and the fear of failure that prevent many us from asking for and processing feedback constructively.

Self-Reflection Questions

At the end of each chapter there are questions designed to help you absorb the material from the chapter. I can't stress enough the importance of investing your time in working through these questions. They will help you translate the book from theory into actionable, real results.

So, what's your intention for reading this book? What do you really want to become? Are you committed to this journey or just mildly interested? Stop and think about that for a minute. When you are ready, grab a drink, get comfy, and let's dive in!

TL;DR: Too Long; Didn't Read

"I would have written a shorter letter, but I did not have the time."

—Blaise Pascal, French mathematician[1]

To be a great disruptive leader who maintains high levels of success, you *must* value your own personal growth and invest the time and energy into evolving on a continual basis. There is no shortcut. If you are serious about becoming a great digital leader, then I highly recommend that you skip this chapter altogether. Move straight on to Chapter 3 and read the book in a linear manner to get the full value from the depth of content provided. However, if you believe you are too busy to do that or require a high-level overview before committing, this chapter is for you.

▨ **Note** In order to concisely summarize the book, this chapter reads more like a textbook. All other chapters offer a richer, deeper guide and include examples to help you put the theory into practice.

---

[1]Blaise Pascal, "Letter CVI," *Les Provinciales, ou Lettres Louis de Montalete* (Lyon: Amable Leroy, 1807). The actual quotation is "Je n'ai fait celle-ci plus longue que parce que je n'ai pas eu le loisir de la faire plus courte."

© James Brett 2019
J. Brett, *Evolving Digital Leadership*, https://doi.org/10.1007/978-1-4842-3606-2_2

In this chapter, I summarize the key concepts of the Unnatural Selection framework to get you up to speed fast. You may then cherry-pick the chapters of interest for more details or skip to Chapter 21, "It's Not Cheating," to download the resources used throughout the book. When you have enough to get started implementing change in your world, read Chapter 20 for more about igniting.

The other chapters in this book provide a more thorough understanding of each topic summarized here. Where appropriate, I point you to the relevant location for more information.

Let's get started!

Becoming a Digital Leader (See Part I)

As we move from a technical role into digital leadership, we often aren't sure what is involved in becoming a great digital leader.

The four key capacities that we must develop to succeed in digital leadership are Tactical vs. Strategic and Delivery vs. Culture. That is, we must be able to respond quickly and provide tactical solutions to urgent situations and we must simultaneously be strategic in our operation. Failure to do either of these well limits our chances of success. Equally, we must build great delivery capabilities that support our organization's commercial model and grow a positive culture that attracts and retains the best talent.

Digital Situational Leadership

Figure 2-1 shows the Digital Situational Leadership model (see Chapter 3). This model plots the four capacities (Tactical, Strategic, Delivery, and Culture) at each end of the X and Y axes respectively, creating the four leadership modes of 1. Get Stuff Done, 2. Futurist, 3. Friend of the Team, and 4. Utopian.

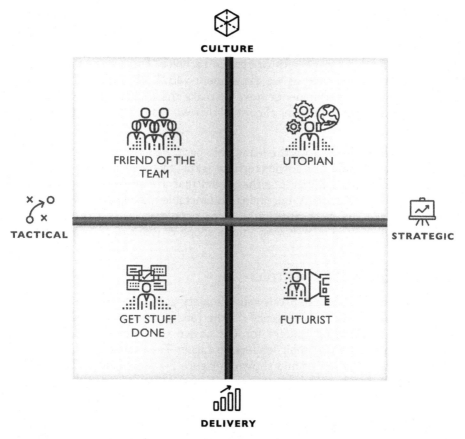

Figure 2-1. The four modes of the Digital Situational Leadership model

For successful leadership, we must be aware of which mode we are operating from at any given time to ensure that we have chosen the most effective one.

It is important to understand our own personal preferences for particular modes. Knowing which mode is our default (or preferred) and which mode is our weakest broadens our awareness and allows us to develop the other leadership modes.

Before we become a leader, we develop our technical skills and expertise as we build our organization's products and services. After spending some time gaining this experience, we are faced with the decision to either follow a digital leadership career path or remain technical. For some of us, we face this choice over and over as we experiment with both options. There are a number of factors that influence how we make these decisions, including our view of managers and the level of control that we wish to have (see Chapter 3 for details).

For those of us who choose the leadership path, we have to make the critical transition from focusing on solving technology problems to focusing on growing people. There are a number of other shifts that are also required, including redefining personal success, becoming comfortable making a decision (versus trying to make the right decision), posing problems instead of prescribing solutions, and moving from having a finite scope of work to an infinite one.

Career Success Pyramid

The transition to leadership can cause anxiety as we try to integrate these shifts and learn new skills—usually on the job. To assist with this transition, I interviewed 40 digital leaders for the advice that they would offer new leaders who are starting their leadership career. The results are summarized in the Career Success Pyramid shown in Figure 2-2 (see Chapter 4 for more information).

Balance leadership and technical **5**

Failure happens, it's how you respond **4**

Redefine personal success **3**

Get a coach and a mentor **2**

Own your career **1**

Figure 2-2. The Career Success Pyramid

The Career Success Pyramid presents five key recommendations developed from over 400 years of combined digital leadership experience. You can focus on one specific recommendation in order to enhance your career or, ideally, start at the base of the pyramid with 1, Own Your Career, and work upward. It can take a number of years to make the transition from a technical specialist to a digital leader, so we must consider what the future holds. What might the world look like in 10 years time and how will our digital leadership need to evolve?

Evolution of Leadership

The pace of change is accelerating at an exponential rate. The major trends of the last 10 years (including high-bandwidth, always-on Internet access, and the saturation of smartphones) have changed society and with it the function of technology in organizations. During this time, technology transitioned from being an IT cost center to a "strategic enabler". As the pace of change continues to accelerate and we move to a digital society, we are likely to see the end of the office block as VR and AR provide for remote team collaboration environments. The rapid adoption of AI will dramatically change how we live and what jobs are available. Before this proliferation of AI, however, we will continue to see an increase in demand for great technical talent that can create the best products for the ever more sophisticated consumer. In summary (see Figure 2-3), the digital leaders of the future will a) build organizations that are digital natives, b) integrate and leverage these key technology trends, and c) develop a deep understanding of people (themselves, their teams, their stakeholders, and their customers).

Figure 2-3. The three components of the digital leadership of the future

Unnatural Selection

It's a complex world, and one solution will not work for every leader in every organization. Even if there were one solution, the pace of change would render it irrelevant very quickly. What is required is a solution that enables digital leaders to evolve faster than the pace of change, where leaders focus on developing a deep understanding of people and ride new waves of change. This is Unnatural Selection (see Chapter 6), at the heart of which is the evolution helix (see Figure 2-4).

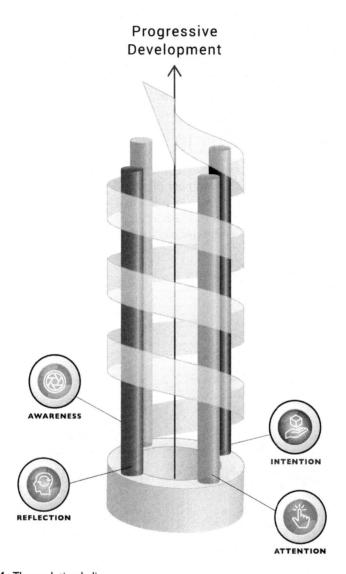

Figure 2-4. The evolution helix

The Evolution Helix is a four-step process of Awareness, Intention, Attention, and Reflection, which, when repeated, consistently fuels our progressive development and evolution. Unnatural Leaders are leaders who embody this process as a habit and constantly improve themselves and their organizations. Let's take a look at each of the four steps.

Awareness (See Part II)

A key objective of the Unnatural Selection framework is to develop your level of awareness; specifically your awareness of people (including yourself) and how and why they do what they do. The key reference model to understand people used throughout the book is the Humans as a Full Stack model (see Figure 2-5). It's introduced in Chapter 7 and explored further in Chapters 9 and 10.

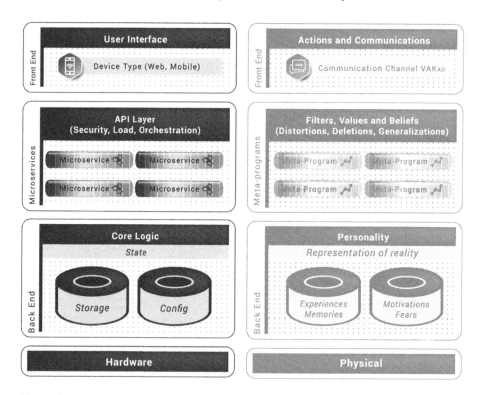

Figure 2-5. The Humans as a Full Stack model

In order to demystify the complexity of human behaviors in an accessible way (to digital leaders), the model draws the analogy that humans work much like the technical full stack, with a frontend (UI), an API layer, and a backend. In the human model, the three corresponding layers are Actions and Communications, Filters, Values and Beliefs, and Personality Types.

As we evolve, we develop our capacity to understand and process the world. While these changes occur constantly and in small increments (much like a mature Continuous Delivery process), developmental psychologists have categorized these changes into groups called stages of development. The three key stages of Expert, Achiever, and Catalyst describe (among other things) what is important to us, our capacity to understand the complexity of the world, how we interact with others, and our emotional responses. These capacities increase as we progress from Expert, through Achiever to Catalyst (and beyond). In Chapter 8, I discuss these capacities in detail and describe how Catalysts are more able to deal with a world that is becoming increasingly more complex and interdependent.

Our human frontend impacts the effectiveness of communications between two parties. There are four main communication channels—Visual, Auditory, Kinesthetic, and Auditory Digital (VAKAd)—and each person has a preferred channel. If a person prefers the Visual channel, they will want to see (or will present) information in a visual format. People with an Auditory preference want to communicate by talking and listening. Communication can become difficult when the two parties involved have different preferred channels. Effective communication involves using multiple channels to ensure that our message is received with the most impact.

Behind our frontend communication layer, we have the equivalent of an API layer (see Chapter 7). In order for our brains to be able to process the world in a coherent manner, our API layer deletes (denies requests), distorts (prioritizes requests), and generalizes (batch processes requests).

Behind our API layer, we have a set of meta-programs (see Chapter 9) that are equivalent to microservices. Meta-programs are patterns of processing in our brain that we have developed over time that impact how and what we do with the information received in our brains. Meta-programs determine things like the size of information we prefer to process, whether we primarily focus on ourselves or on others, and how we understand or relate to authority. To date, over 60 meta-programs have been identified in our brain's "software".

Our backend consists of our core personality structures, experiences, and memories that determine how we respond to the information we receive. The Enneagram (see Chapter 10) identifies nine core personality types or backend platforms. By understanding the nine Enneagram types, human communication channels, and meta-programs, we can gain a deeper understanding of our own motivations and behaviors as well as the people we interact with.

Intention (See Part III)

With an increased awareness, we proceed to step 2, Intention. Intentionality is a critical part of successful leadership (and of leading a quality life). Intention focuses our attention and energy on what is important to us.

> *"Energy flows where attention goes, as set by intention."*

Without intentionality, we run the risk of our attention and focus being pulled in multiple directions as we become distracted by the urgent and unimportant tasks of the day. Intentionality helps us to operate more strategically because we are more aware of what we need to do and why it is important.

So, how do we go about setting the right intentions and being intentional in our leadership? We use the Clarity Process, described in detail in Chapter 11 (Figure 2-6). This simple four-step process begins with owning our career and the choices we make.

Figure 2-6. The Clarity Process

Own: Our Career and Choices

To be successful we must take ownership of our career (as per recommendation 1 of the Career Success Pyramid shown in Figure 2-2) and own the choices that we make (including those we choose not to make). All too often in our careers, we make excuses as to why we can't do something—either we are too busy, can't take the risk, or are avoiding choosing by keeping ourselves frantically busy. These are all choices. When we avoid making a choice, we are still choosing; we are choosing to continue on as we are (and often complaining about it). Unnatural Leaders embrace their power of choice and own their career and their four powers of how they Think, Feel, Communicate, and Act (see Chapter 11).

Understand: What's Important to Us

Now that we have taken ownership, we must get clear on what is important to us at a personal level and what is important to all Unnatural Leaders. We are driven by intrinsic and extrinsic motivators (see Chapter 12), the ratio of which is primarily dictated by our stage of development. Dan Pink's *Drive*[2] (a highly recommended book by the 40 digital leaders I interviewed) identifies three key intrinsic motivators of Autonomy, Mastery, and Purpose. When we experience all three of these in our roles, we are more likely to enjoy and excel at what we do in a sustainable way. Extrinsic motivators include money, cars, houses, and status. While money is essential to live, it alone does not bring us satisfaction and enjoyment.

Our Enneagram type (see Chapter 10) influences what is important to us in all aspects of our life, not just in our careers. It may be that we want to the do the right thing (the Reformer), challenge the status quo (the Challenger), or help people (the Helper). These core desires underpin our very personality and influence what is important and what we focus on as we work toward the goals we have set.

Secondly, there are three key meta-programs (see Chapter 12) that, when understood, help us to determine what is important. These are Quality of Life, Preference, and Attention. The Quality of Life meta-program determines what is needed for us to experience a "good life" and includes the things we have, the things we do, and our way of being.

The Preference meta-program has seven options: People, Place, Things, Time, Activity, Information, and Systems. Preference determines where we like to focus our attention (on the people we are with, the places we go, the things around us), when and how long we spend doing an activity, what information we are gaining, and the big picture involved.

The Attention meta-program determines whether we primarily focus on our own thoughts and feelings (Self) or the thoughts and feelings of others (Other). As leaders, balance in this meta-program is critical in order to lead with vision and empathy.

And, finally our purpose in life strongly shapes what is important to us. Without purpose, we don't have a "true north" to direct our attention.

---

[2] *Drive: The Surprising Truth About What Motivates Us*, Daniel H. Pink, Riverhead, 2011

Four Things That Are Important to All Unnatural Leaders

There are four things that are important to all Unnatural Leaders (see Chapter 12) and *purpose* is the first. The reason I wrote this book is:

> *To positively influence the direction of society so that our children and future generations are able to have a high quality of life.*

If I can influence digital leaders, their teams, and their organizations in a positive way, you will go and build better products, and together we make the world a better place—one I'm proud to leave behind for future generations.

Three things that are important to all leaders are the growth of ourselves as leaders, the growth of our people and teams, and the growth of long-lasting stakeholder relationships. Evolutionary leadership and evolving faster than the pace of change are both grounded in the evolution of these three fundamental activities.

Define and Set Intentions

The final steps of the Clarity Process (see Chapter 13) are to define and set intentions that allow us to focus our attention on what is important. Unnatural Leaders set three intentions: to be passionately curious, to shift from performance management to growth, and to build long-lasting, mutually beneficial stakeholder relationships (see Figure 2-7).

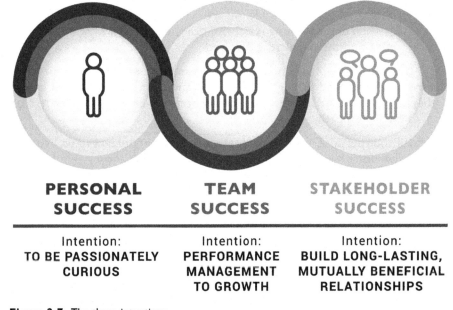

PERSONAL SUCCESS	**TEAM SUCCESS**	**STAKEHOLDER SUCCESS**
Intention: **TO BE PASSIONATELY CURIOUS**	Intention: **PERFORMANCE MANAGEMENT TO GROWTH**	Intention: **BUILD LONG-LASTING, MUTUALLY BENEFICIAL RELATIONSHIPS**

Figure 2-7. The three intentions

We then define and set any personal intentions that help us focus on the things that are important to us individually.

With our intentions set, we move to attention and bring our focus to how we perform our leadership role. We do this to ensure that we deliver on the three key intentions.

Attention (See Part IV)

Step 3 of the evolution helix is Attention. Our three Unnatural Selection intentions focus our attention on the continuous evolution of Self, Team, and Stakeholders.

One of the biggest challenges we face is being distracted from what's important. Leadership is messy; it's full of interruptions, context switching, and juggling of balls. Unnatural Leaders are proactive, not reactive. They take ownership of their time and attention, and they use intention to devise systems that keep them working on the right things, in the right ways to achieve success. Unnatural Leaders take back control of their calendars and plan their time in order to balance tactical and strategic and delivery and culture. It is important to be aware of how our energy levels vary throughout the day so that we utilize the highest levels to make decisions and be creative. An example performance profile is shown in Figure 2-8.

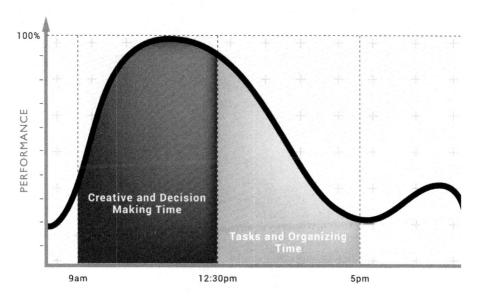

Figure 2-8. Daily performance profile

With our time planned out carefully (see Chapter 14), we focus on framing each and every activity with clarity. Framing is critical to ensure that we are considering the right information, holding the most effective perspectives, and utilizing the most appropriate combinations of the Digital Situational Leadership modes (Figure 2-1). Once we have framed what it is we are working on and why we are working on it, we concentrate on performing and executing to the best of our abilities.

Managing Our State

Outside of the skills, information, perspectives, and leadership modes required to perform well, we must also be able to manage our own physical-emotional state.

Negative states are accompanied by negative emotions (such as shame or guilt) and negative thoughts are less than ideal for high-performance leadership. Energized states, on the other hand, have emotions such as joy, happiness, and elation and positive thoughts that are optimistic, confident, and energizing. The three components that impact our state are our thoughts (internal processing), our emotions (internal states), and our actions (external behaviors). The TEA model, as shown in Figure 2-9, shows how these three components interact.

Figure 2-9. The TEA model

These three components interact with and influence each other to amplify, create, and change our state. We can interrupt negative states by changing our thoughts or actions so that we can access more optimal states for leadership.

As we move our attention to the leadership and growth of our teams, we focus on building a great technology brand that allows us to attract and retain the best talent. A great tech brand consists of seven key components, as shown in in Figure 2-10 (see Chapter 15).

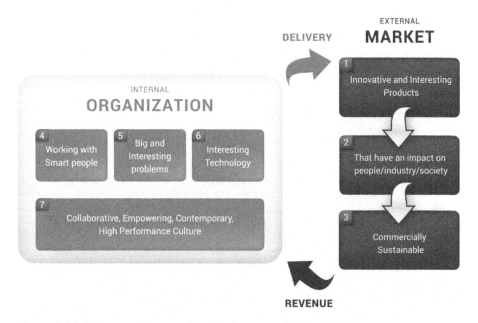

Figure 2-10. The seven elements of building a great technology brand

The first three elements are visible to potential hires outside the organization and include building innovative and interesting products that have an impact and are commercially viable. All three of these elements are important. Products that don't have an impact and/or generate revenue are essentially novelties—they may draw the attention of potential hires, but don't create a brand that top talent wants to become part of.

Internally within our organization, we do our best to hire smart people, use interesting technology, and solve big problems. When we do this in an empowering culture, we have the four key elements that sustain high performance and satisfaction from our teams.

We hold these seven elements in mind as we grow our teams by focusing on developing a deep understanding of each individual, and then coaching them to grow and contribute to the organization. We do this by using the Human Full

Stack model to assist our understanding of their personality and motivators and then we build challenging and exciting development plans with them that focus strongly on learning.

In parallel to paying attention to evolving ourselves and our teams, we pay close to attention to building long-lasting, mutually beneficial relationships with our stakeholders (see Chapter 16). As digital leaders, it's often impossible to develop ourselves and our teams, develop products, grow great cultures, and have the time to maintain strong relationships with every stakeholder. So we begin by utilizing the Stakeholder Relationship map (see Figure 2-11). This provides a framework from which to identify individual stakeholders and categorize how we need to approach each relationship based on their impact on our role and the current strength of our relationship with them.

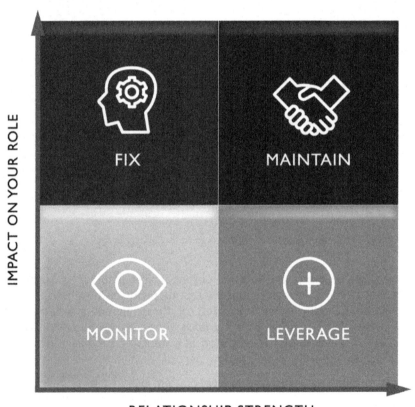

Figure 2-11. The Stakeholder Relationship map

Stakeholder relationships that fall in the upper-left quadrant need to be fixed urgently, as the stakeholder could have a significant impact on us and we don't have a strong relationship with them. Similarly, we can potentially reduce our investment (if we don't have the capacity) in those in the lower-left quadrant to monitoring and light engagement.

As we engage with individual stakeholders, we develop an understanding of what success means for them by asking questions that drive out specific detail about their motivators. It is all too easy to focus on our own success and not take the time to understand our stakeholders. We then wonder why we aren't able to influence and collaborate with them effectively.

When communicating with stakeholders, avoid asking "why" questions that can trigger conflict and instead use "how" or "what" questions, for example "What is it about…? This allows us to gain information about a stakeholder's opinion or perspective, which builds on our detailed understanding of them. This knowledge allows us to create mutually beneficial outcomes as we co-create and pitch strategies to gain the buy-in and support we need. These strategies communicate the business context and drivers first, rather than leading with technical, jargon-laden requests. The latter usually alienate, not engage, the stakeholders.

As digital leaders, we must balance the "right" amount of technical debt. One of the most challenging aspects of this is gaining stakeholder buy-in to pay back the debt already incurred. These conversations usually begin with us asking stakeholders if they would like a new feature delivered or if we can reduce technical debt. A more effective way to do this is to lead with the question, "Would you like feature X delivered, or would you like us to deliver faster?" (see Chapter 16).

It is very important that when things go wrong, (as they inevitably do), we utilize the TEA model to manage our state appropriately and take ownership of our contribution to the problem. Once we take ownership, we switch into problem-solving mode, offering solutions and leading the way forward out of the problem.

Managing our attention can be very challenging and it can take some time to develop the skills and systems that bring about elevated performance, reduce stress, and increase the quality of our experiences (and those of the people around us). As we maintain a high level of curiosity and focus on learning, we also reflect on a daily basis on how the outcomes achieved align with our intentions.

Reflection (See Part V)

The final step of the evolution helix is Reflection. Our goal with reflection is to accelerate the development of our awareness, as we begin another cycle of the helix. Reflection is the fuel for our evolution. We evolve naturally without reflection. However, the pace is considerably slower and it is likely to be less than the pace of change in the world around us.

When we take time to reflect, we consider both the past and the future (see Chapter 19). As we look back on our day or week, we use journaling to keep track of our experiences, lessons, and progress. We journal on a daily basis as we assess our performance and look for insights into ourselves and the world around us. We seek external feedback that allows us to test our assumptions and understand how we are perceived by our teams and stakeholders.

Reflection can give us access to different perspectives, which help raise our awareness. Unnatural Leaders create and respond to change by using the Levels of perspective (shown in Figure 2-12) to contextualize everyday activities in the frames of evolving industries, technologies, and societies and, indeed, how what we are doing (or aiming for) impacts the future of mankind.

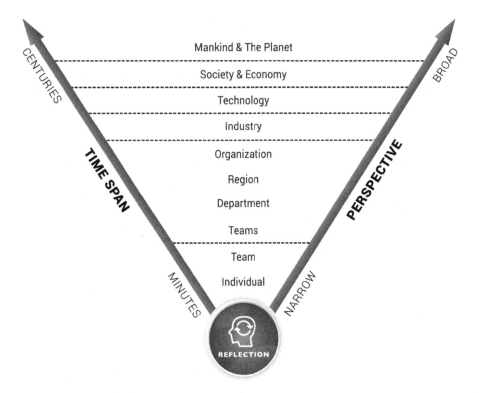

Figure 2-12. Levels of perspective

Key future reflections that we must consider include the impact of AI and VR on industry, society, and mankind. AI's exponential capability will see an equal exponential adoption across most industries as organizations leverage the scalability, efficiency, and effectiveness of these "robots". VR will revolutionize the way we live and work as its capability reaches levels that mean we no longer need to be physically present in city office blocks to perform our roles. The outcome of this will no doubt be a redistribution of cities and living accommodations to areas that are more appealing and/or more cost effective. This movement away from cities will dramatically affect society and the economy as the demand for cities and infrastructure wanes. The decline of the concept of the "city" will have a knock-on effect on the service industries that rely on cities and their workers. Digital leaders (and our organizations) must reflect on the future to avoid being disrupted by these changes.

Chapter 19, "Reflecting Together," contains a set of reflection questions designed to stimulate your evolution through deep thinking about your journey so far and reflections on what you have learned by investing time into reading this book. I also share my own key reflections on the journey of creating this book (the interviews, the writing, and the developmental journey that it has fueled for me). I recommend you read this chapter and attempt the questions after you have read a majority of the book. The questions won't be as effective if you skip to them straight from this chapter.

In summary, Figure 2-13 shows the key components of the four steps of the Unnatural Selection framework.

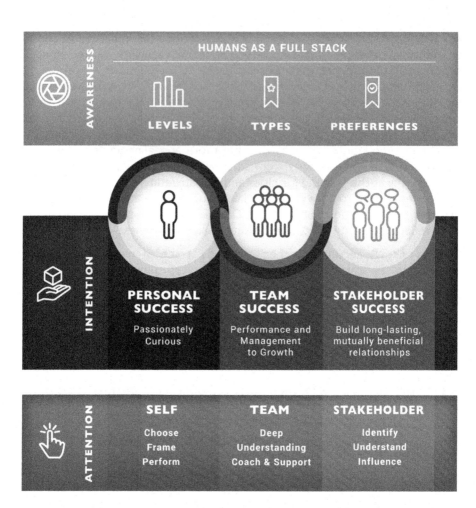

Figure 2-13. The Unnatural Selection framework

Ignite (See Chapter 20)

My call to action to you is to change. Do something different and ignite yourself, your teams, and your community. The book contains powerful and valuable knowledge, but knowledge is useless without action.

Chapter 20 contains six team activities that I suggest you run in order to ignite their (and your own) evolution. You will also find details about how to join our community of Unnatural Leaders, where I hope we can grow, share, and learn from each other.

And finally, I conclude the book by igniting your thoughts of the future and asking you to consider three potential scenarios:

- What if artificial intelligence takes over?
- What if we prepare our children for the digital future?
- What if we genuinely believed every challenge (or failure) we faced was a gift?

I share my thoughts and perspectives on each of these scenarios with the intention of getting more of you to consider the deep impact of the future and how you might thrive in whatever future you end up in.

It's Not Cheating (See Chapter 21)

We're at the end of TL;DR and I hope it has given you a good overview of what we are about to explore in the rest of this book. If you'd like to access the visuals referenced here and in the remainder of the book, you will find all the details in Chapter 21.

If you are a new leader, I strongly recommend you read Chapters 3 and 4, which describe the journey to digital leadership and the career recommendations that will help you get there faster and more effectively.

If you are a senior leader, Chapter 5, "The Evolution of Digital Leadership," sets the context for the rest of the book and is a powerful tool to help you assess how far you have come and where you might need to go next.

If you are time poor and want to quickly develop your understanding of how you and others work, I recommend you read Part II, "Awareness," which bootstraps this understanding by diving deep into the Human Full Stack model.

I hope you enjoyed this brief tour of *Evolving Digital Leadership*—it's not "too long" to read if you value your own leadership.

Becoming a Digital Leader

The real voyage of discovery…consists not in seeing new sights, but in looking with new eyes.

—Pico Iyers, author[1]

You may be a tech lead trying to understand your future career options, or a CTO looking to create and ride more waves, or one of the many roles in between. Whatever role you hold, it's important that we clarify and establish a shared understanding of digital leadership and discuss what it means to be a leader of technologists.

There are many different types of digital leadership roles. This variety comes from a function of the market vertical and the organization's resources, size, and culture. However, one thing is common: all leaders are busy people! We work hard to deliver against "stretch" objectives and maintain high levels of employee satisfaction, while at the same time attending numerous meetings, processing infinite unread emails, and responding to a myriad of unplanned interruptions.

---

[1]Pico Iyers paraphrasing Marcel Proust. "Where Is Home" talk, TEDGlobal 2013, June 2013.

© James Brett 2019
J. Brett, *Evolving Digital Leadership*, https://doi.org/10.1007/978-1-4842-3606-2_3

Juggling all of this successfully requires an awareness of the situation or context. Knowing how the current activity (meeting, conversation, or strategy) relates to the bigger picture, knowing what is tactically and strategically important, and knowing how to respond accordingly is an essential skill.

The Four Capacities

So what are the most important capacities for digital leaders? To answer this, let's first define success:

> *Success for a digital leader involves building a motivated, high-performance capability that tactically and strategically delivers value to customers in a sustainable way.*

That is, digital leaders need to be *tactical and strategic* while focusing on *delivery and culture*. The Digital Situational Leadership model represents these four capacities, as shown in Figure 3-1.

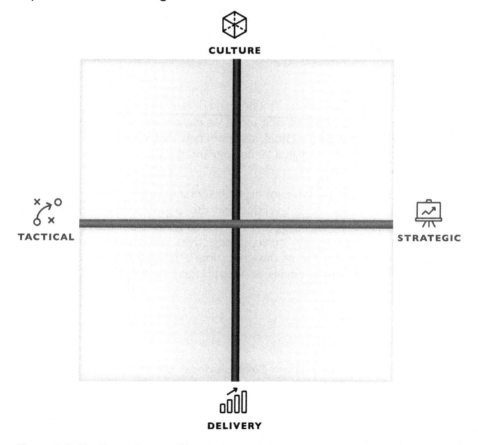

Figure 3-1. The Digital Situational Leadership model

Tactical and Strategic

Development of our strategic capacity is essential if we are to progress successfully from technologists to digital leaders. This isn't a shift from tactical to strategic; it is a shift *from being tactical to being tactical and strategic.* In doing so we deliver urgently needed tactical solutions (or hacks) within the longer-term strategic context. Depending on the role and organization, the strategy may exist, or we may be responsible for creating the strategy and getting buy-in on our own.

For most technologists, we start off in the lower-left corner, focusing on the shorter-term delivery of a single feature, release, or product. As we develop our leadership skills and explore the wider organization, we understand the business model and its constraints more, until we can look into the future, harness technology trends, and steer the organization as one team. The more strategic we become, as we traverse to the right side of the chart, the more strategy becomes about people engagement and influencing others, ultimately leading to securing funding and engaging teams to deliver.

Delivery and Culture

One of the hardest balancing acts digital leaders have to perform is that of building a positive, sustainable culture *and* delivering at speed. Longer-term capability uplift and morale often take time to establish and can't be done overnight. Delivery needs to happen for all businesses, but pushing through delivery at any cost can destroy culture. The paradox here is that as culture gets destroyed, motivation gets destroyed, attrition rises, and delivery performance evaporates all too quickly.

The real kicker here is that cultural decay is quite often a silent killer. It creeps up on organizations and for some leaders the first sense they get is the all-too-late lag indicator of increasing attrition rates. If high attrition rates aren't bad enough, try hiring new talent when the word on the street is that you have a crappy culture. Welcome to your own unemployment! Great cultures are purposeful, empowering, high performance, and practically self-recruiting.

The Four Modes

The two axes (Tactical/Strategic and Delivery/Culture) of the Digital Situational Leadership model create four modes of operation, as shown in Figure 3-2.

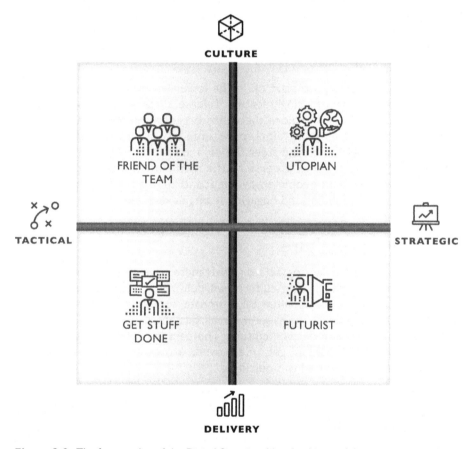

Figure 3-2. The four modes of the Digital Situational Leadership model

Mode 1 (Bottom-Left): Get Stuff Done

Focusing on short-term delivery. It is in this mode where we act fast and get stuff done. There are times when stuff hits the fan, money runs out, systems break, and strategy and culture simply have to take a back seat for a while. Here we hold those things in the background but focus on execution and delivery as a priority.

This mode is probably the most important one to be mindful of, as it has its own gravity, constantly pulling us toward it. It feels comfortable, productive, and busy, and is often the mode of those around us. When we choose this mode, we must have an exit strategy. Leaders who remain in this mode will find their ability to lead at scale severely hampered.

Mode 2 (Bottom-Right): Futurist

As technologists, we often enjoy being in this mode—thinking about the future (but looking at it mostly from a technology and delivery perspective) and spending a majority of our time focusing on roadmaps, trends, and planning for greatness. Answers in this space are relatively more concrete than those that involve culture. The challenge of this mode is linking the vision for the future, logically and clearly back to the tactical work that is being done today.

Engaging teams that will be building the future can also be a challenge as we operate with a delivery focus, which tends to see us act as individual contributors, rather than co-creating with our teams.

Not performing the futurist role becomes a real issue as we ascend leadership roles. Driving the business and leveraging technology for competitive advantage is essential. Leaders who remain more tactical are often overlooked for more visionary, bigger picture personalities who are able to drive change and innovation.

Mode 3 (Upper-Left): Friend of the Team

Short-term focus on culture means that keeping people happy is a priority. It can also mean we are addressing urgent cultural problems that have arisen and require immediate attention. We may take on a role of fighting and protecting a team or individual when others in the organization are pushing delivery in an unhealthy manner. The trap when operating here is what I call the "Happiness Trap", where, like children who are given everything they want, are still unhappy and want more. Structure and discipline are required. Saying "no" appropriately amplifies the experience of the occasions when we say "yes".

Mode 4 (Upper-Right): Utopian

Here we are looking into the future and focusing on building a great culture. Our aim is to create a great, new environment for the great new talent who will love coming to work. Building a future capability is essential for sustained performance. The trick is to integrate our vision of the future back to the current state and connect the two with a strategy that maintains high performance throughout the transition. All too many leaders spend little time in this mode, focusing on the urgent demands of short-term delivery. Great leaders have a people-focused vision and purpose that draws them constantly into this mode. Their vision and purpose drive them to ask meaningful questions about the future and how the organization can positively impact it.

All four modes are essential to success and all are dangerous if we spend too much time locked in one. *Digital situational leadership requires leaders to understand the current situation and maintain agility to move around the four modes as required.* In a particular meeting of stakeholders, ultimate success may mean navigating all four modes over the space of an hour. In another scenario, say a one-on-one meeting, it may mean sitting singularly in one particular mode and focusing our frames and conversation around that. We may find ourselves in situations where it's not clear which mode is appropriate; in that instance, it's useful to try on a mode and ask questions related to it. For instance, stepping into the Futurist role could mean asking about future tech trends and their impact on what's being discussed.

That said, there is more to becoming a successful leader than integrating these four modes of operation. As we transition to leadership, there are some major shifts that need to happen if we are to become great digital leaders!

Some of them are logical and relatively easy to shift to, such as becoming more strategic in operation. Some are intensely difficult and uncomfortable to shift to, such as moving from providing solutions to gritty challenges, to posing questions to your teams.

The challenges and their difficulty vary depending on your personality, context, and experience, but in my 20 years in technology and leadership development, I've seen some common patterns. Conscious of the effect of my own biases, I set out to validate and explore the space further by interviewing over 40 digital leaders, to discuss their journey from technologists to digital leaders.

What you are about to learn is a summary of the key shifts identified during these interviews and is based on more than 400 years of combined experience in digital leadership. It's time to stand on the shoulders of giants!

From Technology to People

Probably the most significant shift required for leadership success is the shift from technology to people.

Coailte Dunne describes this shift as:

> "It's about technologists coming to terms with the fact that they have to interact with people. The further you get away from technology, the more you are dealing with people. The more responsibility you gain the more you will have to lean into influence, relationships and collaboration to achieve your outcomes."

—Coailte Dunne, Agile Coach

For a minority of us, this shift is a release from the shackles of technical complexity and complex problem solving (our heart was probably never really in the technology). For most of us it's a transition that takes some time and usually follows a path that is more or less parallel to that of understanding the nuances of Agile transformations. This process is shown in Figure 3-3.

TECH
- Building the right thing
- Mastery of what I do

PROCESS
- Building the right way
- Effectiveness

PEOPLE
- Who is involved
- Why is it important
- Is there alignment

Figure 3-3. The journey from technology to people

Technology

In the first stages of our career journey, our focus was on technology and building the product the right way. As a developer, we wrote code to solve a problem, refactored it to make it more efficient, secure, or maintainable, and practiced our craft day in, day out. It was beautiful. Then one day, one project, frustration began to set in. Frustration with how things get done around here—the process being followed, the waste, the endless meetings, and the long feedback loops. We may have even had the enlightening experience of "delivering" in a waterfall process. So, as much as we love the craft of building digital technology products, we start to focus some of our attention on the processes being used.

Process

Here we maintain our passion for tech and start to integrate new process skills. We are now focused on building the right thing *and* building it the right way. Enter, the various Agile, lean, and customer-centric movements. As a developer, my passion for Agile came back in 2003 in the UK. I was working on a development team that was introduced to XP practices, a totally new way of working together as a team. As a developer, this shift was initially strange and different, and if I'm honest, a little confronting. There was a lot more conversation to be had and a lot more visibility of what everyone was doing. After getting over the initial hurdle, I loved the empowerment, the clarity, and the teamwork and started to look at the Agile movement as a whole.

For me these movements were incredible for one reason: They made life better. They made life better because they reduced the amount of wasted work we did (either as unused features or as a product that simply wasn't fit for purpose). As technologists, problem solving is our raison d'etre, especially solving problems for other people. We love building products that people use, benefit from, and enjoy. Throwing some work away is a fact of iterative learning and getting a great product-market fit. However, needlessly throwing huge portions away is soul destroying!

In the early days of the Agile movement (going back 10 years or more), the Agile transformations focused on the practices and doing of Agile. This was an essential step in both the coach's and the practitioner's development. Understanding the practices, trying them, and learning from them together as a team is where the magic is. For those who struggled in this phase, we saw what I call "Lipstick Agile," where teams would plaster the walls with post-it notes, time a 15 minute stand-up, and run a four-week sprint, all "managed" by a Scrum Master. Eventually teams would learn that it was the intent and outcomes of the processes that were important not the actual practices themselves: that the processes were designed for people. This is why some teams succeeded and some failed, with what looked like the exact same practices. Process really is all about people.

People

The final stage of the shift is what we technologists often call the "fluffy stuff". I often feel that we lose sight of what organizations are. For me, I prefer the label "Organization" to "Business" because of the implicit focus on people, not revenue and profit.

> Organization: "A group of people who work together in an organized way for a shared purpose."

> —Cambridge Dictionary

Or, in other words, an organization is a collection of people, working and interacting together to build products or services that achieve a goal and purpose. How we organize those people directly impacts the effectiveness of the organization. In the traditional command and control structures of days gone by, we could have easily labeled leaders as organizers (or equally dis-organizers).

Now, as I've said before, this isn't a generic leadership book, so I don't intend to delve into organizational design or the difference between a working group and a team. What is important here, for this book, is to point to the fact that building great technology and products is essentially about understanding our customers, teammates, and stakeholders better, so that we can apply our technical smarts more effectively.

Shifting our attention to focus on people and working with people presents us with our ultimate professional decision point. The fork in the road.

Fork Me!

The ultimate technical career question: Do we stay technical, or go down the people leadership route? For some of us, this decision is simple and almost unconscious. We have a strong and clearly defined view of what we want and enjoy. This enables us to progress down one of the paths and never look back. Our clarity often stems from an early childhood exposure to leadership role models, or a passion for technology and solving technical challenges, taking us down the thought leadership or people leadership paths, respectively.

For others, the path is less obvious. We may avoid or postpone making the decision for a number of years, or traverse back and forth, switching between technical and people leadership until we find a balance that feels right for us.

So let's take a look at "the fork" (see Figure 3-4) so we can understand the options and decide how to approach them.

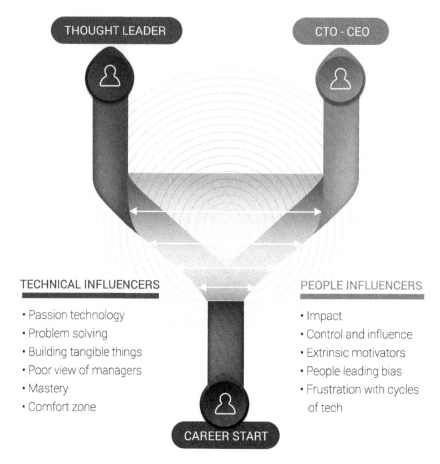

Figure 3-4. The fork

In most organizations, there are two career development paths: the technical path to thought leader and the people leadership path to CTO. The initial stages of the paths are common, with most of us progressing from technologist to senior technologist and tech lead. After this, the paths fork. If you find yourself on the thought leader path, potential roles include architect, community of practice lead, tech evangelist, and eventually thought leader.

For those of us on the people leadership route, the path the may include the following roles: scrum master/iteration manager, product manager, development manager, head of…, and CTO.

I'm not someone who focuses on role titles. They are significant for finding your next role via traditional recruitment channels and the likes of LinkedIn. However, there is usually a fair amount of ambiguity in the title and definitions supplied by an organization. Being a "Head Of" in one organization could mean you are genuinely leading hundreds of people, building great products, intelligently developing strategy, and securing budget and buy-in from stakeholders. In another organization, "Head Of" could be more like a politician and project manager, simply passing down an approved budget and delivering a series of projects.

My advice to leaders who are looking for new roles is to strongly investigate and understand the following two aspects of the position:

- What does success look like for the role? Over what period of time? With what resources? How will everyone measure success?

- Can you work with and respect your boss? Are your styles and approaches sufficiently aligned to enjoy the experience? What can you learn from your boss? This is often one of the keys to respecting your boss.

Role titles aside, let's look at how people are influenced down each path of the fork, with us first looking at the influences to stay technical and head toward thought leader.

Thought Leadership Path

The path to thought leadership involves staying more technical than the people leadership route. There are six key influencers that drive us to stay closer to the technology:

- **A strong passion for technology**

   This may sound obvious, but some of us just love technology. It's our true passion in life. Our passion outweighs the other motivators, such as the desire for senior leadership status.

- **Enjoy solving problems**

   Solving problems can be addictive. That's not to say that those of us who take the people leadership route do not solve problems. Of course we do. The key difference here is that feedback cycles for technical problems are considerably shorter than solving for people dynamics, and technical problems can often be validated with data, metrics, and definitive solutions.

- **A love for building tangible things**

  Building products is an art form and creating tangible things is self-expression at its best. Creating products and solutions that we can touch and feel can provide a certain sense of satisfaction. This satisfaction probably drew us to the field to begin with. Building teams and organizations is a lot more, let's say, "fluffy." For some us, this just doesn't feel productive!

- **Poor view of management**

  This one sucks, it really does! Our poor view of management, or for some, the complete disdain for anyone who doesn't get hands on usually stems from personal experience of being "managed" poorly. (I'll postpone the discussion on the difference between management and leadership for a later day. I intentionally use the term "management" here.) The net result is a poor experience of being managed, leading many of us to hold a view of "why would I want to do that to someone else?" This is often coupled with a belief that all managers do is attend endless meetings and send emails.

- **Mastery of the technical craft**

  If you haven't read Dan Pink's *Drive*[2] yet, it's worth checking out. It was the most commonly cited book by the digital leaders I interviewed. In *Drive*, Pink talks about the three core motivators of Autonomy, Mastery, and Purpose. Mastery, as you might have gathered, refers to an individual's desire to master their craft—to dive deep (enough) into the detail and to feel a sense of satisfaction and accomplishment. A person in this state is unlikely to want to progress out of their role until (their view of) mastery is achieved. A more developed explanation of this subject is covered in the Chapter 8.

---

[2]NY: Riverhead Books, 2011.

- **Prefer to stay in your comfort zone**

    Let's face it, it's warm, cozy, familiar, and feels like home. If the other motivators aren't strong enough to move us *and* we have certain beliefs about discomfort, then we will remain solidly in our comfort zone. This isn't the place to be if we want to evolve faster than the pace of change! It's not wrong, nor is it bad; it's just not embracing the growth or evolution required to be a leader in the future. After all, "Outside of the comfort zone is where the magic happens."

    Are you feeling anxious because you like your comfort zone, but you want to grow and achieve more? Perfect—this book is for you. Keep reading!

For those of us who choose the thought leadership route, we may relate to all six of these key influencers, or maybe just one or two very strongly. This is what makes us choose thought leadership.

For those of us who don't relate strongly to these influencers, let's look at the key influencers that drive us down the people leadership path toward CTO.

People Leadership Path

The path to people leadership roles such as CTO requires a passion for technology and digital but usually in a more hands-off manner. Technical people leaders utilize their experience of building products in teams as a foundation to lead and have more impact on what is being built and when. The five key influencers that guide us down the people leadership path are:

- **To have more control and influence**

    The single most common reason we choose the leadership path is to gain more control and influence over our work, the products we are building, and the objectives that are being set by the organization around us. "I was just sick and tired of working for idiots" eloquently summarizes what I believe most technologists think!

- **Limelight and success**

    Let's be honest, some of us are driven at points in our life to be successful because we want recognition and validation. It's a product of society's conditioning. Ascending the organizational hierarchy is commonly associated with being successful. Conversely, doing the same job for years often implies a lack of effort, commitment, or success. This is changing slowly. Some people have realized that life is about doing the things we love, not what's expected of us. In other words, intrinsic motivation overpowers extrinsic success.

- **Money**

  The other primary extrinsic motivator aside from success is the need to earn more money as we move from being young and single, and become a parent perhaps supporting a family of one or more children. As our family grows, the cost to support them grows, as does the size of the family home. For most technologists in big cities, the cost of housing is continuing to escalate at a dramatic rate. Not to mention the cost of nice cars, international vacations, expensive restaurants, gadgets, and clothing! For some of us, this means choosing a path that leads us to the highest bidder for our time.

- **People leading bias**

  For a minority of us, the decision to lead is a no-brainer and almost unconscious. We take on internal team leadership roles and are easily promoted. The pattern for us is that we experienced some form of leadership as a child, either as a sports team captain, a Scout leader, or had a parent who modeled leadership for us. We tend to be wired for and focus on people naturally because of this. We understand that the dynamics of getting things done relies on people and their interactions. Those with people-leading bias often have a strong desire to help others.

- **Frustration with cycles of tech**

  In contrast to the sustained passion for technology that drives some of us to remain technologists, others move away from technology because of one common frustration: we are discouraged by the constant learning cycle required to remain current and on top of our technical game. I've personally seen hundreds, if not thousands, of new trends, patterns, frameworks, tools, and paradigms in my time. Some people feel like the underlying problem being solved is on repeat and begin looking for new and different challenges.

Deciding Which Path To Take

In summary, it depends on a number of interacting factors as to which path is right for you. Even for those who make the decision easily and are strongly drawn down one particular path, it doesn't always work out the way they want it to.

Some choose the people leadership path because they love leading. However, the combination of company culture, personalities, and events can create an experience that is less than desirable.

Conversely, some people ascend to a leadership role by being great technologists. As they do, they get more and more responsibility and accountability. At a certain point, this added responsibility becomes challenging and uncomfortable and they resign, taking a less senior role in a new organization. The cycle often repeats itself when they are again promoted and have to face their career options and motivators, as shown in Figure 3-5.

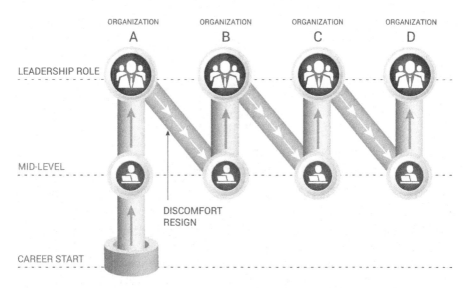

Figure 3-5. The Sawtooth Resignation pattern

Some people move back and forth between the thought leadership and people leadership paths for a while as they either experiment to understand their preferred option or are given opportunities that cause them to switch paths. Path switching can be done (and is done) relatively easily in the early stages of our careers as both people leadership skills and technical expertise are developed in parallel. However, eventually we reach an inflection point (see Figure 3-6) where, once we pass it, switching to the alternative path becomes quite difficult.

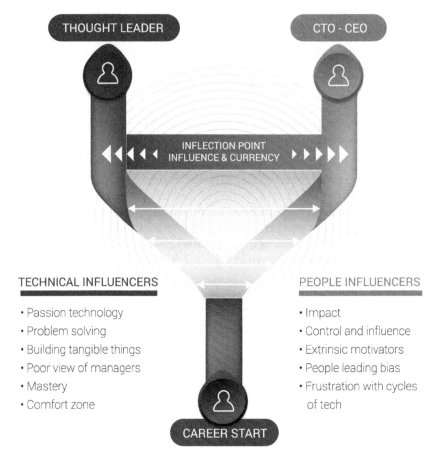

Figure 3-6. The inflection point

This difficulty stems from a lack of expertise of the other track at a senior level, which means we either are no longer technical enough to transition horizontally or we don't have the leadership experience to do the reverse. We can of course, transition over and downward and take on a more junior role than we currently hold and continue our development from there, much like on transition of the Sawtooth Resignation pattern.

Ultimately, both paths require interaction with, and influencing, people. As a CTO or thought leader, success means influencing other technologists and stakeholders in effective ways. This means understanding human assumptions, preferences, motivators, and communication styles. Essentially, we must master the soft skills that do not come naturally for many logical thinkers.

The primary focus of this book is on evolving our people leadership skills to become Unnatural Leaders. That said, the Unnatural Selection framework contains tools that will enable you to evolve faster and improve your people influencing skills, bringing you to the top of your game.

Other Shifts Required for People Leadership Success

Marshall Goldsmith's book, *What Got You Here, Won't Get You There*[3] introduced the concept that the skills and approach you took to get promoted into leadership aren't the same ones that are required for you to keep ascending roles and being successful. Let's have a look at what success means in digital leadership.

From Personal Success to Team Success

Underpinning all of these shifts is the shift in *how we define personal success*. As a technologist, we are essentially individual contributors. As a leader, if success is a version of our personal contribution, this mindset will hold us back from being a great leader. Great leaders realize that success is about making other people successful; it's about challenging our teams, supporting our peers, and celebrating their success alongside our own. *The secret to becoming a great leader is redefining personal success and shifting from an individual contributor mindset to a people growth mindset.*

Heroic leadership in the digital world irritates people! We may feel good in the moment (when we get that pat on the back from our boss), but we will pay the price later when poor team motivation and lack of trust reduce our ability to influence.

Finite to Infinite

A difficult shift to make is from having a relatively finite amount of work to do (to deliver a product) to an almost infinite amount of work to do (in leading a team). As leaders, we need to be able to prioritize what we and our teams should work on. This increased control and influence can be a heavy burden to carry. It means taking control of our time, prioritizing tasks, and saying no to lots of things and people! Wrapped up in this shift from finite to infinite is the way decision making changes.

---

[3]NY: Hyperion, 2007.

From Making the "Right" Decision to Making a Decision

As we progress along the leadership path, the decision-making process moves from us being the expert (needing to make the "right" decision) to us simply making a decision. All too often, technologists search and analyze scenarios, looking for the perfect answer. Experts tend to hold a belief that if they look long and hard enough, they will find the right answer. When we do this as a leader, it can appear to others that we are not making a decision, or that we are stuck in *analysis paralysis*. Great leaders make decisions and experiment wherever they can, reducing large complex problems into a series of fast iterative feedback loops, co-created with the right people in the organization. This brings us to the next key leadership shift, from solutions to problems.

From Solutions to Problems

This next shift is the key for leading highly motivated, self-organizing teams. As a technologist and individual contributor, we are used to digging into the details of complex challenges and solving problems. We got paid to do it and we loved it. Have you ever worked for a leader who took that enjoyment away by telling you how to do your job? They probably told you what to build and/or how to build it. Being told how to do your job is demotivating and disempowering. It often does not provide the best solution either. Leaders inevitably get pulled away from the minutiae of the product teams, and so we should. But this distance impacts our ability (as leaders) to provide the best solution. It's a lose, lose situation: we end up with a poor solution and poor team engagement.

Leaders often ask me how to best lead Agile teams. They complain that their teams don't want them to "control" and "dictate," because Agile teams are self-organizing. Yes and no. Agile teams are self-organizing—however, they are organized around a specific problem (or set of problems) that has constraints (time, money, brand alignment, security, etc.). An aspect of Agile leadership is providing the boundaries for self-organization, while posing problems for teams to solve (see Figure 3-7).

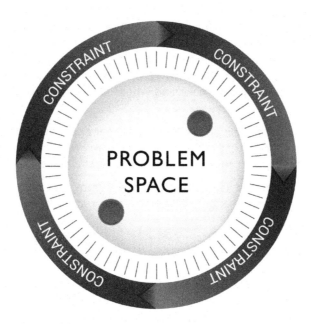

Figure 3-7. Leading self organization teams

This is conceptually simple to understand. The challenge occurs when we are pressured by our own leaders and stakeholders to deliver. We may know (what we believe to be) the best solution for our team to take, but they either can't see it or are taking "too long to find it". The temptation is to jump in and solve the problem (just this once) to get the delivery done. The questions we have to ask ourselves are: What is most important? How might we balance the growth and empowerment of our teams versus faster tactical delivery?

These Leadership Shifts Cause Anxiety

Fear of being incompetent is common for technologists. Having spent our careers mastering our craft and demonstrating competence, the shift into leadership throws us into a new environment where we have to start learning a whole new skillset—one that probably doesn't come naturally to our logical brains. This anxiety is quite normal. What's different in the world of technology is that technologists don't typically talk about their challenges. They struggle on, trying to think their way through, or keeping busy building products while avoiding the people challenges. It seems to me that getting technologists to talk about anxiety is a lot like getting men to talk about emotions! That shouldn't be much of surprise, really, given that the tech industry still suffers from a huge male majority, and anxiety is an emotion.

This anxiety spans more than just the initial steps of the leadership journey. During my interviews, it was common for digital leaders to share how they quietly struggled through their careers trying to answer the following questions: How do I think about my career? What mental models do I use? What decisions do I have to make and when? Is a leadership career right for me or should I stay technical?

I believe the more we talk about these challenges together, the easier it will become. It is my hope that through this book, we will be able to talk more, share more, and support more. We are all facing the same challenges!

In the next chapter, we take a look at the Pyramid of Success: a concise summary of the top five recommendations for a successful for career.

Summary

Making the transition from a technical role to leadership is challenging for a lot of people. Having a good understanding of the shifts required to be a great digital leader makes the transition easier and accelerates the path to success.

Knowing how our peers have approached these decisions and the factors that influence our choice at the fork in our career (sometimes repeatedly) will help relieve some of the anxiety of the process.

Self-Reflection Questions

If you are currently in a delivery role and thinking about making the shift to leadership, consider these questions:

1. What is it about becoming a leader that appeals to you?

2. Can you think about one or more great leaders you have worked for? What was it that made them great?

3. Are you ready to focus on people more than on problem solving?

4. When considering the Digital Situational Leadership model and the four modes of operating: Get Stuff Done, Futurist, Friend of the Team, Utopian:

    a. What do you think would be your preferred (or default) mode of operation?

    b. Which mode do you think would be the biggest challenge for you?

If you have already made the transition to a leadership role, consider these questions:

1. When considering the Digital Situation Leadership model and the four modes of operating: Get Stuff Done, Futurist, Friend of the Team, Utopian:

   a. What is your preferred (of default) mode of operation

   b. Which mode do you least inhabit?

2. What is it that draws you toward your default mode of operation?

3. What is it that pulls you away from your least inhabited mode?

4. What is your current definition of success? Do you need to update it?

5. What is one action you could take to share more about your journey with your peers?

6. What activity could you run with your team to help alleviate anxiety?

Career Success Pyramid

Take control of your own career. No one else can put in more attention, focus, and commitment than you. Leaving this in someone else's hands is a recipe for dissatisfaction.

—Sujeet Rana, CTO

I developed the Career Success Pyramid (see Figure 4-1) with the insights from the 40 plus interviews I conducted with various digital leaders. Although the insights gained were many and varied (giving me enough content for another two books), the following is a summary of the top five most important recommendations. You can address all, or any one of, these in whatever order you choose. However, I urge you to start at the base of the pyramid and lay the foundations for success by owning your career, and then build upward from there.

© James Brett 2019
J. Brett, *Evolving Digital Leadership*, https://doi.org/10.1007/978-1-4842-3606-2_4

Figure 4-1. The Career Success Pyramid

Step 1. Own Your Career

Sujeet's quote at the start of this chapter brilliantly summarizes the starting point of the Career Success Pyramid. Consciously owning your career and owning your decisions is critical if you want to be successful. Yes, luck and opportunity certainly play a part in success; however, the more you focus your attention on what you want, the more it comes into your life.

If you can't decide what you want from your career, then experiment, learn, and play. Pick a goal, set an objective, and aim for it. Maybe it's not the right goal; maybe when you get there you will decide it's not right for you. That's okay. Choose something else. Create your career, create your journey, and don't make excuses. *Success is a place rarely visited by people who see themselves as victims.*

Step 2. Get a Coach and a Mentor

A coach and a mentor are not the same thing! Coaches provide you with deep reflections and insights, and like a mirror, they offer yourself back to you. A coach will help you test your assumptions, point you toward your blind spots, and break through your artificially created mental barriers. Successful digital leaders use coaches to shift their awareness, their consciousness, to new levels, and to move them from emotional reactions to logical responses. A coach will challenge you thoughtfully, not emotionally, and will help you tame and even let go of your ego.

In my experience, leaders who work regularly with a coach, accelerate their development and achieve success faster than those who do not. We will look at stages of development in Chapter 8, "Experts and Achievers," where we will see that once you're in the adult stages of development, there are no guarantees of progression unless you do the work. You have to set your intention, focus your attention, and reflect. Doing this work with an experienced coach will get you ahead much faster.

Mentors, on the other hand, are people in your field of expertise (digital leaders) who generally have more experience than you, and they offer direct guidance and advice on tackling specific challenges. Getting the right mentor can be tricky—mentoring (and coaching) requires a good interpersonal fit. Choose a mentor who inspires you, who you respect, and who you are excited to learn from. Always choose a mentor from outside of your circle and certainly from outside of your organization to avoid any potential conflict of interest.

Crucially, great mentors are well connected and can introduce you to their network of other successful leaders. "It's not what you know, it's who you know." If you're interested in the power of networking, check out Janine Garner's new book, *It's Who You Know: How a Network of 12 Key People Can Fast-track Your Success.*[1]

> "The most successful people in rapid growth environments find and leverage support networks."
>
> —Victor Kovalev, CTO

There is a small subset of people who have extensive digital experience and are qualified personal coaches. They can play both roles when working with leaders and organizations, bringing their deep understanding of people to their digital leadership and their knowledge of digital contexts to coaching. Successful digital leaders of the future will have strong coaching skills that enable them to build dynamic, empowering, high-performance cultures.

---

[1] Milton, Australia: Wiley, 2017.

Step 3. Redefine Personal Success

I touched on the importance of defining your personal success in the last chapter. It's a pivotal component of being successful. To reiterate this, I have included some direct quotes from the leaders I interviewed:

> *"Leadership success to me is about helping people be more awesome at their jobs and more successful themselves."*

> —James Turnbull, CTO

> *"Your job is to not be the best engineer; it's to get the best out of your team."*

> —James Wilson, CTO

> *"Success is balancing the sweet spot of the business' commercial goals and respect for your people."*

> —Leah Rankin, VP Product and Engineering

All these quotes by digital leaders express the same underlying value they place on the success and respect of others. The success of others is integrated into our personal definition of success as we shift our focus from technology to people.

> *"ABC. Always be caring! Care about what matters to individuals and care about what matters to the business. Showing that you care is the best thing you can do as a leader."*

> —David Bolton, Head of Engineering

I'm pretty sure by now (unless you skipped the last chapter) that you've "grokked" that people are critical, so I'm not going to labor this point any more. I will add one comment however, and that is: *You cannot sustainably fake caring about people. If you don't care for your people, you will never be a great leader.* You can't be a great leader without a great team right there with you.

Technologists are smart. Too many claim they have poor people skills and a lack of empathy, but they can still identify quickly when their leader doesn't care about them or the team. Smart people love to learn, and they love to grow. However, that growth is limited when their leader doesn't genuinely care and support them. It's easy for people to quit when there is a high demand for talent, and so they do! So if you don't genuinely care about your people, you might want to sit and think about that for a while. It's not a black and white conversation either—most leaders will say they care about their people, and they do to a degree, but where does that end? What other things are more important to you? When do you trade off people for something else? Is it appropriate?

Step 4. Failure Happens, It's How You Respond

You are going to fail at some point. It's a fact of life, and it's a necessary part of becoming a great leader. Failures cause strong negative emotional reactions; these don't feel good at all. If we process these emotions in a healthy way, they cause us to shift and decide that we are going to change. Alternatively, we may process these emotions and quit. It's also natural to make excuses and blame others to avoid looking at our own failures.

Nearly all the leaders in my interviews experienced a *painful* failure at some point. However, in my opinion, what made the great leaders stand out from the rest was that they acknowledged their part in the failure, reflected on what they could do better, and moved to change and grow. Nearly all of them attribute their current success to the biggest shifts they made after a painful failure. I want you to imagine something for a moment. Imagine if you truly, truly believed that every failure meant success. Take a moment to process that. Visualize what it would be like in the moment to know that a failure was a success. Would there be any more failures?

Remember: It doesn't feel good to fail. You probably fear failure (either consciously or subconsciously) because of this conditioned sense of pain, and so screwing up sucks! Looking like a novice sucks. Getting fired sucks. Let this in. Acknowledge your setbacks with self-compassion and then challenge yourself to grow.

> "The only real mistake is the one from which we learn nothing."
>
> —John Powell[2]

Step 5. Balance Leadership and Technical

One of the biggest challenges we face as we progress from technologist to leader is how technical we need to be. The more senior the leadership role, the greater the pull away from technology. So how, then, do we remain technically competent as a CTO (or any other senior technical leadership role)

---

[2]*The Secret of Staying in Love*: Thomas More Association, 1990

in order to drive technology effectively? I believe the answer to this question relies on the following three components.

- Leadership styles
- Size and type of the organization
- Passion for technology

Leadership Styles

How we lead, or more explicitly, how direct we are when leading, is proportional to how technical we need to be. Figure 4-2 shows the Dictatorship Spectrum. On the left side, we operate in a dictatorial manner and therefore require high technical abilities. On the right side, we operate in an empowering and consultative manner, so our technical ability and currency can be reduced while remaining a high performance technical leader.

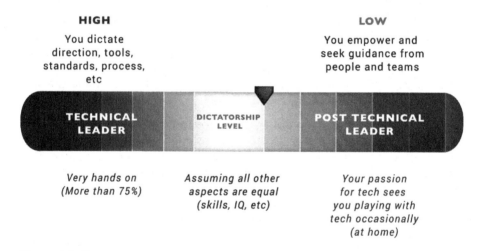

Figure 4-2. The Dictatorship Spectrum

That is, if we are going to prescribe solutions and strategies to our teams, we'd better be great at technology! But this isn't an excuse to stay technical and directive; that just doesn't scale to any size. The more people and teams under our leadership, the more consultative and empowering our leadership needs to be.

In the startup world, the small team size (typically less than 10) often means that the CTO spends a lot of time hands-on. There's no other way around it; startup CTOs generally need to make a hands-on contribution. Conversely, as a CTO of a large organization, our success is not determined by our hands-on contribution. Our role is to guide and shape longer term, strategic enablement of the business and to grow the technical capability around us to the appropriate scale.

Figure 4-3 demonstrates the combination of leadership style and company size as it relates to technical capability.

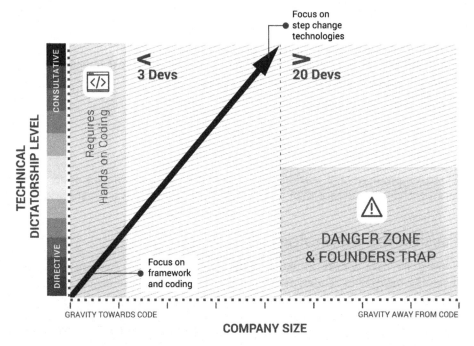

Figure 4-3. Technical direction versus company size

Size and Type of the Organization

In a small organization, gravity pulls us toward contributing directly, due to the lack of other technologists to build products. As the organization scales, the leadership aspect of the role forces a shift, pulling us away from the technology. Being directive is required in small startups—it's how things get done. However, as the organization scales and pulls us away from the technology, we can't stay technically sharp *and* be a competent leader, never mind a great one. If our style remains directive, we will enter the danger zone. We will burn out, act like a jackass, or slow down delivery performance to a snail's pace, if not all of the above!

As we develop our leadership style away from directive, we consult the technical specialists in our teams for specific input and guidance. Rebecca Parsons, CTO of ThoughtWorks (a global consultancy that has attracted thought leaders such as Jim Highsmith, Martin Fowler, Jez Humble, Neal Ford, and many more), utilizes what they call a Technical Advisory Board (TAB). This board leverages the great minds and thought leadership of their global talent to provide direction and assistance to some of the world's leading organizations.

By using a team of highly technical consultants, we can balance people leading and technical input in an appropriate way, leveraging their years of experience with technology and paradigms to challenge and ask questions that reveal the most appropriate solutions for the current context.

The type of organization (not just the size) also impacts the effectiveness of the technical leader. I define three organization types in descending order of required technical competence and currency:

- Technical startup
- Tech product or consultancy
- Non-tech organization

Quite simply, if we are working for a technical organization, we need to be more technically current than if we work for a non-technical organization.

Passion for Technology

If we don't have a passion and love for technology and creation, we won't make the best digital leader, period. There's no room in the digital leadership elite for people who a) have not come from a technology background and b) are no longer passionate about technology. Why? Because we are leading technologists. The best people to lead technologists are leaders who were technologists. They know how technologists work. They know when the wool is being pulled over their eyes, and they know what it's like to be in the trenches.

If we aren't passionate about technology, we probably won't keep abreast of the latest tech trends and therefore will fail to understand both the tool and paradigm shifts happening around our teams. It's all too easy for digital leaders to get busy and then turn around one day and see that the tech world has moved past what we understood. One can usually date the last time a digital leader was hands-on by the way they approach solutions and the paradigms they use.

Passionate digital leaders find time on the train, on weekends, or whenever, to "play" with technology. They seek to understand a new paradigm's strengths and weaknesses and what it's like for the teams that use it as a toolset. Great leaders carve out a portion of their week to pair with technologists. Not to guide them, quite the opposite. They seek to learn from the developers. Victor Kovalev, CTO of Redbubble, makes a point of doing this each week with senior developers, to keep current and experience the coal face, the Gemba, where value is created.

It's a challenging balance to maintain over time. A lot of leaders feel anxious about their diminishing technical skills, some are drawn back into the technology, and most ebb and flow as a natural cycle of being an agile and responsive leader. Find your balance, understand what's needed, and be conscious of your technical dictatorship level.

The Pyramid of Success provides a concise list of five actions to take if you want to accelerate your career success. Each item is simple to understand and yet presents a particular challenge to how we operate and lead. Part III of this book explores intentionality in detail and explains how to set clear intentions for success. It builds on step 1 of the Pyramid of Success. Part V explores reflection and techniques for the healthy processing of failure.

Let's continue our exploration of digital leadership and how it might evolve in the future.

Summary

Becoming a great digital leader and having a successful career comes down to executing well on the five recommendations of the Career Success Pyramid.

Paying conscious attention to your career and seeking guidance from a mentor and coach is the most effective way to accelerate career success.

Self-Reflection Questions

1. Which recommendation on the Career Success Pyramid do you need to focus on to best impact your career?

2. What is it about the recommendation identified that makes it the most important?

3. How specifically will addressing this recommendation shift your career path?

4. What action(s) do you need to take to make this shift?

5. On average, how would you rate your technical dictatorship level (see Figure 4-3)?

6. Do you believe that this dictatorship level is optimal for your current situation?

The Evolution of Digital Leadership

If everything seems under control, you're just not going fast enough.

—Mario Andretti, Formula One, IndyCar, and NASCAR driver

The leadership journey from hands-on technologist to digital leader is an ongoing process. If you're starting that journey now, ask yourself: What the world will look like in 10 years time? There's little value in preparing ourselves for today's challenges if, when we get there, the world has shifted substantially. Maybe you're already a digital leader. If you are, you know how long it takes to build and grow organizational capability and leadership skills. If you don't prepare, plan, and start your personal growth now, you will likely drown in the waves of change, leaving others to shape your future!

Shift of the CTO Role Over the Last 10 Years

Predicting the future is complex and challenging. There are many variables, factors, trends, and events that can dramatically influence how the digital leadership landscape will evolve. One way to predict the change is to look back over time and identify the key shifts and then continue their trajectories

© James Brett 2019

J. Brett, *Evolving Digital Leadership*, https://doi.org/10.1007/978-1-4842-3606-2_5

into the future. Let's look at the market drivers that instigated the current landscape, how organizations have responded, and how CTOs contributed.

The Strategic Shift: Digital Enablement

The last 10 years was the era of ubiquitous mobile and Internet access and the disruption they caused. The iPhone was released in 2007. Soon after that, broadband became fast and cheap, and then 4G came along with its always-on connectivity.

Commercially we saw startup innovators (such as Netflix, Spotify, Tesla, and Amazon) disrupting large incumbents. The huge market shift from physical to digital (DVD, music, and software) was driven by customer desire for faster, easier access. We also had the global financial crisis of 2008/2009, with billions of dollars and thousands of jobs and homes lost. This amplified the demand for cheaper prices.

Large enterprises responded by focusing on customer centricity and efficiency, looking to digital channels and digital enablement as they tried to grow market share, stave off competition, and remain relevant. This response generated a new set of corporate buzzwords, including "omnichannel," "digital-first," "self-service," and "big data," as leaders sought to demonstrate their (somewhat frail) grasp of technology, customer, and market demands.

In software development specifically, the shift was from multiple technologies to multiple paradigms and technologies. The likes of Lean startup, design thinking, and service design established themselves within the realms of everyday process culture, alongside their older cousin, Agile. Cloud-based computing, application programming interfaces (APIs), software as a service (SaaS), and platform as a service (PaaS) became common parlance as they enabled agility and efficiency gains never seen before.

The net result was the escalation of digital leadership roles. CIOs and CTOs became more important. New roles, such as the Chief Digital Officer, emerged as organizations acknowledged the need to reinvent themselves. Great CTOs became more business focused, understanding the nuances of the business model, strategy, and market forces. They widened their view of the organization, to view it as a system, and incorporated a longer term, strategic mindset while simultaneously focusing on short-term delivery and enablement. They leveraged best-fit technologies (mobile, cloud, microservices, big data, and more recently serverless, wearables, artificial intelligence, and Internet of Things—IoT), while Continuous Delivery practices guided the organization's transition (often from legacy systems) to digital- and mobile-first offerings. If your organization isn't here yet, well, now you know where to start!

IT moved from being an expensive, organizational cost center to a strategic enabler, gaining an important seat at the C-Suite table. This decade has been the era of digital enablement.

The Culture Shift: Talent and Process

The focus on digital enablement saw organizations searching for the right delivery and innovation processes and the best talent to deliver these new products and services. The Agile movement provided the much needed focus on cross-functional, empowered teams that delivered customer value in small, fast increments. For the first time, culture became a focus of attention as leaders and practitioners realized its critical role in employee motivation and organizational performance.

The emergence of customer demand for great user experiences and the rise of mobile meant technologists with these skills were in high demand. This demand continued to grow in parallel with the proliferation of the startup movement. The startup culture offered lucrative stock and payout deals, funky office spaces, remote working, casual dress, and a host of other perks, including Mac laptops, free coffee and food, and ping pong tables. Compared to most enterprises of the day, the startup world was a great place to work, and therefore began to attract great talent.

The global battle for talent was on. Demand for technologists was so high that their selection criteria elevated (in a Maslow-like way) from a minimum of interesting work and good pay, to a combination of the following:

- Great products and technologies
- Relaxed and fun culture
- Flexible working and funky office spaces
- Top remuneration and benefits packages
- Awesome working locations
- Meaningful work

Great CTOs understood this and the critical nature of culture. (Autonomy, mastery, and purpose were often respected as the three keys to leading smart, problem-solving product teams). They drove engagement through redefining working policies, building technical communities, hosting meet-up groups, and providing innovation time (such as hack-a-thons and Google's 20% time). Great CTOs developed their leadership and people skills, focusing on growing people and increasing their influence of key stakeholders. Both of these skills leveraged a philosophy of solution co-creation, targeted toward achieving objectives.

Culture shifted from one of "delivery at all costs" to one of creating engaged and empowered high performance. This was the era of talent and process. Figure 5-1 shows these two shifts, plotted on the Digital Situational Leadership model (presented in Chapter 3). Here we see the CTO's strategic shift to Digital Enablement (toward the right) and the Cultural shift to Talent and Process (upward).

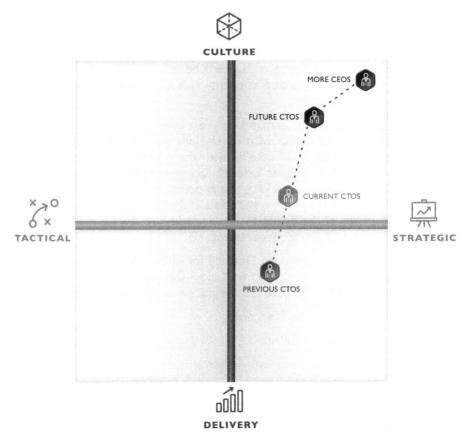

Figure 5-1. The shift of the CTO's role

The Future Role of the CTO (or Digital Leader)

In our review of the last 10 years, we looked at the market drivers that occurred, the responses from organizations, and the role of the CTO as part of that response. We saw how technology drove an era of digital enablement and the subsequent focus on talent and process. What changes and shifts will happen in the future to shape the role and selection process for digital leaders?

Accelerating Pace of Change and Sophistication

The pace of change will continue to accelerate (see Figure 5-2). We are at a point where technology, society, and their integration will accelerate change faster than ever. Put simply: *Today's pace of change is the slowest we will ever see!*

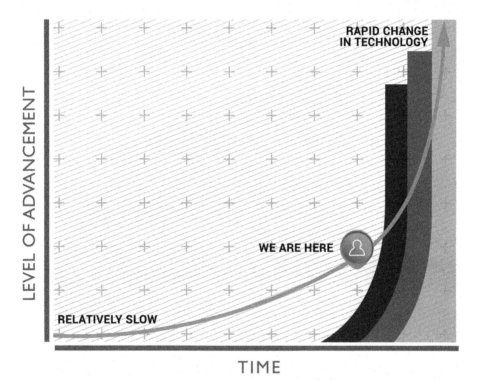

Figure 5-2. The accelerating pace of change

As you can see in Figure 5-2, we are near the middle of the curve, approaching an inflection point that will see the exponential acceleration of change. AI, robotics, VR, IoT, and the connected nature of these devices will radically change our lives, changing how we shop, work, govern countries, and even potentially change our consciousness! (Not convinced? Do a Google search for "Elon Musk and Neuralink".)

Even without the likes of Elon Musk, human consciousness is evolving at an ever-increasing rate. Our capacity to comprehend and hold multiple perspectives is constantly developing, as is our overall awareness. Thanks to advances in neuroscience and a passionate personal development community, we have unprecedented volumes of information that are readily accessible to assist us in developing new levels of awareness.

At any cross-section of time, there will be people and organizations at different stages of adoption. E.M. Rogers' (1971) Diffusion of Innovation theory outlines five categories of adoption, as shown in Figure 5-3. This model has been popularized more recently by Geoffrey Moore in *Crossing the Chasm.*[1]

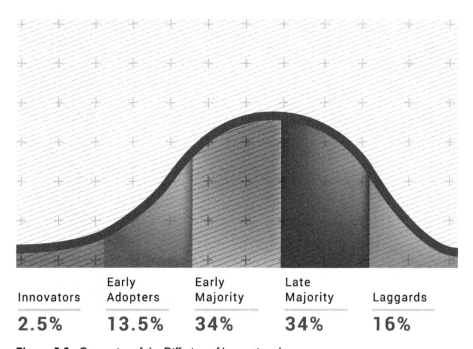

Innovators	Early Adopters	Early Majority	Late Majority	Laggards
2.5%	13.5%	34%	34%	16%

Figure 5-3. Categories of the Diffusion of Innovation theory

We might expect then, that in 10 years' time, the 16% of laggards may still be doing the same as the innovators and early adopters of today. I've witnessed this specifically with the Agile movement. Some organizations are still coming to terms with the very basics of Agile ways of working, which were codified in the manifesto back in 2001.

[1] NY: Harper Business Essentials, 1991

A reasonable place to focus our attention is on the combined categories of early adopters and early majority, the leading 50%. These organizations take their lead from the latest trends and innovators and rapidly respond to the changes they see and predict around them. The three most significant developments I predict are:

- The move to a digital society
- End of the office block (and cities)
- Commoditization of development

The Move to a Digital Society

The pervasiveness of technology will continue. We will continue to track with Moore's law, which states "The number of transistors in a dense integrated circuit doubles approximately every two years". Quantum computing will be at the forefront of this increase in computing power. With this increased power comes smaller size and reduced cost of production, seeing the volume of embedded, wearable, connected devices exploding and technology becoming pervasive in every aspect of society.

Customer sophistication and demand for quality, price, and experience will increase, driving digital further into society and industry. The number of digital businesses (those businesses deriving more than 50% of their revenue from digital channels, products, or services) will dramatically exceed non-digital businesses. The digital natives (the likes of today's Amazon, Apple, Facebook, and Google) will dominate digital and traditional markets, taking over verticals such as food and health.

We will thus see the focus and function of technology complete its transition from IT to digital to simply being the business. In this new digital society, more and more CTOs will become CEOs in implicit acknowledgement of the shift to digital.

End of the Office Block (and Cities)

Virtual reality and augmented reality will develop to levels of sophistication where the need to travel to an office for face to face interaction will no longer be required. Satellite, aerial, and fiber will provide ultra-fast Internet access anywhere on the globe, allowing remote working from a beach house, a forest, on vacation, or even in your subaquatic home. Organizational efficiency and productivity savings will drive widespread VR office adoption, removing the expense of commute times, large offices, workstations, and parking. Further adoption will be driven by the benefits to governments, society, and the environment from the reduction in transportation, which reduces pollution and the multi-billion dollar costs of the transportation infrastructure.

We will see the end of the office block, maybe not in the next 10 years, but it will come!

Commoditization of Development

Developments in AI and robotics will see the commoditization of multiple industries and jobs. Product development at the simpler end of the spectrum will be commoditized and built by intelligent bots. Ten years ago, a developer would handcraft HTML/CSS in a basic editor to produce a functional website. Today those sites are drag and drop and can be built by an 8-year-old. The future will involve conversing with a bot, which will have already assembled everything it knows about the customer, company, and domain (a lot like Watson does today, trawling the Internet and creating personality profiles based on your social media updates). The bot will instantly generate a website based on its findings and the conversational requirements specified. Bots' and AIs' initial takeover of the simpler development will increase over time as their intelligence exponentially improves. As a side effect of the takeover of big sections of industry, cyber-security will become a critical, in-demand skill. The automation of work through technology and the removal of human interaction, will put more and more everyday life into the hands of digital systems, and so their security will become paramount to a safe and reliable world. A recent Cisco report predicted that there will be demand for 6 million cyber security jobs by 2019, with a projected shortfall of 1.5 million candidates!

Extreme Competition for Talent (One Last Time)

Until AI reaches a critical point, the move to a digital society will see an increase in the competition for talent, as existing markets are digitized and new ones are created. There will be an extreme global shortage of talent. Once AI reaches a certain capability level, the demand for human talent across the board will drop and never return, as bots take over the majority of the development work. We are in the very last battle for human talent! Figure 5-4 shows this curve in action. What's hard to quantify is how long this process will take. My gut sense is the demand will increase for at least the next 5-10 years. We will have to monitor the progress of AI and track the increasingly more sophisticated jobs it can complete.

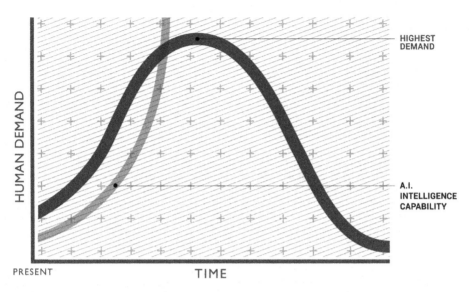

Figure 5-4. The demand for talent versus capability level of AI

Leaders who think this will be a slow and obvious process will be unpleasantly surprised! Technology has a habit of developing quickly and quietly, and then one day, seemingly out the blue, a company releases a game-changing new product, at which point, our only option is to react to the disruption. We must look for the indicators in the market (in this case, the sophistication of jobs that AI bots can complete), capture the opportunities, and ride the wave of change. Don't get drowned by it!

Unnatural Leaders: The Evolution of Digital Leadership

Highly evolved digital leaders will be excellent in the three core competencies (see Figure 5-5).

Figure 5-5. The three components of digital leadership in the future

Deeply Understand People

Understanding what makes people tick, including how they prefer to communicate and what their core drivers are, is the single most valuable competency of an Unnatural Leader.

Knowing how people work and having a deep understanding of how they create their internal version of reality is critical. This is true not only for the people on our teams but, also when we're trying to increase market share with customers, engage with stakeholders and external partners, and gain buy-in from senior executives.

By focusing on the care and growth of people and building a purposeful, contemporary culture, Unnatural Leaders attract the best talent, beating the odds of the global talent war!

Understanding how we (as leaders) work internally—our biases and preferences and being able to choose how we respond to a situation—gives us access to operating in the most effective way possible and rapidly increasing our success rates. Unnatural Leaders view the world as a constantly unfolding and evolving process, one that we actively shape by evolving ourselves. Even as successful, senior leaders, we continue evolving, paddling back out into the swell and looking for new waves to create and ride. Our less successful peers will get washed up onto the beach as they attempt to apply the same old thinking and approaches to new world problems.

Digital Organization

Unnatural Leaders create and grow organizations that are digitally savvy across the whole of the organization. A "digital first" strategy is something that is naturally assumed and not spelled out, and the constant internal utilization of technology to drive innovation and efficiency gains are simply part of the organization's DNA.

Digital organizations don't necessarily provide digital only products and services, but they maximize their use of digital across all functions, including marketing, sales, customer relations, finance, and operations.

Organizations that aren't digital will find themselves out-paced, out-priced, and out-valued by those that are.

Drive and Integrate Key Technology Trends

Riding technology trends is a part of what makes a digital leader great. That has always been the case. Unnatural Leaders do more than that—way more! They identify the key technology trends (such as AI and VR) and strategically incorporate them into the business strategy. They utilize their influencing skills and deep understanding of the business to secure stakeholder buy-in to develop products and services that capture new and existing market sectors.

In short, Unnatural Leaders create the trends for others to ride and integrate!

Unnatural Selection

Unnatural Leaders do Unnatural Selection. Rather than waiting for natural selection to eventually "prune" them from the digital leadership gene pool, they create the future and evolve faster than the pace of change. They learn to ride waves, read currents, develop their strength and fitness, and eventually become the lifeguards of the future as they take over the mentoring and guidance of future leaders who are following in their footsteps.

In the next chapter, I introduce the Unnatural Selection framework.

Summary

Our world and society are changing at an ever-increasing rate. What made a leader successful 10-15 years ago will no longer make a leader successful today and certainly not in another 10-15 years' time.

Understanding people, including ourselves, is the most critical competency we can develop. It allows us to master ourselves, customers, stakeholders, and team. We leverage this increased effectiveness to create and ride the waves of change and avoid being washed up by them.

Self-Reflection Questions

1. How has *your* role changed over the last 10-15 years? Can you map your journey on the Digital Situational Leadership grid shown in Figure 5-1?

2. How do see the changes of the future impacting you personally in your market, industry, region, and country?

3. Which new technology trend or shift in social culture will impact your organization the most? Which will impact you personally the most?

4. How might you prepare yourself and your organization now for these shifts?

5. How deeply do you understand the following (1 being not at all, 5 being a very deep understanding)?

   - Yourself

   - Your teams

   - Your stakeholders

   - Your customers

6. How might your work satisfaction and success levels change if you deeply understood (with a 4 or 5 rating) all four areas listed in the previous question

Unnatural Selection: Evolving Faster Than the Pace of Change

When we are no longer able to change a situation… we are challenged to change ourselves.

—Viktor Frankl[1]

---

[1]*Man's Search for Meaning* (Boston: Beacon Press, 1959)

© James Brett 2019
J. Brett, *Evolving Digital Leadership*, https://doi.org/10.1007/978-1-4842-3606-2_6

The Unnatural Selection framework isn't a prescriptive solution that solves all problems. It is not possible to solve every leader's challenges—they are too complex and varied for one solution to work. Instead, the Unnatural Selection framework is a process that drives our continuous growth, awareness, and consciousness, enabling us to break through our own unique challenges and to drive change in our lives.

Evolving faster than the pace of change means shifting our awareness—awareness of ourselves, of others, and of the world around us. This provides access to an expanded array of perspectives and new understandings of our beliefs, values, preferences, and motivations. Awareness develops our perception of time, to see the present day in the context of an ever-expanding past and future. Our worldview shifts from ethnocentric (our local group or tribe), to world-centric, and eventually to cosmocentric (that of the universe).

Evolving allows us to understand the personal dynamics of our team, stakeholders, and customers and leverage an increasingly wider strategic view of our organization, industry, and society. Evolutionary leaders are inspiring leaders who are able to assess, guide, and shape organizations with grace and ease.

Evolving isn't a one-time process. The Unnatural Selection framework is a process that leaders leverage over the duration of their career. It's specific enough to assist in certain digital leadership challenges and yet broad enough to remain relevant over time. I have no doubt that the framework itself will evolve. It is designed and built for the challenges we face today and in the predicted (short-term) future. Through our community of Unnatural Leaders, we will change the framework as needed, using the feedback and new awareness generated over time. This is a meta-application of the framework on itself.

Just like paddling back out into the swell takes effort, so does evolving ourselves and our cognitive capacities. You have to do the work. You have to want to do the work. I can lead you to water, but you must take a drink yourself.

So how do we "do" Unnatural Selection? How do we evolve faster than the pace of change? It all starts with the evolution helix—the heart of the Unnatural Selection framework.

The Evolution Helix

The evolution helix is a process for developing our awareness with focus, effort, vulnerability, honesty, and self-compassion. It consists of four steps that we progress through in the following order: Awareness, Intention, Attention, and Reflection (see Figure 6-1).

Figure 6-1. The four steps of the evolution helix

Each cycle of the evolution helix is designed to develop and evolve us. This evolution will often be small and incremental; however, there will be times when we get a significant shift in our development in one cycle of the helix. We can consider the four steps of the process (Awareness, Intention, Attention, and Reflection) as a circular process where the reflection at the end of one loop brings new awareness at the beginning the next cycle. However, when we include the vertical development of our expanding awareness, the process takes on a helix shape as we evolve (see Figure 6-2).

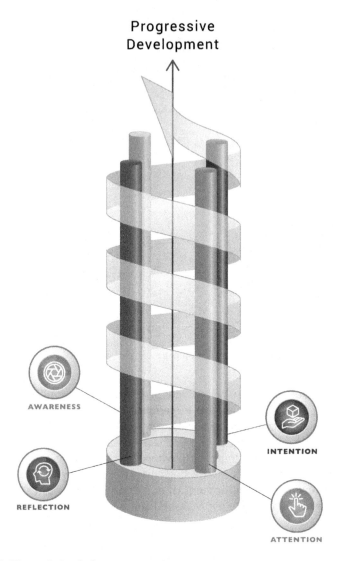

Figure 6-2. The evolution helix

Let's take a look at an iteration of the process and get a basic understanding of each step, starting with Step 1, Awareness.

Step 1: Awareness

We start the process with a particular level of awareness. This awareness is the one that you have right here, right now. It is the awareness that motivated you to read this book and to understand how you might develop your digital leadership skills. We may also be aware of the emotions and energies in our bodies as we go through our day, and how they impact our responses and performance.

> *"Awareness: Knowledge that something exists, or understanding of a situation or subject at the present time based on information or experience."*
>
> —Cambridge Dictionary

We always have awareness. However, when we get busy, stressed, or caught up in life, we can sometimes regress to lower levels of awareness, where we become more reactionary in our actions rather than thoughtfully responding and showing up the way we desire.

For technologists and digital leaders, a common scenario in which this happens is when a particular team member or stakeholder is "just being difficult." We can lose our patience and react with a need to "show him who's right". We do this in a variety of ways, including being overly aggressive, sarcastic, or intellectually beating them down. All too often we get stuck in behaviors that don't serve us well. Maybe we get to win this particular argument, but what happens to the long-term relationship? How does that relationship impact our success? Does the outcome of *winning* this interaction really align with our path to greatness? Maybe or maybe not. Either way, it's hasn't been our choice, has it? Part of awareness is becoming aware of our emotional states and the judgments we are making (of ourselves and others) and then being aware of when we are reacting and not responding consciously.

An increased awareness of what motivates people, how they process information, and how they create their internal mental models of reality is incredibly valuable for leadership success and indeed, in life. It is the primary component of deeply understanding people, which I identified earlier in Chapter 5 and present again in Figure 6-3.

Figure 6-3. The three components of digital leadership success

In Part II, we explore awareness in detail and introduce the Humans as a Full Stack model (see Figure 6-4). The Humans as a Full Stack model increases our awareness of the human levels of development, personality types, and behavior patterns and preferences. This knowledge increases our awareness.

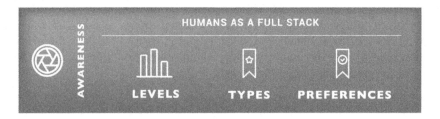

Figure 6-4. Awareness and the Humans as a Full Stack model

Another valuable increase in our awareness comes from gaining clarity on what personal success means to us. Some people are already crystal clear on what success means. However, the majority of us are a little fuzzy and would benefit from investing time defining our personal success and being conscious about what we want in our lives, personally and professionally. We begin this process in Step 2, Intention.

Step 2: Intention

Getting clear on what success means is vital to being successful! Gaining clarity on what we want (and focusing on it) increases our ability to do what's needed to actually achieve it. Intention focuses our attention and our energy, enabling us to respond appropriately to our environment.

Our neurology is bombarded with over 2 million bits of information per second: sights, sounds, smells, temperature, and pressure—most of which is filtered out, allowing us to function without being overloaded. Until you read this sentence, you probably aren't aware of the clothes on your back and the texture and weight of the material (I'm assuming you aren't reading this naked). Our subconscious filters out the details in our daily lives that we don't need.

Another commonly experienced example of this filtering in action happens when we start the process of buying a new car. Have you noticed that, as you finalize your selection down to a specific make and model of car, you begin to see more of this same model on the roads? They were always there, but with our intention to buy one, our subconscious brain put focus on a particular model and now brings them into our awareness.

Our brains filtered out the cars and the clothing on our back because they didn't deem the information useful or relevant at that time. Sometimes our brains filter out information that may indeed be vital to our success. With intention, we adjust these filters to let valuable and related information into our consciousness.

Surprisingly, many people don't actually know what they want, or what success is—success in terms of their role and/or career, for their family, and for themselves. Although success does evolve over time to mean different things, being clear on your current definition of success will bring more of it into your world. In Part III, we use the Unnatural Selection Clarity process (see Figure 6-5) to help develop and set intentions that are appropriate for us and our definition of success.

Figure 6-5. The Clarity process

With new clarity on our individual success, Unnatural Selection recommends three intentions that drive our evolution and digital leadership success. These intentions are focused around the three critical components of success for a digital leader: Personal Success, Team Success, and Stakeholder Success.

Successful leaders balance their focus and attention on developing themselves, their teams, and their stakeholder relationships. A leader must constantly evolve if she is going to create and ride the waves of change. A leader is not a leader if she isn't growing the individuals and teams that follow her by focusing on team success. And finally, successful leaders know that stakeholder relationships are how things actually get done in organizations, and as such, they prioritize stakeholder success. The three intentions that we set for personal, team, and stakeholder success are to be passionately curious, move from performance management to growth, and build long lasting, mutually beneficial relationships (see Figure 6-6). Let's take a quick look at what each of these three intentions means.

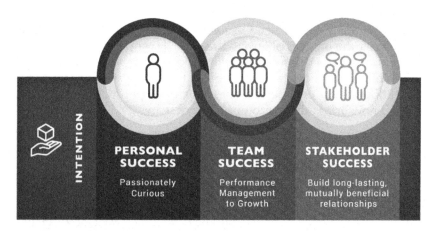

Figure 6-6. The three Unnatural Selection intentions

Personal Intention: Be Passionately Curious

Curiosity allows us to search for new insights or perspectives and then generate new solutions (creating new waves of change). It also allows us to develop the skills we need to identify new waves of change that others have created. Without curiosity, we stagnate and operate from our historic experiences. When we become passionately curious, we enjoy the process of discovery and learning, which helps us evolve.

Team Intention: Move from Performance Management to Growth

Digital leaders often struggle with developing high-performance teams and long-term capability. A big part of that struggle is the lack of investment in the personal growth of the people in their teams. This struggle often manifests itself as a resistance to dealing with underperforming team members. In reality, the under performance is that of the digital leader who has not supported, challenged, or given fast and regular feedback. Our intention here is to flip this situation around and sustainably focus on the growth of our people, starting when they join the organization.

Stakeholder Intention: Build Long-Lasting, Mutually Beneficial Relationships

Long-lasting, mutually beneficial relationships allow digital leaders to execute faster and more effectively across their organizations. Relationships, not process, are how things get done. Mutually beneficial relationships align outcomes across departments and functions and focus on the long-term sustainable growth of the organization.

Our intentions focus our attention on what is important—our self, our teams, and our stakeholders. Our attention guides our energy and determines what we do (and don't do) as a digital leader—it's how we execute.

Step 3: Attention

Attention (described in detail in Part IV) is what we "attend to"—it's how we do digital leadership. Our leadership attention is spent completing tasks, having conversations, delivering presentations, and attending meetings. We might even invest in some form of training or learning (books like this included), which directly impact our awareness and/or skillset.

Without first setting a higher intention, we can fall into the trap of carrying out these actions simply to get them done and tick the completed box. The difference between doing "leadership" and being an Unnatural Leader is that Unnatural Leaders hold a higher intention and don't complete activities for the sake of completing them.

> *"If you don't pay appropriate attention to what has your attention, it will take more of your attention than it deserves."*
>
> —David Allen[2]

---

[2]*Making It All Work* (NY: Viking, 2008)

The attention of Unnatural Leaders is focused by the trinity of intentions we set on self, team, and stakeholders. We use the three attention processes (see Figure 6-7) that assist us in executing each of these intentions in a concrete manner.

Figure 6-7. The three attention processes

Attention to Self

Unnatural Leaders are proactive, not reactive. They take ownership of their time and attention and they use intention to devise systems that keep them working on the right things in the best ways to achieve success. These systems help them overcome the key challenges of choosing what to work on, help them hold the right frames and perspectives on the task at hand, and help them focus on execution and delivery results.

Attention to Team

We focus our attention on our people and teams because we value their growth and development. We attend to their development by understanding each individual's Human Full Stack. We coach and support them to their maximum potential. It is critical that our teams evolve faster than the pace of change if we want our organization to create and respond to disruption.

Attention to Stakeholders

The Stakeholder Attention process guides us through building long-lasting, mutually beneficial relationships. We start by ensuring that we have identified the relevant stakeholders and then develop our understanding of what is important to them. We then align (where possible) to their outcomes and use a range of techniques to positively influence them.

As we execute our Unnatural Leadership, we are likely to perform highly at some activities and less so at others. In order to appraise our performance, we need to reflect on what we do, why we do it, and how it drives us toward or away from success. We do this in Step 4: Reflection.

Step 4: Reflection

Reflection is the process of taking time to sit and think deeply about our past experiences and what the future may hold. We look at our past to assess how well our outcomes aligned with our intentions, and how we might adapt in order to improve our performance and experiences in the future.

Pausing to reflect can feel unproductive to busy leaders. Because of this, so many leaders don't make the time to regularly stop and reflect, unless they are forced to by a significant, painful failure. However, reflection is the key to accelerating our evolution and evolving faster than the pace of change.

Unnatural Leaders use a variety of methods to assist in reflection (see Figure 6-8). This includes journaling, feedback, coaching, mentoring, and levels of perspective (see Chapters 17 and 18).

Figure 6-8. Past and future reflection methods

Reflecting by ourselves is powerful and valuable. Reflecting with external assistance from a coach or mentor can accelerate our evolution by showing us blind spots that could otherwise have taken us months or years to see on our own.

Reflection powers our evolution, and personal evolution is a process of growth. It's practically impossible to grow when we hold a fixed mindset about who we are.

A Growth Mindset

The concept of a growth mindset has been popularized by Carol Dweck, a Stanford psychologist, in her book *Mindset: The New Psychology of Success.*[3] At the core of a growth mindset (see Figure 6-9) is a belief that we, as human beings, evolve over time, and we are constantly growing, learning,

---

[3]NY: Random House, 2006

and developing our capacities. In contrast, a fixed mindset leaves us limited by the belief that our personalities, intelligence, and who we take ourselves to be are fundamentally set in stone.

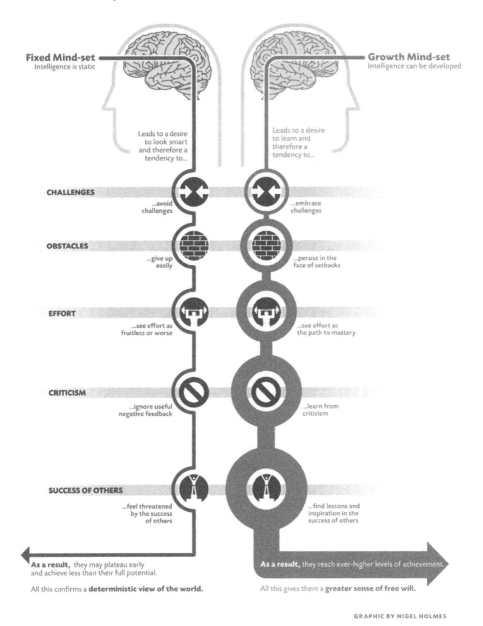

GRAPHIC BY NIGEL HOLMES

Figure 6-9. Carol Dweck's fixed versus growth mindsets (image courtesy Nigel Holmes)

Which one do you believe? If you think people are more fixed in nature and can't change much, ask yourself why you think that? Could it be you don't want to change for some reason? It might be an excuse that masks the fear and difficulty involved in personal change.

Are you the same person you were when you were a teenager? Do you lead the same way now that you did in your first leadership role? The answer is very likely to be no! You aren't the same person you were a decade ago, last year, or even just yesterday!

If we don't grow and evolve, our environment—our business verticals—will grow and evolve past us. I'm sure the leaders of Blockbuster video held limiting beliefs about themselves and their business as the market got disrupted and evolved faster than they did. Change is uncomfortable until we do it again and again, and then change becomes our new normal. As we embrace change, it becomes an interesting and desirable part of our life experience.

Summary

The Unnatural Selection framework (see Figure 6-10) is designed to assist you in your constant evolution—an evolution in which you can create and respond to the waves of change. It focuses deeply on the human, psychological aspects of leadership and bootstraps your evolution by giving you the tools (such as the Humans as a Full Stack model) to grow yourself, your teams, and your stakeholder relationships.

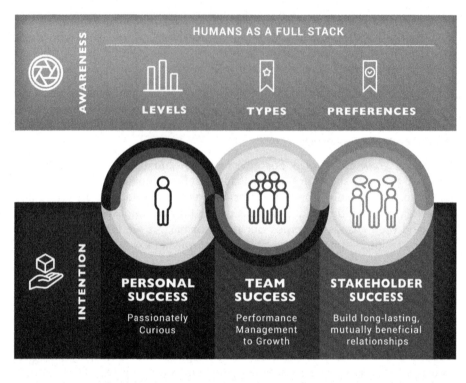

Figure 6-10. The Unnatural Selection framework

The evolution helix is a four-step, iterative process that consists of Awareness, Intention, Attention, and Reflection, which we cycle through on a continual basis as we use the helix to power our progressive development and raise our awareness.

The three intentions of 1) being passionately curious, 2) moving from performance management to growing our teams and, 3) building long-lasting, mutually beneficial stakeholder relationships focus our attention on what is important to sustain successful leadership.

The final step—Reflection—allows us to constantly adapt and improve our performance and to identify and create future disruptions. Reflection develops new levels of awareness that we use in the next cycle of the Intention/Attention/Reflection process.

Self-Reflection Questions

1. Can you think of a time when your awareness shifted? What impact did it have on the way you operated?

2. How much of an impact does getting distracted have on your quality of life and career?

3. Describe a time when you were so focused and intent on something that it was relatively easy to achieve? What intention did you set?

4. Do you consciously choose how you spend your time? Or do you get pulled into reaction mode on a regular basis (urgent versus important)? How might you change this approach?

5. How often do you take the time to reflect and integrate your experiences? What has been the most effective way you have integrated your lessons?

Summary of Part I: Digital Leadership

Becoming a great digital leader is a challenging process. We must undergo a number of shifts in order to make the successful transition to leadership. To assist in the acceleration of this journey, the Career Success Pyramid provides five key recommendations that leverage over 400 years of combined leadership experience.

Once in a leadership role, we can then utilize the digital situational leadership model to consciously assess and choose how much we focus on the key leadership capacities of tactical vs. strategic, and delivery vs. culture.

Over the next few decades, a number of key technical advancements will occur that will change society and industry forever. VR and AI have the potential to bring about the end of the office block (and cities) and the loss of many jobs that exist today. As leaders of digital organizations, we will either lead these waves of change or we will be deluged by the accelerating disruption.

The rate of change is so rapid that it's almost impossible to produce a solution that will remain relevant long enough to have an impact. So, we need to develop tools and frameworks that facilitate our evolution and allow us to adapt as the world around us transforms. The Unnatural Selection framework is one such tool.

The following four parts of the book focus on the four steps of the evolution helix. I start Part II with a deep dive into Step 1, Awareness, and introduce the Humans as a Full Stack model.

Awareness

What is necessary to change a person is to change his awareness of himself.

—Abraham Maslow[1]

Raising our awareness is the first step in the evolution helix (Figure 1) and is the main focus of evolving faster than the pace of change. The awareness shifts you get from the Unnatural Selection framework are mostly achieved in the field as you apply the evolution helix to your digital leadership role.

---

[1]William M. Stephens, *Life In The Open Sea* (McGraw-Hill, 1972), 21.

Figure 1. Awareness, step 1 of the evolution helix

In Part II of the book, we bootstrap the most critical aspect of Unnatural Leadership Awareness: understanding people. Gaining a better understanding of ourselves, our team, our stakeholders, and our customers allows us to respond better, grow faster, influence more, and deliver more effectively.

The chapters in Part II are based on a decade of my experience in coaching, psychology, NLP, Neurosemantics, Leadership Agility, and the Enneagram and over 20 years in digital. Understanding people is a passion of mine—this book and the Unnatural Selection framework is the integration of my experience in both digital and psychology.

I've integrated these two worlds here in Part II and developed the Humans as a Full Stack model, which simplifies the behaviors of a person and makes them understandable to technologists by drawing the analogy to that of a full technical stack, with a frontend, an API layer, and a backend. By the end of Chapter 10, you will have a significantly deeper understanding of how people develop over time, the impact of personality type on responses and behaviors, how we process and filter external information, and the impact these factors have on successful communication.

It's going to be epic!

Humans as a Full Stack

I'm sure the universe is full of intelligent life. It's just been too intelligent to come here.

—Arthur C. Clarke[1]

People are complicated! There are currently around 7 billion people on the planet. 7 billion individuals, all with a unique set of values, beliefs, opinions, preferences, memories, and biases. Not only is that number significant, the human personality and mind is also incredibly complex, making it virtually impossible to accurately predict and understand even one or two people.

The good news is we don't need to. To be an Unnatural Leader, we simply have to know enough about people and personalities to stay ahead. Investing time in understanding psychology and how our brains work, significantly impacts our leadership performance. In true Agile fashion, we focus on developing the most valuable skills and understanding first, and wherever possible, find hacks to short circuit the learning effort.

Humans as a Full Stack (see Figure 7-1) is one such hack. I developed this model to easily explain the human internal processing, which is analogous to a full technology stack. So let's take a look and see how easy it can be to "hack the stack".

---

[1] IRC discussion at Scifi.com (1 November 1996) with Arthur C. Clarke and Gentry Lee

© James Brett 2019
J. Brett, *Evolving Digital Leadership*, https://doi.org/10.1007/978-1-4842-3606-2_7

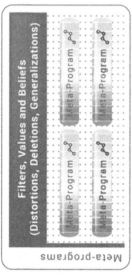
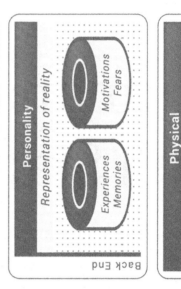

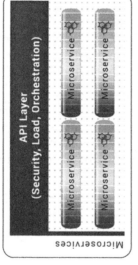
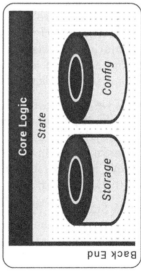

Figure 7-1. Humans as a Full Stack model

Let's first look at the components of the technology stack (the left side) before we explain how it applies to humans (the right side).

Frontend

The frontend is how the users interact with the app, through a visual, audible, or physical user interface (UI). The UI is designed in alignment with an intended (or all-too-often unintended) user experience (UX) and is the mechanism that users see, hear, touch, feel, or even smell. Users interact through a specific device—a laptop, desktop, mobile, or wearable—where each has a customized experience offering, and in some instances dramatically different functionality. In early release products, the experiences often focus on one particular device, leaving others unused or reduced in functionality (i.e., mobile-first offerings) until the product-market fit is validated. An example frontend is a browser-based, online banking web app.

API and Microservices Layer

In a well architected technical product, the core logic is abstracted away from the frontend implementation and accessed through an application programming interface (API) layer. The API layer usually provides a range of services, including load balancing, security, and orchestration of the request to an appropriate microservice. The microservice encapsulates a discrete unit of functionality that accepts a request, processes it, and responds. Often these services will communicate and request data from a backend system, and in some situations translate communication protocols suitable for the backend. In the banking example, services for balance retrieval, transactions, and depositing funds are commonplace.

Backend

Backend systems range from simple data stores to complex (and sometimes legacy) mainframe systems. They often contain considerable business logic and troublesome state management, which heavily utilizes a persistent data store. Banking backends are often mainframe based and responsible for storing customer banking information and records, and they often integrate with the national and international banking systems.

This stack is definitely not a contemporary serverless one. It is more akin to what you might find in most large enterprises today. But this conversation isn't about tech stacks, as enjoyable as they are. Let's progress and talk about the human analogy.

Human Frontend

When interacting with someone, the human frontend is what you see and hear (and potentially feel and smell) during the interaction. It's how they present themselves in dress choices (their UI) and how they speak, move, and respond to your interactions with them (their UX). A person's neurology (their five senses) captures information and requests from the world and then converts that into electrical systems ready for the brain to process.

The more we know and understand the person we're interacting with, the more predictable their response will be. This is, after all, the end game for us! If we can predict their response (or a narrow set of possible responses), we can design our interactions to generate the response we are hoping for.

Like a tech frontend, humans have a preferred, or "more functional," communication channel. Some people are naturally wired to be more visual, preferring to see, draw, and visualize information. Some prefer auditory; they like to talk and listen and are often highly conversational in nature. Others are kinesthetic, where movement is key element of their communication style.

The key here is to know that if you are trying to communicate with someone on their less preferred channel, your effectiveness will be drastically reduced. I personally am wired for visual communications; I find it difficult to remember details that I am given verbally. For example, if someone tells me the pin combination to a door, I will often forget it quite quickly. However, if I write it down and see the code, I find I remember it significantly longer, sometimes years later. Understanding and conceptualizing new ideas and solutions amplifies this difference.

Great communications combine visual and auditory information to ensure the best impact when dealing with numerous people simultaneously, say in a meeting or presentation.

Once a frontend interaction has been initiated, the request is passed to the equivalent of the API layer.

Human API and Microservices Layer

Once we receive a message, our brains filter, distort, delete and generalize the information and call into our meta-programs for processing. As I've mentioned, our neurology is bombarded with over 2 million bits of information a second. We don't have the capacity to process all this information consciously, so our brains filter it based on our values, beliefs, preferences, intent, and mindset. Let's dive deeper into three of these filters: distortions, deletions, and generalizations.

Distortions

Distortions are when we distort an external event and make it less impactful (smaller) or more significant (larger) than it actually is. Maybe someone paid us a small compliment, which we distort into something grander because it makes us feel good and gives us a positive feeling. Alternatively, we might receive feedback that we then distort negatively into personal criticism. Distortions are analogous to the API layer prioritizing certain requests to the services.

Deletions

Deletion is the process by which we subconsciously remove "unnecessary" information from our consciousness. Consider the cars on the road that you never notice until you start looking at a model to purchase and then you see them everywhere! Deletions can be subtler in nature; for example, we may delete a compliment from a person. Maybe we don't think they are being genuine or maybe we believe we aren't worthy of the compliment.

Deletions allow our brains to operate effectively. Without deletions, we would need to process all input received into our senses, which would simply overload our ability to operate and think with any level of clarity. Human deletions are similar to the API layer denying unauthorized access to services. The request for the service comes into the API layer (or brain) and is deleted or blocked from being processed.

Generalizations

Generalizations allow us to process and communicate efficiently. All nouns in language are generalizations. Banana describes a fruit, which is a food, a sweet food, green to yellow in color, and safe to eat. Banana says all those things, in one simple word. It generalizes all bananas and their descriptions. Without generalizations, it would take considerable effort to process the external world, let alone communicate with others.

We also develop our generalizations through the experiences we have. If, for instance, we take two vacations in New York city and it rains both times, we might generalize and say "it always rains in New York". Generalizations usually develop after multiple similar experiences. They can, however, develop after just one sufficiently intense experience.

We can hear a person's generalizations when they talk, and we can read them when they write. When generalizing, a person may use words such as "always," "never," "customers," "developers," and even "leadership" as generalizations.

All generalizations are false, including this one.

—Mark Twain

In the tech stack, generalizations are akin to the system batching up similar frontend requests and providing a single response.

The challenges with all three of these filters are the blind spots they create in service of efficiency. For example, confirmation bias is a phenomenon that stems from distortions, deletions, and generalizations and significantly impacts our leadership ability. Awareness, at its essence, includes becoming aware of the filters that we and others are using.

We now know how deletions, generalizations, and distortions work to filter information from our frontend to our brains. Let's next look at how meta-programs process and translate information in our brains.

Meta-Programs

Meta-programs act as perceptual filters as we attempt to create an internal representation of reality in our minds. Each meta-program is specified as a continuum, with poles at either end. Each pole describes a preference for processing reality. One of the simplest meta-programs to understand is the Cognitive Scale meta-program (see Figure 7-2), which i will use to explain how meta-programs work.

Figure 7-2. Cognitive Scale meta-program

The Cognitive Scale meta-program determines how a person prefers to think about and process the world, either through the big picture (global) or through finer details (detail). "Big picture thinkers" are often irritated by, and tend to ignore, the details in any given situation. People with global tendencies usually write in bullet points and use generalized language. When offered details, they often interrupt and ask for context or a higher-level systemic view of the situation. People with a preference for detail write lengthy documents and emails, can be very specific when sharing information, and often ask lots of detail-focused questions.

Understanding this meta-program, and having the flexibility to adjust our style to think in both big picture and detail, is how we develop our four capacities of Tactical, Strategic, Delivery, and Culture of the Digital Situational Leadership model. We dive deeper into meta-programs in Chapter 9 and learn how to tune and adjust them.

Once information is filtered by our meta-programs, our brains call into the backend, with the modified information payload.

Human Backend

In our human backend, we utilize our personality structures, stored experiences, and beliefs to create an internal representation of our external reality. This internal representation is much like a movie that plays in our minds that has a particular size, color, music, and sound and sometimes smells and temperature. Intense and emotional movies tend to be bright, colorful, loud, and seemingly played on a very large screen at the front of our minds. Other movies are played more quietly on a small screen and maybe in black and white. All of these movies we create are manufactured in the mind and are created specifically by our backend to represent what we perceive as reality.

Like a legacy backend, there is a lot of old logic here, a good deal of which is formed and created in early childhood. Here is where our core personality type sits. We create a perception of reality (from our early experiences), process it, and respond accordingly based on our motivations and fears. Our personality may respond differently to the same request depending on the current load (our stress levels) or erroneous state (our internal representation of reality). We may even respond with the human equivalent of a 500 Server error—a blank expression and no communication!

We will look at the personality types and structures in detail in Chapter 10.

Deobfuscation[2] of humans involves the following steps:

1. Identify the preferred communication channel or neurological input channel.

2. Understand that certain information will be deleted, distorted, and generalized.

---

[2]Convert something that is difficult to understand to something that is simple, straightforward, and understandable.

3. Identify key meta-programs that act as perceptual filters (for yourself and others).

4. Use the Enneagram to understand the motivations and fears of the personality types in order to predict what kind of response we will get back.

Once we have an understanding at this level, we can then choose the appropriate approach to connect with our stakeholders, teams, and customers.

As humans evolve through each stage of development, either from early childhood to adult, or through each of the more advanced stages of adulthood, the whole stack gets a new and improved release of software. Like most good releases, the new release has improved functionality, better processing ability, and potentially some fundamentally new features. Luckily, for humans this new software deployment is not a waterfall, big bang delivery (imagine just how messy that would be). Upgrades to the human stack are rolled out in a small, iterative, Continuous Delivery process. In the next chapter, we take a deeper look at some of these upgrades.

Summary

The "full stack" metaphor in the technical world lends itself well to simplifying the complexities of human behavior. By understanding the three layers that process external input, we can get a deeper understanding of an individual, which dramatically increases our effectiveness as a leader.

Self-Reflection Questions

1. What is your preferred mechanism to process information: visual, auditory, or kinesthetic?

2. What do you think is your boss's (or most significant stakeholder's) preferred mechanism?

3. How might the answers from Questions 1 and 2 impact your ability to be successful?

4. Are you a "big picture" thinker or do you prefer finer details?

5. Write down five generalizations that you make in professional contexts.

6. Which of the generalizations identified in Question 4 are valuable and which might cause problems?

Experts and Achievers

We cannot solve our problems with the same thinking we used to create them.

—Often attributed to Albert Einstein

Bob was the head of product development for a large insurance company. He had been in his role for six months having left a successful technology product company to tackle bigger challenges. Bob was a smart, talented technologist who had made the transition to leadership better than most. His empathy and soft-skills were far above average and he had an outstanding track record, having delivered a number of market-leading products over his career.

In his new role, Bob had managed to secure some significant new hires and build a really competent, technical team to start the product build. The team was co-located, cross-functional, and had all the tools and facilities they needed to build a great product.

Initially, everything went well. Bob helped set the vision and constraints for the product and posed challenges for the team to solve. Secretly, Bob thought that this might be one of those unicorn product builds—the ones where the product-market fit looks great, funding and stakeholder support are secured, and the team is highly competent and engaged.

© James Brett 2019

J. Brett, *Evolving Digital Leadership*, https://doi.org/10.1007/978-1-4842-3606-2_8

Yes, you guessed it, there is a "but". As the team entered their third month of iterations, it became obvious to Bob that progress wasn't being made as fast as he had hoped. The deliveries just weren't being made, with the team caught up in defining and building a technically excellent product. One of the rock-star developers he hired was becoming disruptive. He was forcing his opinions as fact on the more junior developers and shutting down their ideas and contributions almost instantly. Bob stepped in and had the difficult conversation with the developer about his behavior.

As time went on, things didn't improve. The team just didn't seem to be paying attention to, or even care about, delivering on time. Bob tried a variety of techniques and interventions, including one-on-ones and a facilitated retrospective. He observed that the main challenge was prioritization—everything seemed valuable, every architectural aspect critical, and engineering practices were the team's sole focus and priority.

This was an extremely technically competent team who had all that they needed to deliver but just didn't seem to have an eye on performance and outcomes. This frustrated Bob immensely, as he just couldn't understand these really smart, brilliant people. After all, when Bob was last in a product team, cutting code, he was very much outcome focused. His ability to write code and keep the team focused on deliverables is what got him his promotion.

As time went on, the team continued to let deadlines slip, and Bob continued to get dragged into managing the weekly iterations. Over time, Bob's stakeholders began to lose confidence in him, and he began to burn out. Although Bob typically preferred a flat organization, Bob decided to bring in an Engineering Manager to lead the technical team. Although the extra layer of hierarchy allowed Bob to complete his other activities, the command and control style of the Engineering Manager meant the team's culture and morale went from bad to worse. A few months later, the project was abandoned as attrition rate within the team peaked and delivery became impossible.

This scenario is all too common with product teams. What Bob hadn't yet understood was that he had gone through a cognitive upgrade of his own Human Stack (his API and backend) that moved him from the Expert level of development to Achiever level and his team hadn't. In this chapter we are going to look at levels of development and how they impact our performance, both as digital leaders and on the people in our teams.

Stages of Development

It is important to understand these human stack upgrades because they radically affect how we process the world around us, our motivators, and how we interact with our fellow humans. While each upgrade is small and iterative in nature, developmental psychologists have grouped the upgrades into what are called stages of development. Our own developmental stage impacts the frames we use to make sense of the world around us. The developmental stages of the people on our teams directly impact productivity and the culture of the organization.

The numerous developmental psychologists who have studied and researched stages of development each produced models that identify the stages in different ways—some utilize names (Leadership Agility, Bill Joiner), some use colors (Integral Theory, Ken Wilber), others use orders (Theory of Adult Development, Robert Kegan). Figure 8-1 shows the stages as identified and defined by Bill Joiner and his Leadership Agility model[1].

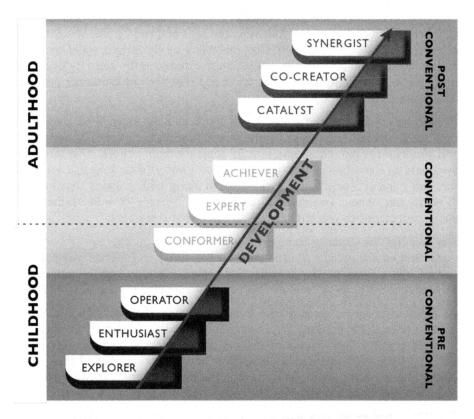

Figure 8-1. Stages of development as outlined in Leadership Agility by Bill Joiner

---

[1]For more details see *Leadership Agility: Five Levels of Mastery for Anticipating and Initiating Change* by Bill Joiner and Stephen Josephs (Jossey-Bass, 2007); https://unnatural.io/link/b81

Each stage is a major upgrade release of our Human Full Stack. If we consider the standard software delivery release terminology, it outlines release numbers using the following format: Major: Minor: Revision. So, mapping back to the stages, each stage is a major release. When we develop ourselves and make a cognitive shift from, say Expert to Achiever, we are completing a Major upgrade (i.e., from 5.x.x to 6.0.0). These upgrades happen over time with smaller developments being released along the way, just as we would move from a 5.8.0 release to a 5.9.0 release before the major release of 6.0.0.

To understand stage development and the stages, let's first take a look at the (easier to understand) childhood stages[2].

When a child is born, she has little cognitive function compared to an adult. However, she quickly develops cognitive capacities and abilities that allow her to function and communicate (between the ages of 0 and 2). She develops her physical abilities such as color vision, the ability to sit upright, walk, and then talk. As her awareness levels progress and she develops the capacity of object permanence, the ability to visually see things that are not physically present. This is the Explorer stage.

Around her second birthday she enters the Enthusiast stage. This stage lasts until age 6 or 7. During this stage, she moves beyond her physical sense of self and experiences herself as emotionally separate from others. This stronger awarness of her physcial and emotional self gives rise to language where I, me, and mine are expressed with strength along with phrases that include "I want" or "mine". The stage often becomes a battle of wills as the child easily expresses her will but can't always get what she wants.

She only has the capacity to see the world from the perspective of her own wants and needs, and she doesn't yet have the ability to generate insights into herself, her actions, or the behaviors of others. Most parents recognize the early part of this stage as "the terrible twos," when tantrums happen frequently.

As children progress through the Enthusiast stage, they develop the ability of representational thinking. Representational thinking allows us to integrate multiple sensory impressions of objects and categorize them (for example, cars and rockets). They also develop their basic understanding of time, from talking about what they might do tomorrow (around age 3), to what parents may have promised for them for their next birthday (around 4 years).

The Operator stage is typical for the grade school years of life. Here the child develops concrete operations—the ability to think about specific properties of objects such as color, shape, and size. This ability allows them

---

[2]For a more detailed description of the earlier stages, read Appendix B of *Leadership Agility* by Bill Joiner and Stephen Josephs (Jossey-Bass, 2007).

to distinguish between imagination and reality. Critically they also develop an ability to regulate their impulses as they anticipate the short-term impact of their actions.

The Conformer stage starts around the ages of 11-12 for girls and usually a year later for boys. Conformers define themselves as part of a tribe or group and often lose their full sense of identity. The price to pay for being part of a group is loyalty and obedience, and as such, they accept norms and rules of the group without question or objection. They learn that to be part of a group, they need to be a likeable person who is "nice," "good looking," and "pleasant". Their black and white thinking now shifts to an "us and them" (rather than I), but they still don't have a sense of a separate adult identity.

Most of us develop into the Expert stage in high school and graduate university to join the workforce at this level. The earlier childhood stages are progressed through in a linear fashion for healthy children, usually advancing at a similar rate guided by the structured school environment. The adult stages, however, have no guaranteed progression—some of us live long lives and die elderly at the Expert stage, while others reach significantly higher stages in their early 20s or 30s.

The adult stages become increasingly more complex to understand and far too deep to cover here. This book is about digital leadership, so I am going to focus on the key stages of the Leadership Agility framework. Leadership Agility takes the stages of development and identifies specific adult capacities required to lead in increasingly complex scenarios. Joiner defines and explains how leaders operate at each stage, and the specific capacities that require development, namely pivotal conversations, leading teams, and leading organizational change.

Figure 8-2 outlines the five stages defined by the Leadership Agility framework.

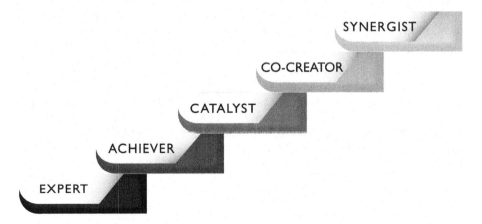

Figure 8-2. The five stages of the Leadership Agility framework

The leadership development journey begins at the bottom, with the Expert stage, and moves one stage at a time. Joiner's research identified that the majority of managers assessed were at the Expert or Achiever stages of development. The actual estimates of the distribution of leaders are 55% Expert, 35% Achiever, and 10% at Catalyst or later[3]. For this reason, I focus on the three levels—Expert, Achiever, and Catalyst—which make up more than 90% of the world's leaders.

The transition from one stage to the next occurs through reflective action. We perform actions, step back and reflect on the impact of the actions, and then adapt our approach. When we are ready to move to the next stage, we do this reflection with the new awareness and intent of the next stage.

For example, when experts become frustrated with the sheer volume of knowledge, information, and data that they need to absorb for their role, they try to work longer and longer hours until they burn out. At this point, they take a step back and reflect on what they are doing. They usually realize that the more they know, the more there is to know, and they begin their progression to the Achiever stage, where information is prioritized based on outcomes and goals.

> The more I live, the more I learn. The more I learn, the more I realize, the less I know.

> —Often attributed to Michel Legrand

The shift to each higher stage transcends and includes all earlier stages. A person at the Achiever stage has full access to the frames, knowledge, and capacities of the Expert (and earlier) stages should it be required. When trying to understand what it means to transcend and include stages, it can help to think about the earlier childhood stages. It wouldn't be very productive if we developed the ability to walk and then lost it at the next stage of development, so we carry that knowledge with us through life.

Each subsequent stage provides a greater perspective on ourselves, others, and the challenges faced. Joiner uses the analogy of a camera and lens that is focused on a specific challenge. At the earlier stages, our lens is a fixed (say 50mm) lens, with a rigid, narrow perspective. The Expert stage then brings the first (limited) zoom lens to our mental camera, giving us a limited ability to zoom out and, when required, zoom back in to the scenario. Each stage adds more and more zoom capability, zooming out to say, a team challenge, then to the organizational context, then to market dynamics, and eventually a global

---

[3] Joiner's research-based estimates, based on four research projects reported by Bill Torbert, totaling 384 managers.

context (and back again as needed). These broader perspectives on how we view the world also include the ability to see character traits, patterns, and structures of both ourselves and the people we interact with.

Try this exercise with me: Take your hands and position them together to create a viewing frame, as shown in Figure 8-3.

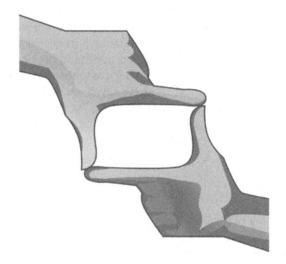

Figure 8-3. Frame your view with your hands

Now place them so that this book (or electronic view of this book) fills the entire frame (this will usually be around 15cm/6in from the book). This view is how we focus on a particular challenge. This limited, constrained view and perspective is akin to one of the early stages of development. All that is in focus and awareness is the book itself—the immediate problem we are trying to solve. If a page of the book fills more than our little frame of reference, we cannot be sure we are even looking at a book.

Now move your hands farther away, to about 1 meter/3 feet from the book. Our perspective now includes more of the book and its surroundings. We may be able to see a desk or table, a computer, maybe a coffee cup, and even a small portion of the room we are in. This higher stage gives us more context and information about the problem we are focusing on. We can now see more of the world and how it's impacting our view of the book, and the other components that were always right there next to book (like a coffee cup), which we didn't initially focus on.

Now, release your hands and take in the whole view of the room you are in, while referring to the book and its location. We can now identify light sources, potentially other people in the room, or other rooms, etc. We now have a wide, "systems view" of the book. With this information available and held in our mind, we can then put our initial frame back in position and focus in on the book, holding an awareness of the room we just saw. This awareness of the bigger picture is developed as we advance through the stages of development.

Coupled with the ability to zoom in and out and obtain broader perspectives, is our ability to comprehend time, both further into the future and back into the past. Early stages, such as Expert, can comprehend time beyond 1 year. But, as leaders, they find it most compelling to focus only up to 12 months ahead. As we progress to later stages, such as Achiever, we expand this focus to 3-5 years. Even later stages are capable of spanning hundreds or even thousands of years. This broader sense of time is critical for a digital leader in order to identify future trends and operate strategically.

Expert Stage

Experts love solving problems. They work hard on problems and when the going gets tough, they work even harder. A common belief that experts hold is that the harder they look for (or refine) a solution, the better it will be. Experts love to demonstrate their competence, and they thrive on the recognition of their contribution to the solution.

All knowledge is valuable and the acquisition of new knowledge and expertise is a key motivator for experts. As such, prioritization can become a challenge for many leaders at this stage of their development. In *Drive*[4], Pink defines the three components of motivation as Autonomy, Mastery, and Purpose. Mastery is a primary focus for those of us at the Expert stage.

Experts have a primary style that is either assertive or accommodating. This style is determined by the individual's personality and flavors their interactions with others. Experts who have an assertive style exercise it more strongly and become more dominant if they feel like they have the authority or a higher-ranking role. Equally their assertiveness is reduced in scenarios where they believe they don't have authority.

There are three areas of functionality that are upgraded with each Human Stack release that are of specific interest to digital leaders: Team Operation, Leadership, and Stakeholder Management. Let's break these down from an expert's perspective.

---

[4]Daniel H. Pink, *Drive: The Surprising Truth About What Motivates Us* (Riverhead, 2011).

Experts as Team Members

Most technologists begin their career at the Expert stage of development, and as such most Product Development teams have a strong representation of experts.

Experts usually find their own problem definitions and solutions the most compelling. Assertive experts tend to argue their position quite strongly. Their arguments can be forceful when they consider themselves to have authority. Experts with the accommodating style still find their solutions most compelling but will tend to defer to others (especially those with authority).

Their focus on mastery and problem solving can often leave achievers frustrated by their lack of outcome and delivery focus. This is amplified by their shorter term, tactical focus, ranging from the present day to around 12 months into the future. For some team members, mastering the technology and/or mastering the delivery process can be more important than achieving customer-oriented outcomes (an achiever's aspiration).

Expert Leadership

Experts implicitly assume that leadership is about expertise and authority. They assume great leaders have deep knowledge of their field and enjoy people seeking them out to provide answers to tough challenges. This is validated when they are promoted into leadership roles having demonstrated expertise in their field.

When an expert is looking for (or being offered) advice, they will first look to the credibility and authority of the source (qualifications, recognized expert in the field, etc.), dismissing anyone who doesn't meet their own criteria of being an expert.

An expert leader operates more tactically and their focus is usually only on the teams and areas of the organization under their direct authority. Their strong problem-solving orientation leads them to solving specific challenges, often missing broader innovation opportunities. Experts prefer an individual one-on-one approach when leading, as opposed to developing a team of direct reports. The one-on-one interactions give them finer grained control of the individuals involved and maintain their own deep understanding of the work being completed. In essence, experts have not yet developed the capacity to think in systems and apply that thinking to their team or businesses.

Expert Stakeholder Management

Stakeholders are generally dealt with by experts on an "as needed" basis, often focused on one or two key stakeholders who may assist or impede their current initiative's success. In essence, the Expert stage stakeholder management is mostly considered a necessary "political evil" to get the job done.

The style and approach they take with stakeholders depends on whether they believe they have authority over the stakeholder or not and whether their natural style is assertive or accommodating. Experts often use a more assertive style when they believe they have authority, and switch to a more passive style when they are subordinate to the stakeholder.

Expert to Achiever Transition

The transition from expert to achiever is often brought about by frustration with acquiring, what seems like, an endless amount of detailed domain and product knowledge. Often this frustration results in a buildup of stress, fatigue, and in some cases burnout. This stress pushes the individuals to question their current mode of operation and the personal cost of valuing expertise so highly. This is akin to the number of defects in the technical stack becoming unmanageable and requiring a major release of functionality or a rewrite to address the suboptimal way the API layer and backend are processing the world.

As experts reflect on their operation (and burnout), their further developed reflective thinking fuels their ability for strategic and systems thinking and promotes an increased awareness of individual subjectivity. Experts shift from doing a task well to achieving outcomes valued by the larger organization. This transition to achiever gives them the ability to prioritize information using concepts such as the Pareto Principle (or 80/20 rule), where 80% of the value comes from 20% of the work or effort.

Achiever Stage

Achievers are goal oriented and focus their energy on achieving outcomes rather than gaining expertise in specific areas. Strategy and strategic operation are core to the Achiever stage of development, as such achievers spend a lot of their time working out strategies for success. The drive toward success and achievement at this stage is motivated by rewards and recognition. The rewards can be either monetary or status-based (public recognition or promotion); therefore role titles are usually important for achievers. At this stage, leaders also begin to understand the individual character traits of those around them and predict the basic behaviors of their team and stakeholders. Achievers see understanding behaviors as valuable and apply this idea to themselves. They are then able to modify their own behaviors to reach their goals. Unlike experts, achievers are aware that leadership is about motivating others and they associate the behaviors of others with their underlying motivations, rather than character traits of a person.

Achievers as Team Members

Achievers in teams love to identify and set team goals and develop processes and strategies to enable the team to achieve their outcomes. Achievers focus on processes that often contain metrics and measures (such as velocity and burn-down charts) to visibly track progress toward an objective.

Achievers can sometimes demonstrate competitive behaviors (both intra-team and inter-team) in order to reach their personal goals.

Achiever Leadership

Achievers believe leadership is about creating challenging and satisfying environments to enable people to contribute to larger organizational objectives. They develop and orchestrate effective teams and deliver against clearly defined goals and strategies. The culture and strategy they develop is customer-centric, with clear rewards and recognition schemes driven by customer outcomes. When under pressure and faced with a choice of delivery or culture, the achievers usually default to delivery in favor of shorter-term wins.

The development from expert to achiever (and the associated shift to outcome-focused behaviors) usually sees Achiever stage leaders bring on a higher capacity for strategy and culture than the more tactical, delivery-focus of the expert. Teams reporting to an achiever are led as a system, facilitated toward outcomes and measured by results.

Under stress however, achiever leaders can regress back to an expert mode of operation, jumping into problem solving mode and micro-managing their teams. We often see this regression to detailed, controlling behavior with tech startup founders. It's what I call "founder's syndrome".

Achiever Stakeholder Management

Achievers tend to see influence as central to leadership rather than authority. They figure out ways to get things done, sometimes outside usual authority relationships, by creating relationships with people that enable their success (i.e., key stakeholders). The upgrade to achiever sees a shift in power style, toward a more balanced approach that is both assertive and accommodating. They will often exhibit both approach during the same meeting.

Achievers develop an initial sense of empathy and understanding that is applied to the way they interact with stakeholders. They pay much more attention to building longer-term relationships with stakeholders than experts do. However, achievers still focus mainly on the relationships that they believe will give them short- to medium-term success.

Achiever to Catalyst Transition

Early on, achievers chase goals and high performance. However, the achiever's developed reflective capacity leads them to realize some of the limiting behaviors that are holding them back from being successful. This realization is combined with a desire to find deeper meaning in what they do and how they lead others and begins their development to the Catalyst stage.

Catalyst Stage

Catalysts develop a broader and more long-term view of their organization and, as such, are more comfortable with change and uncertainty. As with every stage transition, catalysts transcend and include the behaviors exhibited at the Achiever and Expert stage, allowing them to remain outcome focused. However, their attention is now placed strongly on the larger dynamic of human interactions and relationships. Where the achiever's intent was to achieve outcomes, the catalyst desires to create meaningful and satisfying experiences that enable sustainable delivery of outcomes over time. Catalysts appreciate the richness of human life and respect each individual's perspective and journey.

Catalysts as Team Members

Fully developed catalysts are able to access expert, achiever, and catalyst mindsets and behaviors. In a team dynamic, they utilize these abilities to focus on growing and developing teams and nurturing relationships across the wider organization. They often provide a balanced, less emotional response under pressure and will question their own assumptions to understand the motivations of others. Catalysts understand that they do not have (and cannot have) all the answers to all the problems.

Catalyst Leadership

Catalyst stage leadership is visionary and facilitative. They create new environments and contexts where people can creatively develop solutions that benefit multiple stakeholders. Catalyst leadership is the first stage of what is called "post-heroic" leadership—where the primary driver for the leader is in enabling the success of others (rather than their own). Catalysts utilize participative decision making in the teams they lead, sometimes seeking out multiple opinions and striving for consensus as they fully integrate the value each individual contributes.

Like achievers, catalysts create visions and strategies that deliver over short- to long-term horizons. However, unlike achievers, catalysts appreciate the unpredictable nature of the future and set out to build organizations that are Agile in nature and are able to sense and respond to disruptive developments that are not possible to predict.

Catalyst leaders are the first stage of leaders that embody the attributes required for Unnatural Leaders, with the potential to evolve themselves and their organizations faster than the pace of change.

Catalyst Stakeholder Management

Catalysts see others as human beings first and foremost, and secondarily as people who have certain roles, backgrounds, personality styles. They excel at stakeholder management by understanding humans and the importance of maintaining long-term relationships that generate mutually beneficial outcomes across the organization as a whole.

Like achievers, they seek out stakeholders across team boundaries for feedback and contribution, but they also include those stakeholders who are considered difficult and prickly to deal with. When engaging with stakeholders, catalysts can actively balance different styles, both supporting their own perspectives while also enquiring about others.

So What Does All This Mean?

As you read through the descriptions of the three stages of development—Expert, Achiever, and Catalyst—you may have noticed that the achiever most resembles the espoused view of leadership and management in today's workplace. Our western, Wall Street view of business is certainly one of Achiever stage views: a system designed on meritocracy, status, and financial results. The process of starting up a business, growth hacking, and doing an Initial Public Offering (IPO) to the stock market is a classic Achiever stage process that is financially rewarding for those leaders who make it. The challenge with this system is that the cost of success is often paid by employees working long hours for average pay, affecting their health and well-being and with little to no positive social or environmental impact. Put simply, it is often driven by ego and greed, at any expense. (It should be noted that there are individuals who are at the Achiever stage of development and have a set of personal values and beliefs that they prioritize over defined outcomes that will not allow them to participate in this system. Instead, they are often found leading in non-profit or charity organizations.)

When we look at disruption, change, and innovation and the need to evolve faster than the pace of change, what we are essentially talking about is evolving our capacities through this stage. The further we progress through these stages, the broader our perspective. Our attention shifts to people, rather than the technology, process, or personal outcome. We become more self-aware of our personality, assumptions, and biases.

The catalyst's ability to look further into the future (and past) and to appreciate the unpredictable nature of the future and create organizations that evolve through sensing and responding to disruption, put the catalyst in a very strong position to build teams and people (including themselves) that evolve faster than the pace of change. These organizations are based on genuine cultures of empowerment and collaborative problem solving as modeled by the leaders themselves.

Joiner's research identified that the majority of managers assessed were at the Expert or Achiever stages of development. We can safely assume that the majority of leaders that we come into contact with on a daily basis (and indeed ourselves) are likely to be at the Expert or Achiever stage of development.

This is of grave concern given that the connected nature of devices, systems, organizations, and people is accelerating at an exponential rate. This interdependence brings with it a significant added complexity that requires a broader and higher stage of awareness to succeed.

Figure 8-4 shows Joiner's research and how each level is positioned to be consistently effective as the pace of change and interdependence increase.

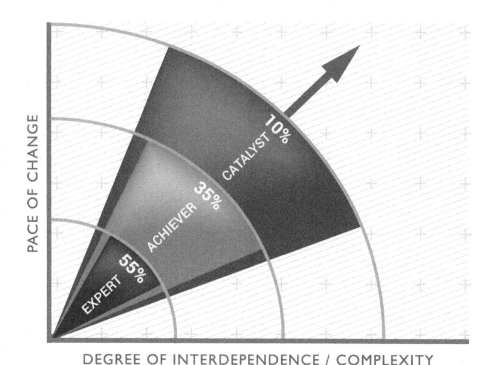

Figure 8-4. Reproduced with permission of ChangeWise, Inc.

Irrespective of your own leadership capacity, developmental stages provide valuable insights into managing our teams and show why some teams struggle with delivery and culture more than others. A team of Expert stage thinkers is generally going to struggle with delivering strategically, and therefore requires help and guidance from you as a leader to expand its perspective on the business environment and its capacity to look into the future.

Longer term strategic thinking, envisioning, and direction setting is more developed at the Achiever stage (or above). Achiever stage leaders use these capacities to guide and shape the future for those who haven't yet developed the ability to conceptualize far enough into the future or find those future focused goals compelling enough to drive their actions.

All too often we mistake a person's inability to focus strategically on the future as a lack of intelligence and therefore as fixed. It is not. It is merely a stage of development and therefore something that can be learned through coaching and training. If we apply stages of development to the Digital Situational Leadership model (see Figure 8-5), it should be obvious that the later stages are more easily able to balance the Tactical/Strategic and Delivery/Culture aspects and push the boundaries of the strategic and cultural components.

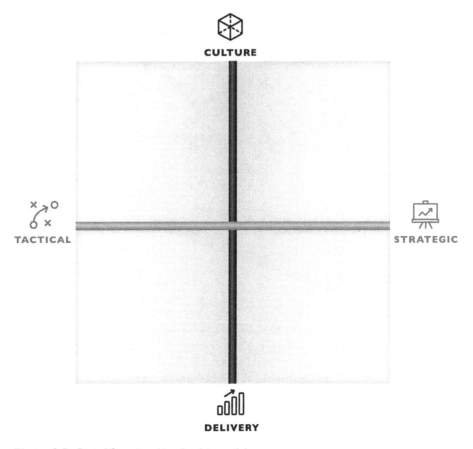

Figure 8-5. Digital Situational Leadership model

Assessing Our Stage of Development

Unfortunately, we aren't that great at assessing ourselves. Nine out 10 people believe they are above average when it comes to their personal looks—obviously, this cannot be true. Something similar happens when we ask leaders to assess their leadership abilities and skill level—around a third rate themselves the same as others, a third below others, and a third above. Therefore, we can assume that only one in three has a reasonable understanding of their leadership abilities.

There are two factors that influence leaders to rate themselves at a higher stage than they are:

- A desire to simply be at the top of the ladder: The developmental stages look like a ladder and we've spent some time talking about how the later stages of development are better positioned to deal with disruption and more complex challenges. Therefore, there is an aspirational aspect for most leaders. This aspiration is amplified at the Achiever stage.

- Understanding the concepts of the higher stages doesn't mean we behave and lead that way. Simply understanding the higher stages doesn't mean that we have embodied the deeper and broader capacities of the later stages. Understanding and aspiring to be higher doesn't mean that we are there (yet).

So, how do we go about making a sound and accurate assessment of our stage? I use the Leadership Agility 360 assessment[5] which, like other 360-degree assessments, surveys the people around us—our teams, our bosses, and our stakeholders. The assessment then reports the stage that we personally believe we are at and the stage that others experience us as being at. This gives us the ability to gain valuable feedback and reflect on how effective we are with each group.

Figure 8-6 shows a small sample of the full report that is generated by the Leadership Agility 360 assessment. Across the top row, we have the three stages of Leadership Agility—Expert, Achiever, and Catalyst—and two intermediate, transition stages—Expert/Achiever and Achiever/Catalyst (which provide a little more granularity for the report). We then have four diamond shaped markers that denote the ratings—Self, Primary Manager, Direct Reports, and Key Stakeholders—and a black circle for all others.

Leadership Agility - Bird's Eye View

	Expert	Expert/Achiever	Achiever	Achiever/Catalyst	Catalyst
Self/All Others			●	◆	
Primary Manager		◆			
Direct Reports			◆		
Key Stakeholders			◆		

Figure 8-6. A sample Leadership Agility 360 summary report

---

[5] https://unnatural.io/link/b82

We can see from this one small section of the report that this particular leader is a late-stage achiever and beginning to make a transition into catalyst. The leader has also rated herself higher than everyone else.

Accelerating Our Development to Higher Stages

It should also be acknowledged that higher stages of development aren't any better than the lower stages in terms of happiness or hierarchy. They simply have more capacity. The increased capacity solves the lower stage challenges we face, such as responding emotionally and assuming our opinions are fact. However, it replaces them with more complicated systemic challenges that span far wider timelines.

That said, each increased stage brings with it an increased capacity for complexity, collaboration, and tackling larger and larger problems. The shift from expert to achiever is essential to basic leadership. The shift from achiever to catalyst brings capacities that position us well to solve global, cross-organizational challenges, and have a positive social impact.

So the question on most leaders' minds is: How do I move to a higher stage more quickly?

There are two ways you can accelerate your development: this book is the first. Becoming aware that there are stages of development and what stage you are currently at is critical. By reading this book and reflecting on your teams around you, your awareness has already shifted significantly.

This awareness and a desire to change can drive you to the second tool to accelerate development—engaging a coach. The right coach operates from a stage higher than our own. They use their wider perspective and view of reality to help expand our own awareness. They do this during coaching sessions by asking powerful questions that cause us to question or see our limited worldview. A great coach doesn't provide answers; they guide us to our development.

Summary

In this chapter we looked at the various upgrades we undergo as our adult development progresses. We identified three key Leadership Agility stages—Expert, Achiever, and Catalyst—and covered how they affect the way we operate in teams, as leaders, and with stakeholders.

We discussed how leadership requires the Achiever stage (or later stage) operation for high performance. The key challenge we face as leaders is dealing with teams at the Expert stage of development.

In our introductory scenario, Bob identified that his team couldn't prioritize and that they were focused on technical excellence (or mastery). Once Bob understands that this is a developmental stage for his team, he can make informed decisions on how to solve the problem. His solution options include getting more involved with the team and providing the prioritization required or hiring new team members who are at the Achiever stage and providing training and tools to assist them in their prioritization of their work.

As an achiever, Bob also needs to focus on his own development if he is going to thrive amidst the change and complexity that is ever increasing. As an aspiration, Bob (and indeed anyone else at expert or achiever) would be well placed to develop an "upgrade" of himself to catalyst.

These upgrades to our API layer, microservices, and backend software happen in small increments until we reach the next stage or a major release. In the next chapter, we are going to look a closer look at our API and microservices layer and how these can help accelerate our development and evolution.

Self-Reflection Questions

1. What stage do you believe you currently operate at? How is this stage impacting your role?

2. How do you think you might identify whether an individual is at the Expert or Achiever stage?

3. Choose 1-3 people who are critical to your success. What stage do you think they are at? What impact is that having on your role and your potential for success?

4. For each of your teams, what stage on average does the team operate at? How might you change how you engage with them now that you have an idea of the stage of development?

Preferences and Patterns

> *The secret of change is to focus all of your energy, not on fighting the old, but on building the new.*
>
> —Socrates in *Way of the Peaceful Warrior* by Dan Millman (1980)

On our human frontend, our communication channel determines the mechanism by which information enters our neurology and is converted into electrical signals for processing by the brain. The brain then presents this information in the mind, creating an internal representation of reality. These representations may be in the form of images, sounds, sensations, and/ or movements and correspond to the representation systems of visual (V), auditory (A) and kinesthetic (K), respectively. We also have another internal meta-representation system—auditory digital (Ad)—which uses language in the mind to process events. These four systems are often written as VAKAd.

Frontend Communication Channel Preferences

Most of us (but not all) have a preferred representational system that favors the related communication channel: visual - sight, auditory - music and sounds, kinesthetic - sensations and movement, or auditory digital - words. We pay

J. Brett, *Evolving Digital Leadership*, https://doi.org/10.1007/978-1-4842-3606-2_9

more attention to our favored channel for information and, in some instances, strongly neglect one or more of the other channels. Figure 9-1 shows the frontend layer of the Humans as a Full Stack model presented in Chapter 7.

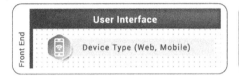 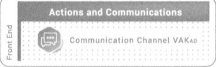

Figure 9-1. The frontend layer

For the majority of the people we interact with, if we want to influence and connect with them, we must use *their* preferred channel to communicate. If they have a preference for the visual channel, we need to communicate with them using images, drawings, pictures, video, etc. If their preferred channel is auditory, then active conversation and the appropriate utilization of sound and even music will likely be most effective.

We can often identify the other person's preferred channel by the language that they use. The sentences they use to describe thoughts and thinking often contain clues to their preferred channel. For instance:

- Visual preference: "It looks right," "I can't see the problem"

- Auditory preference: "It sounds right," "That sounds interesting"

- Kinesthetic preference: "It feels right," "I sense a problem"

We can also gain insight into a person's representational system by observing their eye movements. When a person is processing events (and doesn't know you are looking at their eye movements), their eye direction typically corresponds to the area of the brain they are accessing to process the event. There are six key eye accessing locations, shown in Figure 9-2.

Figure 9-2. Eye accessing cues

V^r

Eye movements upward and to the left generally denote the visual recall of something. When the person looks up to the left they are accessing the area of the brain that recalls visual images stored in memory. In conversation, you can observe a person doing this by asking a question that requires a visual recall, such as "Can you picture your first car?"

V^c

Eye movements upward to the right generally denote visual construction. The person is accessing the area of the brain that constructs new visual images. You can trigger this process by asking the person: "Now picture your first car with pink spots all over it".

A^r

Eye movements horizontally to the left generally denote audio recall. The person is now accessing the area of the brain that recalls sounds, music, or conversations from memory. You can trigger this process by asking the person: "Tell me about the last conversation you had over the phone".

A^c

Eye movements horizontally to the right generally denote audio construction. The person is now using the area of the brain that constructs what it might sound like to have a conversation with someone, or a new sound. You can trigger this process by asking the person: "Imagine what it would sound like if I dropped your laptop onto the floor!"

A^{id}

Eye movements down to the left generally denote self-talk or auditory digital representations. The person is now accessing the area of the brain that has an internal dialogue, where they ask themselves a question and process the answers in an auditory way. You can trigger this process by asking the person: "What did you think of the last movie you watched? How would you rate it?"

Kⁱ

Eye movements down to the right generally denote accessing of feelings of the Kinesthetic representational system. The person is now accessing the area of the brain that processes emotions and what they think about those emotions. This area is generally accessed when one feels strong emotions such as love, happiness, sadness, and guilt. You can trigger this process by asking someone: "How did you feel when …?"

As we converse naturally with someone (either face-to-face or over a video conference call), we can pay attention to their eye accessing cues to help us determine their communication preferences. Equally observing whether they are creating or recalling can help us to determine if they are being truthful. A person who is explaining a conversation they had with a key stakeholder and has eye movements that are primarily in either audio or visual construction will likely not be telling us the whole truth. There is very little need to construct something that has already happened!

It should be noted that, like left and right handed people, the majority of us are wired with construction on the right side (as per Figure 9-2). Some, however, are wired in reverse (flipping the diagram on the horizontal axis), essentially switching construction with recall and A^{id} with Kⁱ. Asking the determining questions provided here helps us to calibrate which way a person is wired before making any judgment and investigating further.

Meta-Programs Layer

Our preferences and patterns of thinking are shaped by the meta-programs we run in our minds. As their name implies, meta-programs are like microservices—small pieces of software that run at a meta level in the brain, creating a frame of mind (see Figure 9-3).

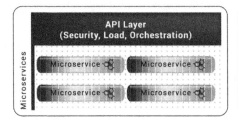 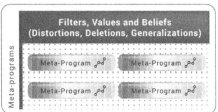

Figure 9-3. The meta-programs layer

Each meta-program colors the way we perceive the external world as we recreate it in the mind, and each is context specific. Michael Hall's neurosemantics work and in particular, his book *Figuring Out People,*[1] identifies and describes the different meta-programs that we all run.

When you take a Myers-Briggs personality assessment, you get a four-letter result like ENTF or INTJ. These four letters represent Myers-Briggs' idea (not mine) of the pivotal meta-programs that describe people. Their assessment confusingly returns one letter for each meta-program that denotes which end of that meta-program continuum they have determined your personality to be at. The first of the four letters is either an "I" or an "E" and indicates whether we have been classified as an introvert or extrovert. Introvert and extrovert are actually the opposite ends of the Rejuvenation meta-program, as shown in Figure 9-4.

INTROVERT   EXTROVERT

Figure 9-4. Rejuvenation meta-program

---

[1]*Figuring Out People: Reading People Using Meta-Programs* by L. Michael Hall, Crown House Publishing 2006

The challenge with the Myers-Briggs assessment is threefold:

- Meta-programs are a continuous spectrum, not a binary choice. In the Rejuvenation meta-program example, an Ambivert (someone who is both introverted and extraverted) would likely get a different letter each time they took the assessment. Every meta-program is a continuum and therefore representing a meta-program result as one end of the spectrum reduces the validity of the assessment.

- Meta-programs are context-specific and therefore change according to context. You may be a big picture thinker at work and quite detail orientated at home or with your car. The assessment needs to be clear on the context of the questions being asked and the results only applied to that context, not all aspects of life.

- There are 60 meta-programs in total that run in our minds, and therefore the meta-programs that are useful to look at depend on what we are seeking to achieve. Later in this chapter, we look at the meta-programs that impact our ability to evolve, interact with, and lead others effectively.

How Meta-Programs Are Configured

Meta-programs are configured by our repeated thoughts and emotions and our mental states that we habituate over time. A lot of these meta-programs are set up early on in our life as our parents rewarded or punished our behaviors in either subtle or direct ways.

Imagine these scenarios: there is a young boy aged 6. His mother tells him that if he keeps his bedroom tidy for the whole week, he will get an extra dollar pocket money as a reward. The little boy is motivated by this as he is saving up for the latest and greatest toy he's wanted for so long. So he agrees to the deal and tidies his bedroom. His mother comes into his bedroom every Saturday morning and inspects it for tidiness and, if he passes, he gets the dollar.

In scenario A: The mother comes to his bedroom each Saturday morning, opens the door and glances in from the doorway to see if the floor is cleared of his dirty clothes, that there are no dirty dishes or glasses on his desk, and that his toys are all put away out of sight.

In scenario B: The mother comes into his bedroom and opens each desk drawer, looks under the bed, opens the cupboards and checks that everything is neat and tidy and in its correct place and neatly organized. She may even wipe her finger over surfaces and check for dust or grime.

Over time, (maybe years) the mother in scenario B (either consciously or unconsciously) programs the boy for detail. That is to say she configures the child's Scale meta-program for the detail end of the spectrum. In scenario A, the boy is more likely to be global orientated because these are the formative years of the boy's life. This configuration gets set quite solidly and unconsciously and he begins to value detail (or not) and apply it to other aspects of his life. It may even draw him into a detail-oriented career such as accounting. His value of this detailed way of being is then projected onto others, such that he likes and appreciates others that he sees as diligent, structured, and therefore doing a good job!

Neither end of the spectrum (detail or global) is better than the other. What tends to cause challenges for us is when we are fixed (or driven) at one end of meta-program, which then impacts our life in a negative way. Highly global people often complain about the boring minutiae and trivial details of life and avoid them, sometimes at great personal and professional cost. Equally, highly detailed people are frustrated by global people who talk so vaguely they just can't understand what the conversation is about or what is being asked of them.

The key to evolution, and indeed to a better life, is to be aware of the existence of meta-programs, to be aware of the ones that drive us, and to be aware of the ones that impact what we are trying to achieve. The great news is that meta-programs are re-programmable! Like habits, they take time and effort, but we can change them. Sometimes they change on their own without any conscious effort from us. Sometimes they take real focus, determination, and time to shift.

So, let's explore the essential meta-programs for our journey together and learn how to shift and upgrade them.

Convincer Meta-Programs

This book, in part, is about convincing you of the need to change, that I have something valuable for you to take away and use, and that, with intention and attention, it is possible for you to change dramatically.

Convincing people, whether it's a stakeholder, peer, or spouse, can be very hard at times. The relationship involved brings elements such as trust and respect, which are absolutely essential to influence and convincing. However, there are a set of four meta-programs that, when understood, help us realize how to best convince someone. Let's take a look at them next.

Relationship Comparison: Matching or Mismatching

This is the relationship we have with new information received. Do we match it with what we already know and look for how it's the same or how it differs from what we already know? It's my direct experience that a majority of technologists mismatch new information with our pervasive response of "Yes, but". This mismatching helps us look for exceptions to the rule, for faults, or for how it might be wrong as we test the robustness of the data. To test this meta-program with someone, you may ask them "What's the relationship between your first job and your current one?". People wired for matching will first identify the similarities in the roles. Mismatchers will immediately identify the differences. In instances where a person is wired strongly at one end, they may not be able to identify the issues at the end other end of the spectrum.

When convincing someone, strong mismatchers can present a challenge. We may need to be ready with a thorough set of answers to their objections or we could mismatch their mismatching early on. If we were to lead with a sentence such as: "You aren't going to say yes to this but...," a compulsive mismatcher will hear that sentence and instinctively want to say "yes" to the request.

Convincer Representation: Looks, Sounds, Feels, or Makes Sense

This meta-program has four points on the spectrum, rather than the usual two. This meta-program processes information differently based on the values we place on our experiences. We develop different emotional strategies for how we feel convinced. These are often related to our primary representational systems or communication channels, which are visual, auditory, kinesthetic, and auditory digital. Those of us with a preference for auditory digital, for instance, will have a level of internal self-talk as we make a decision and decide on the validity of something. Most people use language that explicitly points to this process. When they are convinced, they will often say "Yes, that looks right" or "Yes, that sounds right".

The key to working with this meta-program is to be aware of the other person's preference and, if need be, adapt your style (your preference) to meet theirs, matching their language and biases. For visual people, drawing a concept on a whiteboard and asking them if it looks right is usually far more effective than talking to them and asking whether it sounds right.

Convincer Demonstration: Number of Times or Length of Time

Quite simply, this meta-program describes how some people require new concepts or information to be repeated multiple times before being convinced, whereas others require the new concept to sit with them for a period of time. Being convinced doesn't simply consist of whether something looks or sounds right; it involves how we make choices and the processing of decision making. An essential part of this is the specific trust involved. The more trust, the less repetition or length of time is required to make a decision.

Some need a concept to be repeatedly exposed to them numerous times before it seems real and trustworthy. Others need the idea of the concept to solidify over time.

Authority Source: Internal or External

When making a decision about external information, where does our authority come from? If it's external, we allow others to direct our choices and validate what is right or wrong, useful or not. If it's internal, we decide on our own. Those of us with internal authority tend to be more difficult to convince, especially if we are at early developmental level such as Expert, where self-awareness is not fully developed.

Take a moment to reflect and understand your own convincer preferences. Are you mismatching what's being presented here in this book? Do the visuals throughout the book convince you more? Do you need to read some sections a few times, or enjoy the book concepts for a period of time? Do you have a strong sense of internal authority? Is it accurate? What does understanding this mean to your relationships at work and at home?

When you have thought about these, ask yourself this question: Are these temporary strategies you have for learning and decision making working for you? If not, skip to the "Tuning Meta-Programs for Success" section and then come back here when you are ready for more.

Meta-Programs for Evolving Faster Than the Pace of Change

I can lead you to water but I cannot make you drink. You have to want to evolve; you have to want to change. You have to put the effort in, to paddle back out into the swell and ride that next wave. This sustained effort is fueled by our personal motivators.

Our personal motivators are critical in driving our effort to change (or not) and whether we evolve faster than the pace of change. Setting meaningful goals that align with our motivations allows us to focus our effort and energy on what we want. We set a stake in the ground for an outcome we desire and often we declare a time frame in which to achieve it. For some of us this works really well, for others not so much. For some, it works well for certain goals, but then not for others. The key to setting goals and intentions that work is to understand how we are individually motivated.

There are four key meta-programs that impact our motivations to evolve, set goals, and achieve them, and they are discussed in the following sections.

Nature: Static or Process

I introduced the concept of the growth mindset in Chapter 6. The Nature meta-program filters how we perceive who we are, whether we are static (fixed) or an evolving (growth) process. This program is usually set early on to be quite fixed (or static) for most of us in the western world. Over time, as we progress through the stages of development to Achiever and Catalyst, the meta-program moves toward Process. At even later stages of development, the Nature meta-program moves almost completely to Process as we see ourselves, others, the world, and indeed the universe as one unfolding process.

If you are strongly fixed at the static end of the spectrum, you are going to struggle to find the motivation to change, as you don't believe you can. The good news is you are reading this book and you have come this far, so something inside of you wants more and knows this isn't true. Keep reading, keep going; you're doing awesome!

Motivation Direction: Toward or Away From

Understanding our motivation direction is fundamental to our quality of life. Humans are generally motivated toward something—a goal or desire—or away from something such as pain or fear.

If your motivation strategy is "away from," you won't be moved to do this work until you have to. Maybe your job is threatened; maybe your business is crumbling around you or maybe you can't find any work. You may be also be in a successful business looking into the future and have anxiety about your market's disruption and competition. Away from motivation is very strong, usually stronger than toward motivation, but it's not a pleasant experience.

Being motivated "toward" something—something we want to do to create a different future for ourselves, others, and the planet is inspiring, positive, uplifting, and a lot less stressful. The key here is to focus on the future and create what you want to be motivated toward.

What is it that is motivating you to become a better leader?

Scenario Type: Pessimist or Optimist

I think most of us are aware of this concept. Are you optimistic about the future and think that all will go well? Or are you a pessimist, processing what might or will go wrong. Socially, optimists are more positively regarded; they are upbeat and engaging people to be around. What most people don't understand is that optimists can make highly ineffective leaders. People who are overly optimistic take bigger risks, tend not to plan as much, and may not take action when it's needed, because they think all will be okay. The key, as with most meta-programs, is to have a healthy balance of optimism and pessimism. To believe that you can change and evolve, that your new vision of the future can be achieved, and maybe there will be challenges ahead that you need to account for and action.

Goal Striving: Skeptic-Optimization-Perfectionism

The Goal Striving meta-program filters how we approach a goal. Are we skeptical about achieving it? Do we optimize for most efficiency or do we try to achieve perfection? There is a direct relationship between the developmental levels and how we do Goal Striving. Experts tend to run a Perfectionism Goal Striving program, and achievers an Optimization strategy. Often, the most appropriate for leadership goals is optimization. Perfectionism has its place, but generally not at the higher levels of leadership.

We can all benefit from adjusting, even slightly, just one of these motivational meta-programs, whoever we are. Unnatural Selection is about dialing these meta-programs in and creating the best mental frames and state of mind for excellence and success.

Tuning Meta-Programs for Success

Meta-programs are flexible. With effort we can tune and adjust them; in fact, we are constantly tuning meta-programs either consciously or subconsciously as we grow throughout our life. Our meta-programs are not our fixed destiny. They are, however, incredibly valuable because of their discrete and tangible nature. This discreteness and the fact that we can adjust them makes them an incredibly powerful tool for us to use in our evolution.

The six-step process (modified slightly from Michael Hall's, *Figuring Out People*) to tune or adjust our position on a particular meta-program is as follows:

1. *You have already begun to become aware of meta-programs and how they are structured.* This awareness changes your subjective experience into a more objective system to understand. Objectivity is key to shifting what and who we believe we are—our personalities.

2. *Identify which meta-programs are causing a challenge.* Are you finding that you are mismatching people and concepts excessively and it's caused you professional and personal issues? Then the Relationship Comparison meta-program would be a good choice to focus on.

3. *Understand clearly each end of the meta-program scale and hold them in mind.* You need to be conscious that all meta-programs are constructed in the mind and are not concrete or immovable. If we consider the Relationship Comparison meta-program, we have Matching and Mismatching at either end. Some people match most of what they experience while others mismatch. If some people match and others mismatch, then we know that this way of operating is programmed and not fixed and concrete.

   We then think about and imagine what it would be like to operate at each extreme end of the spectrum. We imagine scenarios where we match everything others say and do. We experience what it's like to be a matcher. We then flip to the other end of the spectrum and imagine what it would be like to mismatch everything. We experience being a mismatcher. In doing this process, we see and experience the polarity of each end of the spectrum.

4. *Describe your new preferred style of operation.* Where would you like to be on the meta-program spectrum and why? Do you want balance between Matching and Mismatching? When you have the right balance, what will life be like to have that balance? What will operating in a balanced Matching-Mismatching manner bring you? What might you lose by operating like this, and is that okay?

5. *Make a conscious decision to change.* Knowing why you want the change and deciding to make the change is critical. It sets a clear intention that directs your energy and attention to what you want.

6. *Try it on for a period of time.* Try on this new way of being with this meta-program and see how it feels to operate with balance. Define this trial period and give yourself permission to experiment—to see what it's like to play with the new aspects of the meta-program. To gain flexibility of meta-program, it often helps to try on the other extreme for a while. As we try on this opposite way of being, we get to experience the stark contrast of Matching (if you were a Mismatcher). After the trial period ends, decrease your focus and effort on matching but, the experience is integrated back into how you operate. The amount of integration depends on the effort and value we place on operating in this new way. For some leaders, the integration requires further cycles of the trial period to fully integrate and gain flexibility.

A Meta-Program Tuning Example

A common meta-program that leaders tune is the Attention meta-program (see Figure 9-5). It is a valuable meta-program to tune, as it strongly impacts how effective we are as leaders. This meta-program describes how much we focus our attention on ourselves versus on others.

Figure 9-5. Attention meta-program

At one end we place our attention on ourselves, focusing on what we need and want and on our opinions. At the other end, we focus on the needs, desires, and views of others.

Being stuck at either end tends to cause challenges—solely focusing on self is essentially narcissistic in nature and often leads to poor stakeholder relationships and poor team engagement and productivity as we force through our agendas, demands, and viewpoints.

Being solely focused on others can lead to tactical operations, as we service our team or more indecisively as we focus on the multiple needs of our stakeholders. Unnatural Leaders balance this meta-program, holding a sense of what they want to achieve (their vision, their goals, etc.) while simultaneously focusing on the growth of their people and building lasting relationships with stakeholders.

Steps 1-3

We have understood meta-programs and how they operate (Step 1) and we have identified that the Attention meta-program is the one we want to work on (Step 2). We have outlined the two ends of the meta-program as Self and Others and defined what operating at each end means (Step 3). We continue Step 3 by diving deeper into this to understand what it means for us personally to operate at either end. For this scenario, let's assume that we are operating (like a majority of leaders) close to the Self end of the spectrum, so we chose to imagine what it would be like to operate at the opposite end—Others.

Step 4

During this step, we articulate what it means to have balance and attend to Self and Others. In a leadership context this balance usually leads to a more engaged team, improved stakeholder relationships, and outcomes that aligned across all of these goals. This means our operation now involves more conversations and enquiries into what others want and need for success. As we promote others, we may lose some of our (perceived) high profile visibility in the organization, which we accept in accordance with our new definition of personal success.

Step 5

Having completed Steps 1-4, we now have a sense of what we want and what it means to operate in this new meta-program. Step 5 is where we make a commitment to ourselves to try this for a period of time (Step 6). If for whatever reason we cannot make a full commitment (maybe we don't want to give up that visibility or invest the time in others right now), then we stop here, or reset what we are willing to commit to as a trial change.

Step 6

We try on the extreme other end of the meta-program, focusing solely on others and letting go of what we need or want as appropriate. We may spend a majority of our time reconnecting with our people and teams and engaging in active listening to understand and support them better. We consciously chose to let go of our habituated patterns and opinions and experience what it's like to strongly focus our attention on others for a fixed period of time.

This step takes commitment and focus to complete. Our habits and the expectations of others may try to pull us back into our old ways of being. We have to want to change, to put the energy into change. Evolving ourselves as digital leaders and as humans comes down to making these shifts on a constant basis.

At the end of the trial period, we reflect on the experience in order to integrate it back into how we operate. Operating (even artificially like this) at the other extreme pulls our balance toward the middle as we exit this trial period, thereby introducing a more balanced and flexible nature to our meta-program.

Of course how we operate and respond includes the logic, rules, and structure in our backend personality structures. Our meta-programs filter and adjust information flow and then call down into our backend to complete the response. We cover this in detail in the next chapter.

Being an Introvert Is Not an Excuse for Having Poor Social Skills

Many technologists are introverts, but it doesn't mean that we have poor social skills. Technologists are often labeled "nerds" by those around us. If we look at the dictionary definition of "nerd," it actually calls out a lack of social skills:

> *"A person, especially a man, who is not attractive and is awkward or socially embarrassing."*

— Cambridge Dictionary

Being a nerd has nothing to do with being an introvert, and introversion has nothing to do with social skills. There are plenty of extremely social and successful people who are introverts. Introversion, as we identified early in this chapter, is one end of the Rejuvenation meta-program, as shown in Figure 9-6.

INTROVERT   **EXTROVERT**

REJUVENTATION META-PROGRAM

Figure 9-6. Introversion on the Rejuvenation meta-program

Introversion indicates how we rejuvenate. Quite simply, when introverts are tired and drained, they will want to go somewhere quiet to relax to re-energize. An extrovert might want to find a bar with lots of people and energy to recharge and relax. Neither the extrovert nor the introvert is naturally gifted with good social skills. Sure, extroverts are often great talkers, but I'm sure we have all experienced those extroverts who talk too much! While being outwardly facing, their social skills can still leave something to be desired.

It is my direct experience that technologists and some digital leaders use the (assumed) fact that they have no or poor social skills as an excuse to not build relationships with people in their organization, industry, and customers. *Saying you have poor social skills is not an excuse for having poor social skills*. Interacting with unfamiliar people may feel uncomfortable at first, and you may actually have less than average social skills (by some abstract definition of average). However, those skills, like any other, will not improve without work.

Unnatural Leaders don't use their current social skill level as an excuse for not engaging with people. They embrace the opportunity to develop those skills because they want success and they know sustained success comes from growth.

Summary

In this chapter we looked at how we represent external reality in our minds by processing information through our preferred communication channel(s) of VAKad and the meta-programs we run in our minds. A person's preferred communication channel can significantly impact how effectively their communication is received, so it's wise to strive to understand and communicate in their preferred channel.

There are a total of 60 meta-programs and each one consists of a spectrum with one or more points on that spectrum. We tend to face challenges in our leadership when we are "stuck" at one end of a meta-program. Fortunately, we can re-tune our meta-programs and adjust the way we operate.

We looked at the key meta-programs that impact how we become convinced about a particular concept and whether or not we evolve faster than the pace of change.

Meta-programs are incredibly useful tools to create change as they provide a discrete view of how we do the complexities of thinking and being. They form a significant part of how we do "us," but they aren't the only part. Meta-programs process information received and call down into the backend-personality structures to complete the internal representation of reality and develop a response.

In the next chapter, we take a look at the final component in the Humans as a Full Stack model—backend personality types.

Self-Reflection Questions

1. What is your preferred communication channel (Visual, Auditory, Kinesthetic, or Auditory Digital)? How does this impact the way you communicate?

2. Which meta-program that you run is impeding your professional success most? How might you re-tune it?

3. For the key people in your life, what meta-programs have you observed them running? Knowing this, how might you adapt your communication to achieve better results?

4. How might your team respond to you experimenting (or shifting) one of your meta-programs to the other end of the spectrum? What might you do to alleviate any challenges?

Personality Types

Ego takes everything personally.

—Eckhart Tolle[1]

The backend of our Human Full Stack reflects our core personality structures (see Figure 10-1). External information is received through our preferred communication channel(s) and filtered, distorted, or deleted and then processed by our meta-programs in the API layer. The meta-programs then call our backend personality structures, which create and hold our external representation of reality. Our unique personalities are forged through our genes (nature), our upbringing (nurture), our culture, and our experiences. This dynamic combination creates a truly unique, individual personality in each and everyone one of us. This makes our job as digital leaders extremely complex as we endeavor to interact successfully with our customers, stakeholders and teams.

---

[1]Eckhart Tolle, *A New Earth* (10th anniversary ed.), (NY: Penguin Random House, 2016)

© James Brett 2019
J. Brett, *Evolving Digital Leadership*, https://doi.org/10.1007/978-1-4842-3606-2_10

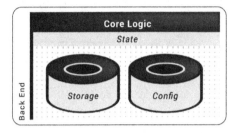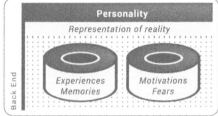

Figure 10-1. The Human backend

However, to be successful, we don't need to understand the 7 billion or more unique personalities of the people on our planet. In fact, most of us don't have the time to dive into understanding the key people in our lives (our partner or parents). Yet, what really amplifies our chances of success is getting a basic understanding of the deep motivations that drive a person's behaviors, thoughts, and emotions.

Let's see how this plays out. If a member of your team is deeply motivated by intellectual ability and demonstrating capability and competence, he will often present a very logical personality that thrives on cognitive rigor and knowledge, and, in some cases, can appear quite "emotionless" (Mr. Spock anyone?). This type of person can often be one of the smartest people in the room, having spent their life developing their gray matter. They can also irritate others with their need to intellectualize and analyze every situation, down to the make-up and origins of that rather bland coffee cup in your hand.

Contrast this with someone who is deeply moved to help others and connect emotionally with them. In a team environment, these people often provide a valuable support network to others. Their challenge is to avoid burning themselves out helping others, leaving little or no capacity for their own personal productivity and self-care.

As we encounter a person (be that a stakeholder, executive, peer, or member of our team) who demonstrates particular personality traits consistently, we may begin to think about the different styles we can employ in our interactions with them to achieve our desired outcomes. The key is to use a personality framework that honors the richness of the human being, while allowing us to hack through the personality stack, demystifying the people who we are looking to grow, influence and engage with in a more sophisticated manner.

The Enneagram

I've worked with hundreds of people using the *Enneagram* over the last five years. I've also run numerous Enneagram training programs, presentations, workshops, and one-on-one coaching sessions that introduce the Enneagram and how to use it for professional and personal success. Each person who has been through one or more of these engagements has reported back that learning the Enneagram was a significant experience for them and impacted the way they think of themselves and interact with others.

The Enneagram has a long history, the basic symbol dating back a few thousand years. The Enneagram Personality system evolved in the 1970s through the work of the Chilean developmental psychologist, Claudio Naranjo. Naranjo developed the main body of work for Enneagram Personality Types, elements of which have been adapted in more recent years by Don Rhiso, Russ Hudson, and others.

The Enneagram is effective for digital leaders for two key reasons:

- The depth and accuracy of the system is unsurpassed, showing preferences, motivations, thought patterns, mind, body, gut integration, and the shifts that happen for each type under stress and relaxation.

- There is a vast, easily accessible body of knowledge available online for when you are ready to drive your own personal development to the next level. The resources available range from books, to YouTube videos, to informative articles, and even online courses.

The richness and complexity of the Enneagram presents a particular challenge for me in writing this book. With such a broad and deep body of knowledge, communicating just enough of the most valuable aspects of the Enneagram is a balancing act. What I cover in the rest of this chapter is a summary of the nine personality types, their response patterns, and their leadership styles. These three topics give us a veritable treasure chest of knowledge to use in our interactions and personal evolution. Once I've piqued your interest, you can continue learning about the enneagram through other channels.

The Enneagram Symbol

The word Enneagram is Greek for nine (ennea) and gram (written or drawn). Essentially it is a personality system that has nine personality types arranged around the outside of a circle, as shown in Figure 10-2.

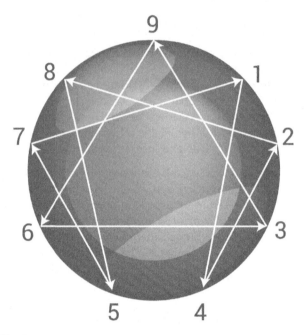

Figure 10-2. The Enneagram

The nine types are arranged in a clockwise order around the outside and each one has an arrow pointing away from it and another pointing toward it. These arrows indicate the transitions that happen when each type is either under stress or in health. For Enneagram Type 1, for instance, we can see that the arrow pointing toward it comes from Type 7. This means that when Type 1s are relaxed, they take on the healthier aspects of the Type 7. Conversely, the arrow pointing away from Type 1 points toward Type 4, which means they take on the unhealthy aspects of a Type 4 when stressed.

Let's take a closer look at each of the nine types.

Type 1: The Reformer

Reformers (see Figure 10-3) are conscientious and ethical, with a strong sense of right and wrong. They seek perfection and feel a dutiful obligation to change and improve things for the better. They are often highly organized and provide detail, quality, and diligence to teams.

Desires and motivators	Response Patterns	Leadership Styles
Desire to be good, to have integrity	Aim for perfection	Lead by example
An extreme sense of personal moral obligation	Black and white thinking	Focus on quality and excellence
Fear of being defective or corrupt	Dutiful obligation to make things right	Can make others feel judged or inferior

Figure 10-3. The Reformer

Reformers can be critical of those around them. Their perfection seeking can come at the cost of delivering value early or personal burn out, working extremely long hours to get the job done to their own high standards.

At their best, they are wise, discerning, and noble.

Type 2: The Helper

Helpers (see Figure 10-4) are the most relationship-focused type. They're empathetic, supportive, and sincere. Their people and relationship focus helps build healthy cultures, but can become overly focused on the happiness and support of others, losing sight of the need for productivity and outcomes. They often take on people support, coaching or mentoring roles in organizations, providing much needed individual growth for those in the organization they assist. Their focus on others can see them burn themselves out, at which point they can become stressed and demanding. At their best they are altruistic and have unconditional love for others.

Desires and motivators	Response Patterns	Leadership Styles
To feel loved	Provide praise and flattery	Strong connections with people
Search for intimacy	Focus on relationships	Supportive and motivating
Fear of disconnection	Caring, empathetic and dutiful	Can burn themselves out

Figure 10-4. The Helper

Type 3: The Achiever

Achievers (see Figure 10-5) are self-assured and charismatic. They are ambitious, outcome focused, and highly driven to success. They bring a focus on goals and productivity to teams and organizations, which can sometimes see them detach from what they perceive to be unproductive scenarios, including some team building activities.

Desires and motivators	Response Patterns	Leadership Styles
To feel valuable	How they will be seen	Performance focused
Search for validation and acceptance	Focus on outcomes and success	Goals and structure for success
Fear of being worthless	Charismatic and assertive	Avoidance of emotions

Figure 10-5. The Achiever

Achievers often ascend quickly to leadership roles and can balance out an overly perfectionist technical culture. Also known as chameleons, they have the ability to read situations and can adapt their style to achieve success. Achievers often over associate with status and roles, in their need to feel valuable. At their best they are self-accepting and authentic role models for others.

Type 4: The Individualist

Individualists (see Figure 10-6) are self-aware, sensitive, and reserved. They are often creative types drawn to technology through the art of creating products (either as designers or developers). They love to deep-dive into the meaning of things and value work tied to a bigger meaning and purpose. Motivation can be a challenge for individualists, as they often avoid what they see as mundane, ordinary activities that may be detailed in nature. They are often ideators and innovators, connecting seemingly disparate topics in new inventive ways. Under stress, individualists can be moody and difficult to manage, wanting special attention from the people around them.

Desires and motivators	Response Patterns	Leadership Styles
To be authentic	Desire to express themselves	Creates meaning and purpose
Search for identity and purpose	Focus on outcomes and success	Goals and structure for success
Fear of having no significance	Will want to know WHY they need to do something	Avoidance of mundane

Figure 10-6. The Individualist

At their best, individualists are inspired and highly creative and are able to renew themselves and transform their experiences.

Type 5: The Investigator

Investigators (see Figure 10-7) are alert, insightful, and curious. They are deeply motivated by intellectual ability and demonstrating capability and competence. They will often present a very logical personality that thrives on cognitive rigor and knowledge. Independent, innovative, and inventive, they can also become preoccupied with their own thoughts and imaginary constructs.

Desires and motivators	Response Patterns	Leadership Styles
To be competent and capable	Take a systems perspective	Create effective organizations
Search for mastery	Knowledge is power	Research and deliberation
Fear of helplessness or incompetence	Intellectualize the situation and understand HOW	May detach and become aloof

Figure 10-7. The Investigator

The leadership challenge for investigators is to shift from the enjoyment of information and solving problems to that of growing and enabling people. At their best they are visionary pioneers, sharing their knowledge and insights.

Type 6: The Loyalist

Loyalists (see Figure 10-8) are committed, reliable, trustworthy, and excellent troubleshooters. They are usually future focused and are able to foresee challenges and bring their team together to solve them. However, loyalists can get caught in cycles of analysis paralysis, which often leads them to be anxious and stressed.

Desires and motivators	Response Patterns	Leadership Styles
To have support and guidance	Analysis of options and what might go wrong	Group problem solving
Search for security and safety	Detailed planning	Empowering leadership style
Fear of being without support or not belonging to a group	Focus on their group and seek advice	Can have cycles of indecision

Figure 10-8. The Loyalist

Loyalists focus on culture and being part of a team, tribe, community, or organization helping to foster a collaborative way of working. They often seek guidance from strong sources of authority to help guide them through their self-doubt. At their best, they are internally stable, courageous champions of teams and culture.

Type 7: The Enthusiast

Enthusiasts (see Figure 10-9), as their name suggests, are enthusiastic, optimistic, and spontaneous. Their fun-loving nature brings energy into their environment and they are often the ones driving new innovation and big-picture thinking. Their energy can become scattered under stress, seeing them struggle to complete the many activities they have started.

Desires and motivators	Response Patterns	Leadership Styles
To be satisfied and content	Excitement and energy	Drive innovation and new ventures
Search for fun and fulfilment	Positive focus on the big picture	Create excitement in people
Fear of being trapped or in pain	Can become distracted	Long term execution can be a challenge

Figure 10-9. The Enthusiast

They are usually practical and fast thinking, focusing on keeping busy and moving. At their best, they are grounded (focusing on meaningful goals) appreciative, and satisfied.

Type 8: The Challenger

Challengers (see Figure 10-10) are confident, assertive, protective, and straight talking. They are decisive in action, but can also be demanding and controlling. Challengers want to control their environment and shy away from any personal vulnerability. This often sees them quickly reaching leadership roles and then struggling to lead at scale, where vulnerability and engagement of others plays a significant part of success.

Desires and motivators	Response Patterns	Leadership Styles
To protect themselves	Gain control or protect	Lead from the front
Search for survival	Moved to action	Decisive and empowering
Fear of being harmed or controlled	Can become vengeful	Can be demanding of people

Figure 10-10. The Challenger

Challengers are extremely protective of the people in their "tribe" and can become vengeful if they perceive either themselves or their tribe as being under attack. At their best, challengers create change, lead from the front, and help improve the lives of others.

Type 9: The Peacemaker

Peacemakers (see Figure 10-11) are calm, stable, and trusting by nature. They often go along with others to keep the peace, sometimes losing sight of their own preferences. They see similarities in the world and use this to create harmony where they go. Like loyalists, peacemakers help create harmony and positive cultures, often smoothing out the ripples caused by the challengers.

Desires and motivators	Response Patterns	Leadership Styles
Peace of mind and wholeness	Look for similarities	Build a collective mission
Search for harmony	Put others first	Create a harmonious culture
Fear of less, separation and fragmentation	Disconnect and daydream	Can be passive-aggressive

Figure 10-11. The Peacemaker

Peacemakers can struggle with energizing themselves and can come across as stubborn or passive aggressive to others.

At their best, they are all embracing, bringing people together and healing conflict where appropriate.

▓ **Note** You can find a set of nine Enneagram posters to download as part of this book's material at https://unnatural.io/link/b101.

Backend Processing

The Enneagram defines nine personality types. These are our human backend systems that process requests received from our API layer and meta-programs and provide a response. We can think of the nine types as nine different backend codebases. Each of the nine codebases has a set of motivators and particular ways of responding and leading. Each person whom we interact with has forked one of these original nine codebases by the age of seven and developed their own personalized branch of the original Enneagram type codebase (see Figure 10-12).

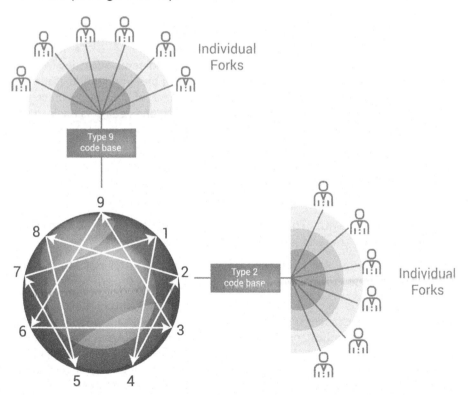

Figure 10-12. Forking of the Enneagram type codebase

This concept is important because even though two people may be the same Enneagram type (the same original codebase), they don't usually respond exactly the same. They do respond according to the same base behaviors of the original codebase (Enneagram type), but with individualization that is coded from their unique human experience. These experiences instill different beliefs, values, and memories that configure each person's meta-programs differently.

However, two people of the same Enneagram type (or original codebase) will behave and respond relatively similarly compared to that of the responses from two different Enneagram types. For example, consider a scenario where Bob asks two of his direct reports—Mark (Peacemaker – Type 9) and Dave (Challenger – Type 8)—the same question: "What do you think we need to change in our team dynamic in order to improve performance?"

Mark's response is "Well, I'd like to confirm with the team first, but I think we could allow members of the team to vote on the work we do, or maybe run more retrospectives to allow the team to tune performance."

Bob challenges this with "Hmmm, we have already tried that and it didn't work, because the team never came to an agreement and spent too much time in discussions."

Mark responds with "True, yes that's right. It's a tough one, I'm not sure. There are lots of little things we could try…"

Mark's peacemaker response pattern is to agree and see similarities in what Bob is saying. He struggles with seeing the world in black and white, right and wrong, and making a clear stand because of his fear of creating conflict and disruption. He instantly tries to deflect the question and redirects back to the team, so as not to become the source of any aggravation.

In contrast, Dave responds: "Steve (another team member) is the problem. You need to fire him. Steve just isn't competent enough and doesn't act like he's part of the team. In fact, I question his loyalty to the team full stop. I've had multiple arguments with him and he just doesn't see reality."

Bob challenges this with "Thanks Dave, but could it be that it's just a clash of your personalities that's causing you this frustration?"

Dave responds with "Are you saying it's all my fault now? It's not. I'm the one that gets stuff done around here. If you don't fire Steve then I am going to quit."

Dave's response is in stark contrast to Mark's (as is often the case with peacemakers and challengers). Right out of the gate we can sense that Dave wants control and is holding some vengeance against Steve. His suggestion is forcefully made and very black and white—fire Steve! When challenged by Bob he becomes defensive and threatens to quit, looking to gain control of the situation. It's common for challengers to consider themselves to be right and they tend to struggle with vulnerability. Challengers also protect their own inner circle. Here we can see that Dave dislikes Steve in part because he doesn't see him as a team player.

Here we have the same scenario, same leader, same team, and two individuals: Mark who forked the Peacemaker (Type 9) backend codebase and Dave who forked the Challenger (Type 8) codebase. They both add value and present Bob with a set of challenges to deal with. Bob probably needs to work with Mark on his decision making and self-authority, while with Dave he may choose to work on softening those aspects of his character. Bob may even choose to use Mark and Dave as role models for each other as the focus on the growth of this team and the individuals within it.

Common Technical Types

There isn't a strong dominant type that is drawn to technical work. That said, investigators (Type 5) are very commonly found in engineering roles. Their cerebral nature draws them to any field where they can enjoy problem solving and analysis. The creative, art-like nature of development (either software or hardware) also sees a number of individualists (Type 4) expressing themselves in design and code. Equally, reformers (Type 1) are drawn to testing, quality, and compliance type roles. All types can be found in teams. As a leader, the key is to find balance across all types and put people into roles where they will thrive.

Which Balance of Types Makes a Great Team?

This is the most common question leaders ask me, once they understand the basics of the Enneagram. Team dynamics are immensely complex and the demands on the team change over time, so there really isn't a "best team" type composition. Like strengths and weaknesses, a high-performing team will generally have a good balance of all skills required. The same applies for personality types. Each type brings with it a set of strengths and weaknesses. Without any context of the team, the only advice I give is: A sub-optimal team is skewed toward only one type.

Common Leadership Types

Anecdotally the two types that I see most often in senior/executive leadership roles are achievers and challengers. That's not to say other types don't become leaders. They absolutely do. However, western business appreciates and rewards these two types with leadership positions because:

- Achievers, by their very nature, are focused on achieving success. They live by goals and outcomes and are very well suited to the performance demands of most organizations. Their charismatic, chameleon-like nature also enables them to inspire and lead in multiple different ways, suiting the needs of the people and context.

  The achiever leader has to guard against what I call the *performance paradox trap*. Their singular focus on performance can cause them to ignore the more personal scenarios, such as conflict and employee morale, as they see time spent solving these as unproductive. Failing to deal with these often leads to severe team underperformance and eventually into the performance paradox trap of ever-decreasing performance.

- Challengers lead from the front and love getting lots done. Challengers are what some might call natural leaders. They want control and aren't afraid to make decisions (based on gut instinct). Their passion for traction and disruption (challenging the status-quo) often allows them to disrupt existing markets and start new ventures.

  Challenger entrepreneurs who are trying to scale their business often face the challenge of transitioning from solving problems themselves to communicating the problem and context to their teams and allowing them to generate the appropriate solutions. Conscious awareness of this pattern, coupled with coaching, can easily help challengers overcome this.

Apply to Self First: Understanding Our Own Personality Type

The first step in any evolutionary work is to apply the principles to one self. Understanding ourselves allows us to understand better what we are motivated by and why. Bringing this into consciousness can often lead to a realization that some of these (subconcious) motivations are no longer relevant, and in some cases are pulling us away from what we really want.

Once we have identified our core type, we can then begin to look at the inter-personal differences in style and motivations and design a strategy to align the two for mutual benefit.

Assessing your Enneagram type can be done in a number of ways, including online testing, coaching, and various other typing tools such as cards. The most common mechanism is the online test. I use two providers for this—The Enneagram Institute[2] and Integrative Enneagram Solutions.[3] Both providers offer a basic test for around $15 US; however, Integrative also offer in-depth reports for professionals (which I use in my digital leadership coaching programs). Select the one that you feel most aligned with and take the test.

Once you have your results, allocate some quiet time to absorb them and, if required, read further into the type descriptions. Do you identify with what the report is saying? There are some instances where the Enneagram assessments struggle to find your type based on your answers (loyalists are often mistyped). The key here is to read more deeply into the nine types until you find the core patterns that resonate with you. Some of these patterns you may not like and you may not want them to define you. That's perfectly normal. It's common for people to dislike their own type the most (with the exception of enthusiasts and challengers).

Once you have identified and understood your type, reflect on what that type means for you and your life and how it might impact what you are aiming to achieve. How do you operate differently from your boss, your stakeholders, and the members of your team? How does your type impact your relationships with your spouse, friends, and family? What types might they be? What might you change in order to bring more of what you want into your life?

Identifying Others' Types

There are two categories of people that we need to understand deeper—people who work under our leadership (e.g., our teams and direct reports) and those who don't (e.g., stakeholders and our leaders).

---

[2]https://unnatural.io/link/b102
[3]https://unnatural.io/link/b103

For those who work under our leadership (in particular those who report directly to us), I strongly recommend running Enneagram sessions together as a team. During these team sessions, explore the Enneagram system and the nine types. You'll discover each team member's Enneagram type and how each type behaves in a team and responds to conflict. These sessions increase team and individual awareness, which reduces frustrations and increases communication and productivity.

The vast majority of people who we want improved interactions with won't have been involved in an Enneagram assessment or workshop, and therefore we won't have access to their typing scores. So we need some clues to help us understand which of the nine types they might be. The first place to start is to look at the way the nine types respond and lead.

The response patterns and leadership styles of the nine types are summarized in Table 10-1.

Table 10-1. The Response Patterns and Leadership Styles of the Nine Types

Type	Response Patterns	Leadership Styles
1 – Reformer	Aim for perfection	Lead by example
	Black and white thinking	Focus on quality and excellence
	Dutiful obligation to make things right	Can make others feel judged or inferior
2 – Helper	Provide praise and flattery	Strong connections with people
	Focus on relationships	Supportive and motivating
	Caring, empathetic, and dutiful	Can burn themselves out
3 – Achiever	Care about how they will be seen	Performance Focused
	Focus on outcomes and success	Goals and structure for success
	Charismatic and assertive	Avoidance of emotions
4 – Individualist	Desire to express themselves	Create meaning and purpose
	Creativity and ideation	Inspire creativity
	Will want to know why they need to do something	Avoidance of mundane
5 – Investigator	Take a systems perspective	Create effective organizations
	Knowledge is power	Research and deliberation
	Intellectualize the situation and understand how	May detach and become aloof

(continued)

Table 10-1. *(continued)*

Type	Response Patterns	Leadership Styles
6 – Loyalist	Analysis of options and what might go wrong	Group problem solving
		Empowering leadership style
	Detailed planning	Can have cycles of indecision
	Focus on their group and seek advice	
7 – Enthusiast	Excitement and energy	Drive innovation and new ventures
	Positive focus on the big picture	Create excitement in people
	Can become distracted	Long-term execution can be a challenge
8 – Challenger	Gain control or protect	Lead from the front
	Moved to action	Decisive and empowering
	Can become vengeful	Can be demanding of people
9 – Peacemaker	Look for similarities	Build a collective mission
	Put others first	Create a harmonious culture
	Disconnect and daydream	Can be passive-aggressive

Let's look at a scenario where our fictional character Bob (from Chapter 8) is holding a one-on-one with a new stakeholder named Jenny, who also recently joined the organization.

Bob and Jenny are at a local coffee shop and are talking through the various initiatives and challenges they are both working on. Bob's reason for asking Jenny for coffee was to build a longer-term relationship with her. Jenny's role in the organization is to lead the call center that supports the products that Bob's team develops. As such, Bob considered Jenny to be a customer too. (Nice work Bob.)

Bob had recently learned the Enneagram system and strongly identified with his Enneagram type score of the achiever. Through this discovery process, he has realized that he has a tendency to drive people hard toward outcomes and, on occasion, avoid conflicts that seemed to him to be a waste of time.

Aside from his desire to build a relationship with Jenny, Bob also wanted to figure out what Enneagram type Jenny might be and apply his newfound knowledge for a better outcome. (Be careful Bob, don't over-focus on outcomes.)

As they chatted over coffee, Bob observed that Jenny knew every member of her team personally and obviously valued the personal interactions she had with them. Jenny had focused her side of the conversation on getting a better understanding of who Bob was a person and how she could help him.

He found her to be very pleasant and positive, often complimenting him on his achievements and viewpoints of the organization. When Bob asked Jenny why she had left her previous organization, she complained about the workload, the long hours, and juggling the demands of the people in the organization. Worse still, she received no appreciation or recognition from her leader, who quite insultingly gave her below average performance feedback for not delivering against her own personal objectives.

Bob began processing this and believed he had understood Jenny's Enneagram type—have you? If not, take a moment to assess the story against the Enneagram types.

Bob had correctly identified Jenny as a helper. Jenny's focus was definitely people—she had focused on understanding Bob and already had a good sense of her team at a personal level. Jenny also had a positive and flattering conversational manner. Bob assumed that Jenny's challenges at her previous role had, in part, come from her desire to help others, which caused her to burn out. He finalized that assumption when he heard that her efforts were not appreciated.

Bob now had two valuable pieces of information: he knew that he was an achiever and that Jenny was a helper. This meant he would have to be really conscious of his performance focus, which at times ignored the people involved, and that, in his interactions with Jenny, he needed to focus on appreciation for her assistance and clearly ask for help when he needed it. The Enneagram goes a lot deeper than this somewhat superficial level, but as you can see, this basic knowledge can make the difference between a strong and productive relationship and a poor, conflicting one.

It's not always easy to type other people correctly. Most Enneagram types respond to appreciation, and a lot of leaders (irrespective of their type) get to know their teams. What we see on the outside as a behavior isn't always directly indicative of a person's Enneagram type. A more productive and safer way to build this relationship would have been for Bob to directly share his newfound Enneagram knowledge and his own type. Sharing at this level would have demonstrated his commitment to personal development and an openness to share and collaborate. It would then give Bob and Jenny the chance to directly discuss what type Jenny might be.

If you are making private assumptions as to someone else's type, always be aware that they are only your assumptions and may not be accurate. As Bob's relationship with Jenny develops over time, he has the opportunity to validate and check his assumptions as he varies his approach accordingly and gets to know more about Jenny's personality.

One other approach we can use to type a person (which is implicit in this scenario) is to understand the basic motivators of each type.

The Nine WIIFMs (or Nine Motivations)

WIIFM stands for What's In It For Me? A question that each of us asks (sometimes consciously but often subconsciously) during our professional interactions. At the earlier levels of development (achiever and earlier), "What's In It For Me?" is a primary driver for how we behave.

It's so easy to become engrossed in what *we* want and what's in it for *us*, that we forget to focus on what's important to the other person. If we ignore what the other person is looking to achieve (what they want), they will soon pick up on this and begin to disconnect from the relationship. They may even begin to demand and force their outcomes more explicitly as the relationship dissolves into a power struggle (we've all seen those haven't we?).

Utilizing our knowledge of the Enneagram, we have a concise list of nine core WIIFMs, one for each of the types, as shown in Table 10-2.

Table 10-2. The WIIFMs for Each Enneagram Type

Type	WIIFM
1 – Reformer	How can I do the right thing and change things for the better?
2 – Helper	How can I help someone or the group?
3 – Achiever	How can I be successful?
4 – Individualist	How can I express myself?
5 – Investigator	How can I demonstrate my competence?
6 – Loyalist	How can I support my group's needs?
7 – Enthusiast	How can have I have fun?
8 – Challenger	How can I do something that challenges?
9 – Peacemaker	How can I find harmony and calm?

For example, individualists are generally looking for a way to express themselves and be seen. This can look similar in nature to the achiever who needs to be seen and validated. However, the difference between the two is the achiever wants the success and status to be seen, whereas the individualist wants to be seen as a unique and authentic human being (which for them does not require any level of success).

We can also see here how the WIIFMs of the two examples of Mark (a peacemaker) and Dave (a challenger) align with the scenario and how they responded.

Once we understand the other party's type, we have the keys to unlock their core motivators, their WIIFM, and their response patterns. We can then utilize this information to create a better relationship with them, grow and support them or, more generally, develop our level of empathy for those around us.

Curiosity Is Key

A childlike curiosity is the secret to evolution. What if? Why? How? These are the questions we asked almost endlessly as children. As adults, we often lose this intense curiosity and questioning from a fear of looking stupid or incompetent, or because we believe that we already know the answers to those questions. We may indeed have an answer that's appropriate, but is it the best? Can we do better? Elon Musk cites his success to his ability to reason from first principles and question what the majority of leaders have taken for granted. In his interview with Kevin Rose,[4] Musk said:

> First principles is kind of a physics way of looking at the world. You boil things down to the most fundamental truths and say, "What are we sure is true?"... and then reason up from there.
>
> Somebody could say, Battery packs are really expensive and that's just the way they will always be... Historically, it has cost $600 per kilowatt hour. It's not going to be much better than that in the future. With first principles, you say, "What are the material constituents of the batteries? What is the stock market value of the material constituents?"
>
> It's got cobalt, nickel, aluminium, carbon, some polymers for separation and a seal can. Break that down on a material basis and say, "If we bought that on the London Metal Exchange what would each of those things cost?" It's like $80 per kilowatt hour. So clearly you just need to think of clever ways to take those materials and combine them into the shape of a battery cell and you can have batteries that are much, much cheaper than anyone realizes."

Musk got curious, real curious, about why a kilowatt hour cost $600. He got curious about why the cost of space rockets was so high, and what would happen if they were re-used. His endless curiosity and passion has driven him to become one of the world's most significant leaders. He is rapidly creating our future. His companies—SpaceX, Tesla, Solar City, and Neuralink—are all redefining the markets where they play. They are creating tsunamis—from first principles!

---

[4]Innomind, "The First Principles Method Explained by Elon Musk," YouTube video, 2:48, posted December 2013, https://www.youtube.com/watch?v=NV3sBlRgzTI

What is it that you have assumed or taken for granted when it comes to yourself, your teams, stakeholders, products, and customers? What if you got really curious about your own assumptions, biases, and motivations? What might you be able to do differently with this new level of awareness?

Summary

While every human being is unique and offers a rich depth of complexity, we can use the Enneagram to understand the nine core motivational types. These motivations strongly affect a person's thoughts, emotions, and behaviors. Once we understand a person's type (or backend original codebase), we can choose to adjust our style and approach for greater influence and success.

There is no best Enneagram type, nor is there a worst type. Each of the types brings with them a set of strengths and weaknesses. Certain types naturally perform well in certain scenarios and under-perform in others. The more outward types of the achiever, enthusiast, and challenger are generally easier to type as they tend to communicate more openly and more often.

We don't change our core Enneagram type over time. We configure our type by the age of around 7 and that configuration remains set for the rest of our lives. What we do, with effort into our own development, is become healthier in our type and become more liberated from the negative aspects of our type.

We have merely scratched the surface of the Enneagram in this introduction. There is so much more richness and depth to the tool that I encourage you to continue your research. To better understand how people react under pressure and how to identify when they are doing well, my suggestion is to explore the integration (in health) and disintegration (in stress) of the nine types but, in particular, your own type. A deeper exploration of the three triads—Gut-Anger, Heart-Image, and Head-Fear—is also highly recommended as it provides the next layer of clarity on how each type operates and which centers of intelligence they use most.

Self-Reflection Questions

1. Which of the nine types do you think most describes you? What attributes of that type do you resonate with?

2. For your type (identified in Question 1), follow the stress (pointing away from your type's number) and health arrows (pointing toward your number type's number) to the two types that you integrate and dis-integrate to. What can you learn about your personality style in these emotional states?

3. How might you adapt your style or operation in order to achieve higher levels of success?

4. List five important people in your life and see if you can identify their Enneagram types (you can include friends and family). How might you change your interactions with them knowing this?

Summary of Part II: Awareness

As we raise our awareness, we gain a greater perspective on ourselves, others, and the challenges faced. If we don't have a sense of where we are, how the environment is changing, and the opportunities that present themselves, successful leaders will all too often get washed up on the shore.

Awareness always allows us to see the waves of change, to choose the one we want, and to paddle back when we need to as that wave comes to an end.

The waves of change are driven by people—by us. Whether we ride a wave or get washed up on shore is determined by our awareness of ourselves and the people around us. Understanding human biases, motivations, responses, and leadership styles is essential to being strategic, leading our teams, creating great products, and building great stakeholder relationships.

In this part, we explored the Humans as a Full Stack model and the following four key components that impact how a person behaves and responds:

- Their level of development (Expert, Achiever, or Catalyst)

- A person's preferred communication channel (Visual, Auditory, Kinesthetic, or Auditory-Digital)

- Their meta-programs running in their mind

- Their personality type and the nine Enneagram types

These four components raise our awareness and drive us toward success by delivering against these three outcomes:

- Increased level of self-awareness and tools for evolving further

- Development of our empathy and understanding for others, which increases quality of life for them and us

- Increased digital leadership effectiveness by improving how we respond, lead, and engage with stakeholders and customers

In Part III, we take a look at Intention, which is Step 2 of the evolution helix.

Intention

> *"Would you tell me, please, which way I ought to go from here?"*
>
> *"That depends a good deal on where you want to get to," said the Cat.*
>
> *"I don't much care where—" said Alice.*
>
> *"Then it doesn't matter which way you go," said the Cat.*
>
> *"—so long as I get SOMEWHERE," Alice added as an explanation.*
>
> *"Oh, you're sure to do that," said the Cat, "if you only walk long enough."*
>
> —Lewis Carroll, *Alice's Adventures in Wonderland (1865)*

Having intent helps us cut through the distractions of our busy lives and focus us on what we want to achieve. Intention works at the conscious and subconscious levels of the brain, activating areas that affect what is filtered in and out of our awareness.

Intention (Figure 1), step 2 of the evolution helix, builds on shifts in awareness (or stages) and then significantly shapes where we place our attention (step 3) and what we do.

Figure 1. Intention, step 2 of the evolution helix

The chapters in Part III begin with taking a look at the importance of being intentional. We leverage key elements of Parts I and II to help us understand what is important to us and how our Enneagram type and meta-programs impact our motivators and what we determine success to be.

We then explore the three elements that are important to Unnatural Leaders and the intentions they set to become and remain successful digital leaders.

Intention: The Secret to Success

Intention is one of the most powerful forces there is. What you mean when you do a thing will always determine the outcome. The law creates the world.

—Brenna Yovanoff[1]

Hollywood movie director James Cameron's unique combination of technical skills (special effects), artistic flair, and drive for perfection have helped him create the world's biggest box office smash hits, including *Terminator 1* and *2*, *Titanic*, *Avatar*, *Aliens*, and *The Abyss*.

---

[1]Brenna Yovanoff, *The Replacement* (Razorbill/Penguin Group, 2010).

© James Brett 2019
J. Brett, *Evolving Digital Leadership*, https://doi.org/10.1007/978-1-4842-3606-2_11

What is the secret to his incredible success, time after time? His intention! When creating movies, Cameron's intention is to "Push the boundaries of what is possible with cinematic digital effects." Never content with making movies with the current technology, Cameron's vision often requires the development of new cutting-edge technology that allows him to create realities on-screen that have never been seen before.

Intentionality drove Cameron to create the two most successful movies of all time (by box office revenue). The 1997 film, *Titanic*, drew in $2.19B globally and won 11 Academy Awards. *Avatar* (2009) made over $2.78B worldwide, making Cameron the most successful 3D movie director of all time.

Both of these movies cost millions of dollars and years to make. Cameron blew *Titanic*'s budget to over $200M (making investors extremely nervous before general release). *Avatar* went a step further, costing $300M in total production costs, and was a work of passion for Cameron for nearly a decade.

The significant costs incurred for both of these movies came from Cameron's development of new cinematic technologies. For *Titanic*, Cameron's directorial vision meant he had to film in the deep ocean depths of the shipwreck. At the time, there simply wasn't the recording technology available that would withstand the immense pressures of the deep ocean. So he went to work creating it—adding years and millions to the price tag—but Cameron's intent was so strong, he would not compromise. For *Avatar*, Cameron spent two years developing a new 3D camera system that set the benchmark for all 3D movies to date.

Cameron pushed the limits of what was possible at the time. Where most directors would have lowered their expectations or compromised the film's direction, Cameron pushed forward, sometimes dragging his stakeholders with him, and his overwhelming results are more than just dollars or fame—they are tsunamis of change.

> *The way James operated hit me hard. It opened my mind to the idea that it didn't matter what had or hadn't been done before, or how seemingly insurmountable the task. If you really want something, you go after it. You create a new reality. Fearlessly.*
>
> —Jessica Alba, Actress[2]

Cameron is a disrupter; he creates the future (his future). He doesn't wait to ride the waves created by others. His attention and energy are sharply focused by his passionate intention to push cinematic boundaries. Intention has fueled Cameron's meteoric rise to success.

---

[2]Jessica Alba, "How James Cameron Taught Me to be Fearless," LinkedIn, June 7, 2017, https://unnatural.io/link/b111.

What Is Intention and How Does It Make Us Successful?

At first glance, intention is a simple enough word to grasp. The Cambridge Dictionary defines intention as "something that you want and plan to do". So what's the big deal? Why is intention such a critical and challenging part of the Unnatural Selection framework?

Well, without intentionality our focus can be pulled in multiple different directions either by external influences or self distraction. Being busy doesn't mean we are being productive, effective, or bringing into our lives the things we desire. We all have very busy lives, yet few of us are true disruptors.

Without intention, this busyness can give us a false sense of productivity or can make us feel drained and tired, much like a hamster running endlessly on its wheel that's going nowhere fast. I'm sure most of us can associate with that hamster-wheel feeling at some point in our lives.

In leadership, it's common for our business to be more tactical in nature, and it can pull us toward operating in Mode 1—Get Stuff Done—of the Digital Situational Leadership model. The Get Stuff Done mode is where we spin endlessly on our wheel, dealing with urgent issues, giving in to interruptions, and responding to requests from our teams and stakeholders. If we allow ourselves to stay here for too long, we will soon face poor performance feedback from our leaders, who will likely criticize our lack of strategic, long-term thinking. This may reduce our chances of promotion or even of retaining our current position.

Operating and behaving in this manner is what I call Intention Deficit Disorder.

Remember this mantra: "***Energy flows where attention goes as set by intention***".

When we set an intention, it directs where we place our attention. Our energy then goes into the things that have our attention. A clear and compelling intention helps us determine what we do and don't do. Like a good product vision, intention helps us say "No" and focus on what we need to do to achieve success.

Our attention is focused by the intentions we have. If, say, we have the intention to help children develop healthy mindsets, we look at how we might find the capacity to coach and educate them. Our attention is then focused on how we find the time to invest in these activities. In this scenario, we currently spend a reasonable portion of our time each week on household chores and cleaning. With our intention, we able to choose (because we have the income level required) to engage a cleaner to take over these activities to enable us to attend to what we are passionate about.

Being intentional consists of two steps:

1. **Setting an intention:** Intentionality requires us to make a choice and get clear on what we want. To do this we need to take time out of our busy day and understand what is truly important to us and prioritize these things. Once we are clear on what is important, we are then able to set intentions that guide us toward what we want to achieve and what we want in our lives. You would be surprised how many leaders do not have a clear intentions. For some of us, this process is challenging. Working with a coach can help us to get clear on the what is important and why.

2. **Holding the intention:** Holding the intention is the hard part! By holding the intention front of mind, it keeps us focused on what we want so that we can continuously make the decisions and choices that keep us on the path to success. Sustaining this over a period of time can be challenging, especially if your organization or your default operating mode is Get Stuff Done. Holding an intention requires us to consciously revisit our intentions and priorities, so that we remain clear on what's important to us in the longer term, bigger picture.

Let's look at a specific example: Have you ever decided to eat more healthy food or lose weight? If you have, you no doubt set an intention for yourself. Let's assume that our intention is to gain more energy and vitality.

As we enter the kitchen to make ourselves dinner, this intention informs the food choices we make. The intention, when powerful enough, guides us to select fresh vegetables and clean foods where previously, we may have been drawn to the pizza. However, if our intention isn't truly meaningful enough for us, we will be pulled back into your old habits quite quickly.

Equally, as we change contexts and head out for our weekly grocery run, our same intention guides the food we buy. After all, it's hard to eat healthy when there aren't healthy options in the fridge. Our intention encourages us to make healthy choices and ignore or limit our selection of unhealthy, convenience foods.

The great thing about intention is that it doesn't just work on the conscious, obvious scenarios outlined here. There is an area at the base of our brains called the Reticular Activating System (RAS). It's the part of our brain that does our API-layer filtering. It filters out information that it believes is not important to us. The RAS determines what is important by what we focus on most. It determines what is important by the intentions we set. So, as we switch contexts to our commute home, we may make the decision to walk home to get some exercise. On our walk home, our RAS filters in the special offers available at the gym on the high street billboards, even though we were not actively looking for them. These adverts were always there, but now with intentionality, our brain is automatically, subconsciously bringing them to our attention.

So imagine what your career would look, sound, and feel like if you dialed in the intentions that supported your view of success. What would these intentions bring into your world that you have been missing so far? How might your actions, decisions, and behaviors change with new empowering intentions? If you are eager for more and want to find out how to go about setting and holding these intentions, then read on and I'll show you the Clarity Process. However, if you are unsure or skeptical, take some time to understand where this is coming from. Try asking yourself these questions:

- How has being skeptical served you well in the past? Is it appropriate here?

- Can you acknowledge your uncertainty and remain open to receiving more information and learning?

- What is (or might be) more important to you than reading and implementing the ideas in this book?

Remember, it's okay to feel wary, skeptical, and unsure about what I'm saying. In fact, the resistance you may be feeling is a normal part of the self-protection process that helps us avoid the feeling of disappointment in the event of not achieving our goals.

The Clarity Process

There are four steps in the Clarity Process that guide us through intention setting. The four steps are shown in Figure 11-1.

Figure 11-1. Four steps of the Clarity Process

The Clarity Process begins with us owning our career and our choices. Once we have taken ownership and are ready to take action, we need to understand and get clear on what is important to us as Unnatural Leaders. We then need to clearly define personal success and finalize the process by setting our intentions. In this chapter, we are going to explore the first step: Own.

Owning Our Career and Choices

Owning our career is the foundation of the Career Success Pyramid (discussed in Chapter 4), which is shown in Figure 11-2. If we don't own our careers, then no one will. What do I mean by owning our careers? At a fundamental level, it's about taking responsibility for where we are in our life, planning where we want to go next, and then doing something about it.

Balance leadership and technical **5**

Failure happens, it's how you respond **4**

Redefine personal success **3**

Get a coach and a mentor **2**

Own your career **1**

Figure 11-2. Career Success Pyramid

Intentions are future focused; they are things that we want to happen in the future. Therefore, the way that we process time has an impact on our ability to set future intentions. The Time Zone meta-program defines our preferences for processing time, as shown in Figure 11-3.

Figure 11-3. Time Zone meta-program

We all have a preference to focus on either the past, present or future. Planning our careers comes naturally for those of us whose minds are wired to focus predominantly on the future. For some, we look to the future with optimism and enjoy the potential of what may come; for others, our future focus can be more pessimistic and can create anxiety around what may or may not happen.

For those of us who are wired for experiencing time by being in the present moment or by constantly looking backward into the past, it can be more of a challenge to set and hold a future-focused intention, as our minds are constantly pulling us away from the future. Like the future-focused preference, the past-preference also has positive and negative biases.

Those of us who process time with a past-positive bias enjoy creating photo albums of our experiences and spending time reminiscing and recalling happy memories. For those of us who have a past-negative preference, we often suffer from regret, guilt, and shame, remembering the things that went wrong, or blaming ourselves for what we did wrong in the past.

Whatever our memories are, however negative they are, there is nothing that we can do to change the past. All we can do is show up today in the present moment and make decisions that impact our present and future.

Our goal as Unnatural Leaders (and healthy human beings) is to process aspects of the past that inform and guide us and place a majority of our focus on the present and future. We often have to make a conscious choice to do this. Leadership is about making and owning our choices each and every day, so let's take a deeper look at choice.

Choice

Choice is a very important and powerful thing. For many of us, we resist "owning" our choices, and instead take the easier route of blaming others for our challenges and mistakes. Choice isn't just about external events either; choice is about choosing and owning our own emotional state too. Have you ever heard someone say "He makes me so angry!" or "She really wound me up." The reality is that no other person can "make us angry". We have to choose to be angry in response to our observations of the other person's actions and communications.

I'm sure you've experienced one of those days where you are on top form—happy, energized, motivated, calm, and generally rocking it. On those days we hardly even notice the "irritating" actions of certain people, and if we do, we carry on without giving them a second thought. Yet on other days, when we feel tired, grumpy, and stressed, those same people seem to impact us in a significant way. The difference isn't in what they do; it's in how we react or respond. Unnatural Leaders are aware of their immediate, internal reaction to a scenario and can cognitively choose a response. This response may be the polar opposite of their initial (emotional) reactions.

When we truly own the choices we make, we no longer have any excuses.

Let me say that again—when we truly own the choices we make, we no longer have any excuses.

There are no excuses! For most of us, this is extremely confrontational. It means we have a new level of responsibility for our actions and our reactions—and this can feel very uncomfortable. It's a lot easier to blame others for our current situation, feelings, and responses than it is to own them.

Try this out now: Think of a current or recent scenario where you become frustrated, angry, or stressed about someone. Did you blame them? Did you respond appropriately? Are you still feeling negative? What would it be like if you owned your state and your response and moved on in a positive manner?

We Always Have a Choice

Choice can never be taken away from us. As a rather extreme demonstration, consider a scenario where, if I were to hold a gun to your head and tell you I would shoot you unless you stood on one leg, you would still have the power to choose to stand on one leg or not. You may not have any pleasing options, but you do have a choice. Even with a gun to your head, I cannot make you stand on one leg unless you choose to.

We complain all too often in our roles (and indeed in our lives) that we have no choice, or that we simply have to do something. It might be that our boss directs us to follow a strategy we don't believe is right and he simply won't listen. So, we have a choice to make. Once we empower ourselves with the power of choice, we actually have multiple responses to choose from:

- Follows his directives and do as he says

- Refuse and quit

- Refuse and escalate the situation

- Follow his directives calmly and look for another job in the process

- Follow his directives calmly and use our longer-term influence on our boss and stakeholders to change direction

Note. There was no option called "Sucking it up and moaning about how bad our job and/or boss is". When we own our choices, the need to complain disappears.

When we own our choices, we own our four powers.

Four Powers

The four powers (see Figure 11-4) are incredibly simple to understand. However, I can tell you from my own direct experience of being coached and in coaching others, fully owning all four of them is one of the hardest things to do. Owning them is a continuous, daily process. We don't simply go through owning our powers once and then we are done. We have to own them each and every day (which is why this is so challenging)!

Figure 11-4. The four powers

We have two internal powers that other people cannot see: Our thoughts and our feelings (the left side). We also have two external powers that they can see: our actions and our communications (the right side).

Owning Our Internal Thoughts

Owning our thoughts means choosing what we think about, how we think about things, and choosing to adjust our thinking when it's appropriate. When we don't own our thoughts, we can get into cycles of negative thinking that disempowers us. We ruminate over a past failure or become anxious about the future.

Equally, we may have an overly optimistic style of thinking that causes us to plan less and assume that what we want to happen, will happen. The outcome of this is that we experience failure in areas we might have predicted had we chosen to spend more time thinking about the risks and challenges ahead.

How we think is a choice and if we own our power of thought, we take responsibility for thinking the way we do and change it when required.

Owning Our Internal Feelings

Human beings have feelings and emotions. In 1980, Robert Plutchik identified eight basic emotions: joy, trust, fear, surprise, sadness, disgust, anger, and anticipation. Plutchik plotted these emotions on the Wheel of Emotions (see Figure 11-5).

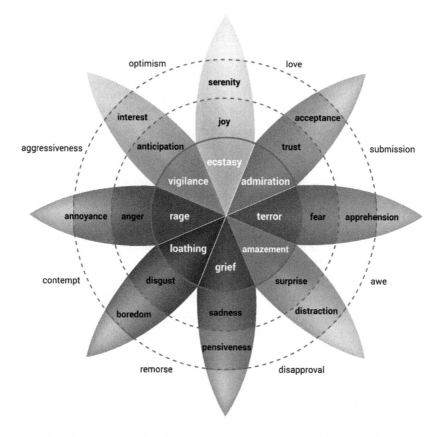

Figure 11-5. Robert Plutchik's wheel of emotions

The closer the emotion is to the center of the wheel, the more intense it is. Emotions such as joy and sadness are plotted opposite to each other, showing a consistent spectrum and how the emotion changes with intensity from serenity through to pensiveness.

Plutchik developed his model to include the more discrete sub-emotions that are derived from the eight basic emotions shown on the first ring around the center. The wheel of emotion gives us a concise model of what emotions exist and how they relate.

So what is an emotion? An emotion or e-motion is energy-in-motion—energy that is moving through our body. When we think about the intense emotions, we can often feel the energy in areas of our body. For example, a lot of us feel anxiety as an energy in our stomachs. How we experience and respond to emotions is impacted by our Enneagram type, and outlined in Table 11-1

Table 11-1. The Enneagram Types Relationship with Emotions

Type	Relationship with Emotions
1 – Reformer	Often have an anger emotion that drives them to want to change themselves and the world for the better.
2 – Helper	Are relationship focused and focus on and express emotion, in particular love. They can become angry or annoyed when they don't feel appreciated.
3 – Achiever	Are driven toward success, often ignoring the emotions around them, but paradoxically being driven and making decisions by their own emotions, although they are mostly unaware of this fact.
4 – Individualist	Love the intensity of both positive and negative emotions and often require emotion to move them to action. Fours often take situations too personally.
5 – Investigator	Tend to be the ones who engage least with either their own or other emotions, preferring to reason the logic of the situation. They do fear being seen as incompetent.
6 – Loyalist	Often fear the future (anxiety), which drives them to cycles of indecision and search for support and guidance.
7 – Enthusiast	Enjoy being positive and hold a positive emotional state. They avoid negative emotions and pain wherever possible.
8 – Challenger	Have a fear and anger of being controlled and often focus this anger (vengeance) on a person they deem to be attacking them.
9 – Peacemaker	Avoid emotional intensity in preference for stillness. They suppress their own anger, which often comes out as passive aggression.

Owning our emotional state involves owning the energy in motion that is in our body and knowing that we have the choice to react or respond to that emotion. For those of us at the development stage of Expert or below, our emotions are us, and therefore our reaction to the emotion is difficult to control. At the later stages of Catalyst and above, we see emotions as transient states that can be observed as they pass, thus giving us greater ability to choose our response rather than react.

You may be familiar with the technique of counting to 10 before responding. This is a technique often used by people at the earlier stages of development to help them control their reactions.

Another useful technique that allows us to respond rather than react is to ask clarifying questions of the other party to test any assumptions we have made. Often our incorrect assumptions are the root cause of our own emotional response. When we enquire at a more detailed level, we can determine if our initial response was appropriate. The questioning process allows us to gain a deeper and broader insight into the person and the context. This enables us to understand the drivers and motivators of the other person and why they communicated or behaved in a particular way. This more detailed and developed perspective regularly generates a level of empathy that tones down our original emotional reaction.

Owning Our External Actions

Our actions are our behaviors—the things people can see us do. Internally we think and feel certain things and we make decisions and choices that influence our actions. We may choose to drive over the speed limit (action) based on our desire to get to our destination on time. We make this choice knowing the risks involved in doing so and the potential that we might get caught by the police, or worse still, be involved in an accident. When we own our choice to speed, we take full responsibility for breaking the law and the risks involved. If we get caught, we don't blame the police officer for giving us an unnecessary ticket or complain about being victimized.

Equally, we may have an intention to get into shape, so we make the decision to put in two extra sessions at the gym each week and we follow through. Our actions are a positive move to get to the gym more to achieve our goal. As you can imagine, most of us are very good at owning our positive actions, and not so great at owning the actions that go wrong, or even inaction (which is still an action that involves sitting on the couch and watching TV instead of hitting the gym).

Owning our actions is taking full responsibility for the choices we make and the actions we perform and accepting any outcomes or consequences that occur from them, both positive and negative.

Owning Our External Communications

We have a number of different communication mechanisms. The two biggest ones are verbal (what we say) and nonverbal (our body language).

When we own our communications, we own what we say and how we say it. Only 7% of our communication is through words. A further 55% of our communication is through body language, with the remaining 38% being the tone, range, and speed of our voice.

All too often I see leaders focus on the words they use and ignore the other 93% of communication and then wonder why we aren't achieving the influence or impact we want.

It's too easy for digital leaders to resort to emails, text messages, and various other forms of electronic communication out of convenience or when we want to avoid having a face-to-face conversation. This may or may not be an effective way of communicating with the other party (or parties), but owning our communication choices involves us owning the medium we use to communicate and the content and tone of the message.

Owning Our Four Powers Is Challenging and Empowering

Owning all four of these powers, all of the time, is incredibly challenging. To make matters worse, our monkey mind often plays games with us by blaming us for not owning our powers, potentially creating a negative spiral of thoughts and emotions. Being a great leader involves taking risk and trying new things, some of which will fail. Those failures can be very unpleasant to experience. However, a mark of a great leader is to process the failure (and feedback) and grow from the lessons. Great leaders step back up, own their four powers, and then carry on.

Paradoxically, ownership of our powers is both challenging and empowering. When we step into full ownership of our powers, we are no longer a victim to anyone or anything. We understand that we can control the way we think and feel and that it is not dependent on our external environment and the people we interact with on a daily basis.

Remember, not choosing is still choosing. Often we convince ourselves that there are too many unknowns, or too many options or that we just don't have time to sit down to plan and make decisions. That is a choice! We are choosing to continue on as we are. We are choosing to stay comfortable, to not address the problem and create a solution. Maybe we're even choosing to stay miserable and unhappy. Are you starting to see how confrontational the process of owning your four powers of choice can be?

Summary

Setting career intentions and defining a path (whether short or long) is where the magic is. It assists us in combatting one of the biggest challenges to success—distraction. Knowing that we always have the choice of what we do, how we think, and how we feel is incredibly empowering. We can choose a wave to ride or create our own wave. We can then choose to paddle back out for more waves or we can chose to give up and stop. It's always a choice.

The key to making the choices that stick is to align them to what is fundamentally important to us at an individual level. Choices and intentions that don't propel us to success are often in conflict with other things we value (e.g., watching TV on the sofa instead of going to the gym points to the belief that being healthy isn't as important as relaxing).

In the next chapter, we take a look at Step 2 of the Clarity Process—Understand—and how we determine what we value as individuals and what is valuable to all Unnatrual Leaders.

Self-Reflection Questions

1. How would you rate your current level of ownership of your career on a scale of 1-5 (1 being no ownership, 5 being fully committed)?

2. Assuming you didn't answer 5 to the last question, what is it that is holding you back from full commitment? If you did answer 5, what is that has driven you to be fully committed?

3. Recall a scenario where you reacted in a less than ideal manner. If you had fully owned each of your four powers (Thoughts, Feelings, Communications, and Actions), how would you have responded? What impact would it have on your career if you could do this the majority of the time?

4. Where in your life are you not making the best choices? Remember than not making a choice is choosing not to choose and choosing to carry on with the current situation. How might you take more ownership of these choices?

Understanding What's Important

If it is important to you, you will find a way. If not, you'll find an excuse.

—Often attributed to Ryan Blair, American entrepreneur and author

Step 2 of the Clarity Process (presented in Chapter 11) is to understand what is important to you (see Figure 12-1). The objective of this chapter is to help you create a list of what is important to you in your life. The list you create will be specific to you and your situation, but it will contain elements of what all Unnatural Leaders deem important. However, for the items on the list to be compelling, it is crucial that it is *your* list—not the company's list, or your boss' list, or your colleagues' list. The items must be valuable to you!

Figure 12-1. Understand, Step 2 of the Clarity Process

© James Brett 2019
J. Brett, *Evolving Digital Leadership*, https://doi.org/10.1007/978-1-4842-3606-2_12

To figure out what is important, we will start by looking at the difference between extrinsic and intrinsic motivators and how our Enneagram type impacts what is important to us. We will then progress further up the Human Full Stack and explore three meta-programs that shape our idea of a quality life.

Once we have our list, we will complete Step 2 of the Clarity Process by looking at the three things that are important to all Unnatural Leaders and how they drive us toward digital leadership success.

The Challenge

For some of us, the challenge is that we don't know what we want. It might be that we find it hard to plan for the future because we don't know what our options are. For others, we might not like being constrained by making one single choice and prefer to keep our options open. Sometimes we know what we want, but people in our social circle expect something else from us, and we feel obliged to fulfill their expectations.

Often money is a driver and is either an integral part of our intentions or conflicts with them. Our society considers success as status and wealth. It measures our success by luxury cars, big houses, the latest gadgets, designer clothes, and extravagant vacations. We might value these too, and so we make career choices that chase the dollar but pay the penalty of dissatisfaction with our jobs.

What we need to understand is that success is an inside job. Success is a combination of our internal thoughts and feelings—it's not a concrete thing that we obtain from someone or somewhere else. Winning a competition, becoming a CTO, or buying the house we've always dreamed of, all do one thing: they trigger positive emotions inside us and we "feel" successful.

Success means different things to each of us, and it changes over time and through our stages of development. At the earlier stages of development (where many of us are at the start of our careers), we struggle balancing extrinsic (social) and intrinsic (desire) motivators. Let's explore the difference between the two.

Extrinsic Motivators

Extrinsic motivators drive us to engage in something in order to receive some form of external reward. The rewards can be either tangible or intangible in nature. Common tangible rewards include pay rises, cars, houses, and trophies. Intangible rewards are psychological rewards and include promotions (higher status), praise, and public acclaim.

All too often we perform activities that we don't fully enjoy to receive these external rewards. For most of us, the reality is that we have to work to earn a wage that we use to pay for our accommodation, food, and living costs. Therefore, there is usually a level of extrinsic motivation that is required to live. Where we start to create problems for ourselves is when we chase bigger and bigger external rewards by working harder and longer in jobs that we don't enjoy.

Intrinsic Motivators

Intrinsic motivators propel us toward something that gives us an internal reward—satisfaction, fulfillment, and gratification. Examples of intrinsically motivated activities are painting, drawing, or reading. It may be that what we do also attracts an external reward—if we sold our painting we would receive money as an external reward. The key difference is whether or not we paint primarily for the enjoyment of painting (intrinsic motivation) or the financial reward (extrinsic motivation).

In *Drive*,[1] Pink identifies three core intrinsic motivators:

- **Autonomy**

   We are driven internally by a desire to control our destiny. We want to be able to choose what we do, where we do it, when we do it, with whom we do it, and how we do it. This involves leaders posing challenging questions and giving the team space to generate solutions, rather than micro-managing and prescribing solutions that we think are appropriate. When we have autonomy, we feel empowered and in control of our lives. This will also lead to a feeling of satisfaction in a job well done.

- **Mastery**

   Developing our skills and expertise in something we are interested in or care about is a key motivator. 100% interest goes a long way to 110% effort. Mastering our craft (particularly at the Expert stage of development) is critical to our motivation levels. Digital is a cerebral industry and expertise and intellect is a highly regarded commodity in building products and services.

---

[1]Daniel H. Pink, *Drive: The Surprising Truth About What Motivates Us*, (Riverhead, 2011)

- **Purpose**

  We want to know that what we do, the products that we build, are of benefit to others. When what we do has a positive impact on other humans, we deem our work as having meaning and purpose. Without meaning and purpose, we quickly become demotivated and our chances of achieving success diminish rapidly.

Pink defines people that are primarily driven by intrinsic motivators as Type I people, and those that are driven more by extrinsic motivators as Type X. His research shows that in the long term, Type Is always outperform Type Xs as their energy and motivation is a renewable resource. As leaders we need to be consciously aware of this fact.

Our level of development and personality type determine how strongly we are driven by extrinsic motivators. Earlier developmental levels such as Expert and Achiever are motivated more by extrinsic motivators. Intrinsic motivators are present at all stages. However, as our development progresses, external rewards become less and less meaningful.

As our developmental level progresses to late-stage Achiever, Catalyst, and beyond, our values and beliefs become more integrated, and we start to become more driven by our intrinsic motivators and values. Meaningful work and impact become more and more important to us. We also start to define our purpose in life. How we define purpose depends on our unique personality and perspectives. For some of us, our purpose is to have a positive impact on the planet; for others, it's to help the underprivileged; and for others, it's to create a harmonious home life for their family.

The Midlife Crisis: The Painful Transition from Achiever to Catalyst

Transitioning from Achiever to Catalyst can often be a painful and lonely process. Western society has collectively progressed to an Achiever-level of development. This means that there are strong external motivators for us to keep up with the Jones', and so, as we progress beyond this stage, society can hold us back. When we develop into the early stage of Catalyst, our values and worldview shift and we, as a result, no longer appreciate or want the things that society is structured for.

We are no longer driven primarily toward financial success and materialism and instead want to contribute to meaningful work, have a positive impact on others, and leave behind a positive legacy. This causes us to critically question the actions of organizations and leaders that disrespect race, class, and gender, or damage the environment. In some cases, we completely reject "normal" society and what it stands for, becoming quite angry at the world.

Note   In psychology, we call this stage (with its anger aimed at the Achiever society) Mean Green. Where green is the label given by Integral Theory[2] for this stage of development.

As we reject society's way of being, it looks to others (at Achiever level and earlier) like we are having a midlife crisis—we are not. To society, it looks like we are going off the rails and "losing our minds" when, in reality, what we are doing is developing our consciousness further toward a more integrated values and belief system that is driven primarily by intrinsic motivators. I prefer to call this process a *midlife awakening*.

What makes this a lonely process is the lack of connection we feel with our friends, family, and social circles who still value expertise, achievement, and conforming to society's norms. Our social circles become either frustrating or boring as our worldviews and the people in our circles begin to misalign. This can, in some instances, pull us back into Achiever, where it's easier to keep doing what we always did and what everyone else expects of us.

There are many actions we can take to help ourselves through this transition, but I believe the two most important are thus:

- To develop our social circles to more reflect our changing worldview.

- To enlist the services of a coach who will assist us in our understanding and processing of our shift to Catalyst. Coaches and coaching organizations often have a community of people who are making similar transitions and who are focused on similar personal development journeys.

The Achiever to Catalyst transition aside, let's utilize the Human Full Stack as a tool to understand what is important to us by looking at how our meta-programs and personality type influence our motivations.

---

[2]Integral Theory is a developmental framework developed by Ken Wilber.

Human Full Stack

Our Human Full Stack (see Figure 12-2) impacts what is important to us, particularly in our backend personality layer where our core motivators sit. Our Enneagram type (discussed in Chapter 10) defines a set of motivations and fears that transcend shorter-term desires such as career promotions. Our meta-programs layer and the meta-programs we run also impact how we set and hold intentions; they determine how we make choices, how we interpret a situation, how we experience quality of life, and they define our overarching modus operandi.

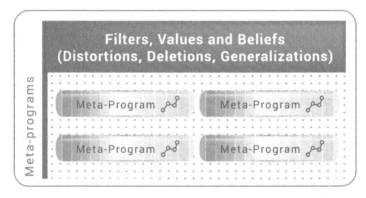

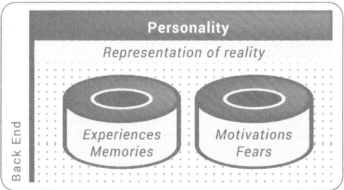

Figure 12-2. Meta-programs and backend of the Human Full Stack model

Backend Motivators: Enneagram Types

Knowing our Enneagram type's core motivators helps us develop a deeper understanding of what might be important. These motivators can be used to shape new intentions or refine existing ones to give more impact and meaning. If we set intentions that oppose our Enneagram motivations, we are likely to struggle to achieve success as the two forces pull us in different directions. Table 12-1. outlines the primary things that are important to each Enneagram type.

Table 12-1. What's Important to Each Enneagram Type

Type	Core Motivation	Things That Are Important
1 – Reformer	Do the right thing	Perfecting skills; changing things for the better
2 – Helper	Help a person or group	Connect with and help people on a personal level
3 – Achiever	Be valuable	Achieving outcomes
4 – Individualist	Express themselves	Creativity and variety
5 – Investigator	Demonstrate competence	Intellectual stimulus
6 – Loyalist	Be part of and support a group	Loyalty, connection, and guidance
7 – Enthusiast	Have fun	Innovation, variety, and options
8 – Challenger	Challenge the status quo	Control, power, and getting things done
9 – Peacemaker	Harmony and calmness	Physical and mental wellness

As you can see in the right column of Table 12-1, for each of the nine Enneagram types, we reference what's important to us to enable us to identify what we need in our lives to feel satisfied and successful. We then set powerful intentions that align with what we deeply desire.

Let's look at the individualist (Type 4) as an example. (This is my Enneagram type.) As this name suggests, the individualist's core motivator is to express themselves as unique and different. This desire influences their choices to include creativity and variety. Creativity draws individualists toward activities that allow for expression such as product creation, strategic visioning, business building, art, music, etc. Creating something new and different is an enjoyable process for Type 4s and has added significance if what they create is meaningful to them.

Individualists generally don't like being controlled or having to conform to normality—how can they be individuals if they are the same as everyone else? Avoiding normality sees them search for variety and avoidance of the mundane, routine aspects of life.

Use Table 12-1 and your Enneagram type to help identify what is important to you and what you must, therefore, consider when thinking about the future and setting your own empowering and meaningful intentions.

Let's now take a look at the next layer in the Human Full Stack—the meta-programs layer and the key meta-programs that affect what's important to us.

Three Meta-Programs That Impact What Is Important

There are three key meta-programs (see Figure 12-3) that impact what is important to us: Quality of Life, Preference, and Attention. These meta-programs shape our representation of the world and influence our highest frames in many ways, which are discussed in the following sections.

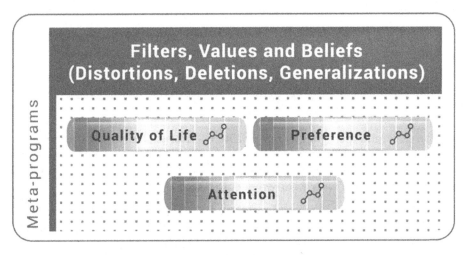

Figure 12-3. Three meta-programs that influence what's important

Quality of Life: Be-Do-Have

The Quality of Life meta-program (see Figure 12-4) affects what is required for us to have a satisfied life: We feel satisfied with life when we are *doing* certain things, or with the things that we *have*, or *being* in a particular way.

Figure 12-4. Quality of Life meta-program

If we experience satisfaction through the things that we *do*, we tend to enjoy experiences, dinners, vacations, activities, etc. We are happy when we are busy doing new and interesting things. The things that we do are important.

If we experience satisfaction through the things we *have*, then we feel satisfied when we have the things that we want: a house, car, kids, clothing, gadgets, and status. Having material possessions, riches, and status are important for those with a *having* preference.

If we experience satisfaction through *being*, we enjoy spending time with people, animals, nature, and activities such as reflecting, meditating, and creative self-expression. *Being* ourselves and/or *being* with others is important.

All of three of elements are appealing at certain times. However, at any stage of life, we often find that we determine our satisfaction primarily through one of these elements. When we know which is our preference, we can leverage this to set more powerful intentions and goals. Alternatively, we can also set intentions that include elements of all three.

Preference: People, Place, Things, Time, Activity, Information, and Systems

The Preference meta-program helps us identify our core motivations by determining what type of things we look for when we have peak experiences. The Preference meta-program has seven points—People, Place, Things, Activity, Information, Time, and Systems—as shown in Figure 12-5.

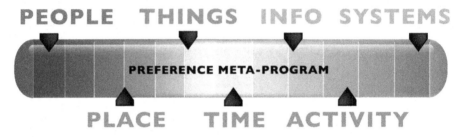

Figure 12-5. Preference meta-program

A preference for *people* means that our positive experiences are usually around people and who we share them with. Unsurprisingly, those of us who have this preference are often social beings. When we have a preference for people, we dislike being on our own and can suffer from loneliness more than others. People are important and, as you can imagine, will be central in the intentions we set.

A preference for *place* means that we focus on where we are, our location and geography. This preference usually gives us a high awareness of our surroundings and environment. In some instances, we search for new and exciting locations, in others we want a familiar or safe place.

A preference for *things* brings focus to what is in our environment and we take pleasure from both the tangible things (gadgets, car, house) and intangible things (qualifications, status). In a professional context, this preference tends to mean we enjoy working more with things rather than people.

A preference for *activity* means we prefer to keep in motion and keep busy. We enjoy the how of doing things and get energized by being in motion and getting things done. Those of us with a preference for activity don't often focus on our own emotions, instead turning our attention to tasks and the actions needed to complete them.

A preference for *time* means that we focus on how long something will take, how long we will remain in a location or when will we return. "Time is money" is a belief that people usually hold when they have this preference. These people are often always aware of the day, date, and time.

A preference for *information* means we seek out scenarios where we can learn new facts and concepts and figure out how we can apply this new knowledge. We are less concerned with who we are with and where we are as we learn new information, and are more focused on the source of the information and how to apply our new lessons.

A preference for *systems* means we like to look at processes and the interconnected nature of things. We look for cause and effect and how things function, even when those systems are human systems. People with a preference for systems tend to think big picture, and can easily see how all the nuanced details fit together and impact one another.

The final meta-program describes where we mainly focus on our attention as we go through life.

Attention: Self or Other

I introduced the Attention meta-program (see Figure 12-6) in Chapter 9 as an example of tuning meta-programs. As we move through the world we process information, relate to people, and perform actions. The Attention meta-program determines whether we focus on our own thoughts, feelings, and choices as we go through life (self), or focus on other people's thoughts, feelings, and choices (other). Because this meta-program fundamentally determines whether our priority is to attend to our self or to others, it is critical when determining what is important to us. If a person is wired strongly toward others, they will struggle to complete the self-reflection questions in this book without involving someone else to assist them. Equally, a person strongly wired for self may have a more limited view of themselves and capacities as they only process their singular perspective.

Figure 12-6. Attention meta-program

As you can imagine, balance in the Attention meta-program (the ability to focus on both self and other) is critical for successful leadership. If we have a strong preference at either end of the spectrum, it often leads to unnecessary challenges, especially around team engagement, building a compelling strategy, and communicating with others, for example.

The final technique we are going to look at to discover what's important to us is to understand the highest mental frame we are holding.

The Highest Frame Governs the Game

Sometimes we know what we want (or at least we think we do) or we know what we want but we aren't sure why we want it. In coaching, we use a technique that looks for what's most important to a person by identifying the "highest frame" they are holding in a particular situation.

The highest frame can be described as the highest level of meaning we have given to something. This highest frame (or mental view) directs our actions and contains what is most important to us.

If you have been in the Agile world for a while, you may have come across the five Whys process, originally developed by Sakichi Toyoda at Toyota Motor Corporation. The Five Whys process is an iterative inquiry process that seeks to find the root cause of a problem. The approach was developed to help get to the cause of a defect or problem in the manufacturing process and has been adapted to the software development world through the application of Lean techniques.

In coaching, rather than looking for the root cause of a problem, we follow a similar process to find the highest frame of meaning the person is holding, by asking a similar series of why questions.

Here's a coaching scenario from one of my clients, who we'll call Jane:

> **Jane**: "I'm really frustrated and can't seem to get motivated by my work."
>
> **Coach**: "Why?"
>
> **Jane**: "Because my boss won't promote me and I really want to move up to a Director role."
>
> **Coach**: "Why?"
>
> **Jane**: "Because I really need to earn more money."
>
> **Coach**: "Why?"
>
> **Jane**: "Because I really value family and I want to have a baby. Having said that, I don't think I could take time off from this job."
>
> **Coach**: "Why?"
>
> **Jane**: "I don't think my boss would support me if I focused on my family more."
>
> **Coach**: "Why?"
>
> **Jane**: "Actually, I'm frustrated because I don't feel like my values align with the organization any more, and I probably need to find an organization that better aligns with who I am before I plan for a baby."

After this conversation, Jane realized that her and her boss had misaligned values (her highest frame), and Jane's desire for a family would not be supported where she was. She decided to leave her role and move to another organization and leader that were more aligned with her core values.

It can take some coaching skill and time to work through this process, but it's worth the investment to understand the core motivation driving a behavior.

In this scenario, it may be that leaving the organization is the best action to take. Alternatively, Jane could have a candid conversation with her boss and discuss her motivations and desire to start a family in order to validate her assumptions (the lack of her boss's support). Irrespective of the outcome, Jane has gained significant insight and clarity about what is highly important to her.

We can apply this process to understanding the motivations and meaning-making of our teams and stakeholders. It is incredibly powerful in one-on-one scenarios in gaining a deeper understanding of what drives a person. However, caution should be exercised when using this process with others. As you might imagine, it's quite easy for the other person to feel interrogated when being asked "Why?" over and over. In coaching, we tend to ask "and why is that important to you?" or "and what does that mean for you?" instead of just "why?". (We cover this in more detail in Chapter 16.) However, in this chapter, we are applying the five Whys technique to ourselves as a tool to drill down into our core motivations and to help us understand what is important.

Purpose

What is your life purpose? Do you know? Is there something that drives you, both professionally and personally? Purpose is essentially our single highest intention that binds together what we value most with all other intentions, creating a complete and single way of being.

Elon Musk's purpose is:

> To make the human race a multi-planetary species.[3]

His way of "being" leads him to single mindedly focus all his time and energy into achieving this life purpose. Indeed, what higher purpose can there be than to protect the human race against its potential destruction caused by the limitations of living only on a single planet—Earth.

---

[3]SpaceX, "Making Humans a Multiplanetary Species, streamed live on September 27, 2016, 1:58:21, https://unnatural.io/link/b121

His purpose drives his intentions and prioritizes his energy and attention on SpaceX and Tesla. He knows that every step he takes with these companies takes him one step closer to colonizing another planet, either through the development of space rockets or energy supply and advanced manufacturing techniques.

Without a purpose, we go through life mostly doing disjointed and un-related activities—the exact opposite of Elon Musk. You may find this way of life enjoyable and you may not want or need anything else. However, if you feel like something is missing, something to make sense of what you are doing, then defining your purpose can help. Finding our purpose can be a challenging and lengthy process. In my experience, engaging a coach can help you find clarity.

Make a List

We have now looked at three tools we can use to understand what's important to us:

- Aligning to our Enneagram type's core motivators
- Understanding where we sit on the three meta-programs of Quality of Life, Preference, and Attention
- Knowing our highest frame of meaning

Before we continue, make a list of the things that are important to you personally by applying these techniques. You may end up with a short list or a really long list. It will probably take quite a bit of time and effort to really dig deep into these things. I started the process with post-its on a wall, and evolved the list over a number of months, so don't be discouraged if you can't do this in one sitting. Invest the time and make your list. If it is a lengthy list, try to prioritize the top 5-10 items to gain better clarity.

What Is Important to All Unnatural Leaders?

In this chapter, we looked at various ways of unpacking the Human Full Stack to get a better understanding of what is important to us in our lives. At this point you should have a list of these items, some of which may be related to your digital leadership journey and some may not. Now that we have this base understanding, let's take a look at the four things that are important to all Unnatural Leaders (see Figure 12-7).

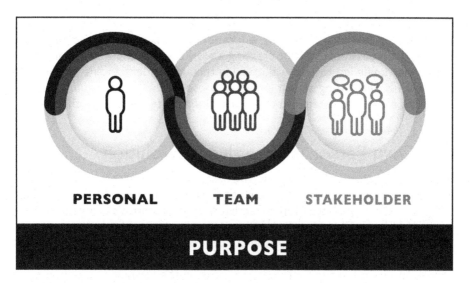

PERSONAL   **TEAM**   **STAKEHOLDER**

PURPOSE

Figure 12-7. What's important to an Unnatural Leader

Purpose

Unnatural Leaders have a purpose, or at least a basic concept of the impact they would like to have on their organization, their industry, the world, and the human race. Their purpose provides context and the fuel that drives their growth and evolution. Each leader articulates this in their own specific and personal way.

As an example, I describe my purpose as:

> *To positively influence the direction of society so that our children and future generations are able to have a high quality of life.*

What makes this meaningful for me is that I believe the future is uncertain. With the advent of artificial intelligence and other technical advancements, I believe that our society could head in a number of directions, and some of those directions are ones that I would not want for my children. I believe that the world is ever increasingly being run by technology-led organizations, and as such, digital leaders are the focus of my attention. If I can impact digital leaders, their teams, and their organizations in a positive way, I can build a more positive future and a world I'm happy to leave behind for the children and future generations.

My purpose, however, does not limit me to just working with digital leaders. It also drives me to look at the education system and how we raise our children. I am passionate about creating a world where children are given the skills and knowledge to lead a better life through understanding how to run their own brains (using similar tools to those in this book), which in turns generates more compassion in the world and a better future for all.

Our Own Personal Growth and Evolution

Unnatural Leadership is about evolving faster than the pace of change. If our growth and evolution are not important then we'll fill our days with busyness and fail to focus our attention on activities that promote our evolution (for more details see Chapter 14). We have to value and embody our evolution and not simply pay lip service to the concept of it. Sometimes our growth can be painful when we fail or receive negative feedback. However, when we value growth and have a growth mindset, we focus on the learning that comes from that setback. Over time, we fear failure and negative feedback less as we come to appreciate it as a fundamental element of our growth and success.

The Growth of Our People

If bringing out the best in your people isn't important to you, then you probably aren't operating as a leader and instead are working as a manager. Nowhere in this book have I defined the role of Unnatural Manager (there are enough of those already).

Unnatural Leaders care for and place importance on their people. It's important to Unnatural Leaders to cultivate environments for their people to thrive, flourish, and grow. This growth is integrated with high-performance delivery and creates leading-edge cultures.

The Growth of Long-Lasting Stakeholder Relationships

Unnatural Leaders value people and stakeholder relationships. We understand that people are how things get done and that people are important in every context. Unlike tactical leaders who battle with stakeholders in order to push through their own agendas, Unnatural Leaders value long-term stakeholder relationships that benefit both parties. They can't help but see the silos (and the unfortunate side-effects of archaic organizational structures) and where possible, they transcend these to create relationships that drive organizational success and impact.

Configuration of the Unnatural Leaders Full Stack

Now that we have explored various tools to understand what is important to us as Unnatural Leaders, let's bring this all together and look at how an Unnatural Leader's stack is configured.

Unnatural Leaders are primarily intrinsically motivated. They clearly understand what is important them and what work is meaningful. This guides and shapes what they do and plays into their highest frame.

An Unnatural Leaders Backend Configuration

An individual's Enneagram type doesn't change, even as we evolve, and therefore we aren't able to reconfigure our core type. (As we discussed in Chapter 10, there is no right or wrong Enneagram type.) What Unnatural Leaders do is to clearly understand their Enneagram type at a deep level, and can bring to their conscious awareness the patterns, focus, and motivators that drive them. Unnatural Leaders understand the aspects of their type that power them to success and the aspects that may cause challenges. They align and integrate what is important to fully actualize their potential and the potential of others in their organization.

An Unnatural Leaders API Layer Configuration

An Unnatural Leader's three meta-programs are configured in the following way:

- **Quality of Life—Being and Doing**

  Quality of life for an Unnatural Leader is typically biased toward being and doing and away from having. They experience a high quality of life through the experiences they have with people, self-expression, and enjoying the human aspects of life.

- **Preference—People**

  As Unnatural Leaders develop their leadership capacity they shift their preference toward people and away from what probably made them successful earlier on in their careers: Activity and Information. This is part of the journey described in Chapter 3. Relationships are central to Unnatural Leaders and this is echoed in the people focus of the three elements they identify as important (self, team, and stakeholders).

- **Attention—Balance Between Self and Others**

  Chapter 9 discussed the benefits of gaining balance on the spectrum between self and others in the Attention meta-program. Unnatural Leaders are able to hold their attention in the middle of the spectrum and shift to each end as needed, allowing them to define what is important to them while also incorporating what is important to others to create effective team environments and the best outcomes during negotiations.

What underpins the configuration of the Unnatural Leaders stack is a high degree of focus on people (including themselves). Gaining a deep understanding of how we operate is critical to experiencing a high quality of life and reaching our full potential. The focus on people, whether it's the people in our teams or the stakeholders we engage with, allows us to have a more significant and positive impact on the organization, industry, and society.

Summary

A majority of us aren't crystal clear about what we want. Most of us have never invested the time and energy to understand what we want, let alone why we want it! Getting clear on what this is for you will enable you to set intentions which are personally compelling and drive your evolution in a positive manner. They are the fuel for your evolutionary rocket.

Our level of development has a significant impact on what we want and what we view as success. Our society is primarily at an Expert-Achiever level of development, and as such, success tends to be about enjoying our work, mastering our craft and achieving goals. Does this resonate for you? Or do you find yourself beginning to long for something more purposeful?

Our Human Full Stack influences what we deem to be important. It does this through our intrinsic and extrinsic motivators, our core Enneagram type and meta-programs. By understanding how you place importance on things, you now have a framework that will allow you to dive deeper into your own personal motivators and those of the people around you (which are almost always different!).

Understanding what is important to you is key to experiencing a satisfying life. When you can articulate what is important for you (and why), you can then create conscious intentions that bring more of those things into your life.

Likewise, understanding what is important to others is key to influencing and leading them to deliver high-impact, meaningful work as individual contributors or as part of a team.

Note   In the next chapter, we build on the list you made here. Do you best to complete it before moving on.

Self-Reflection Questions

1. What extrinsic rewards do you currently need (or want) to feel successful and have a high quality of life?

2. For each of the three meta-programs (Quality of Life, Preference, and Attention), try to determine where you sit on the spectrum. If need be work with someone close to you and ask for personal feedback.

3. Do you have a purpose that you are inspired by? If so, write it down in one or two sentences. If you don't have a purpose, write down what you are passionate about and think about how the outcomes of what you do have an impact on people that is wider than your role and organization.

4. On a scale of 1-5 (1 being not at all, and 5 being extremely important), rate how important the following are for you right now:

    a. Your own personal growth

    b. The growth of your team(s) and people

    c. The growth of long-term stakeholder relationships

5. For the three items in the previous question, which was most and least important to you and why?

Successful Intentions

The first responsibility of a leader is to define reality. The last is to say thank you. In between, the leader is a servant.

—Max de Pree[1]

You now have an understanding of what's important to you, and to all Unnatural Leaders (our own personal growth and evolution; the growth of our people and teams; and the growth of our stakeholder relationships). Now it's time to define your concrete intentions, which help to bring into your world what you have placed value and importance on (see Figure 13-1).

Figure 13-1. Define, Step 3 of the Clarity Process

---

[1] *Leadership Is An Art* (NY: Crown Business, 2004).

© James Brett 2019
J. Brett, *Evolving Digital Leadership*, https://doi.org/10.1007/978-1-4842-3606-2_13

The Three Intentions of Unnatural Leaders

We will start by defining the three intentions that all Unnatural Leaders set to help to actualize personal, team, and stakeholder success. Following on from this, you can use the same process to define any intentions that you need to set, based on the list you created in the previous chapter.

Intention 1: Passionately Curious

Albert Einstein famously said, "I have no special talents; I am only passionately curious."

We all know that passionate curiosity wasn't the only thing that allowed Einstein to make the discoveries and scientific contributions to science that he did—he was incredibly intelligent too! What Einstein is alluding to with this quote, is that the fact that humans can do great things when they are both passionate and curious about a subject.

Being passionately curious creates a sustained energy and interest in things we are focusing on (see Figure 13-2). The passion drives our sustained focus, while curiosity opens our minds and perspectives to ask questions and dive into areas that we may have otherwise missed or dismissed.

PERSONAL SUCCESS

Intention:

TO BE PASSIONATELY CURIOUS

Figure 13-2. The intention: to be passionately curious

Unnatural Leaders have a passionate curiosity for the world around them and for the development of themselves and others. They are excited by the potential of their own growth, the opportunities that it might bring, the impact that they will have, and the legacy that they will leave. They are curious about how and why they operate the way they do and how this affects their performance and the performance of those around them. The original passion they had for technology and problem solving is now focused on the process of self-evolution and actualizing their full potential (which includes the development of others).

Let's go back to our wave surfing metaphor but this time from a perspective that has little to no passion or curiosity:

Our leader is standing on the beach, looking out at the ocean preparing to surf the waves of change. As she stands there she is filled with fear and anxiety about how well she will perform. She stands on the beach, for what seems like an eternity, looking for a wave that looks perfect but just never comes. The longer she waits, the less she wants to go. The less she wants to go out there, the more mentally painful the whole experience becomes. As her stress builds, her muscles and posture tighten and her breathing rate increases. She is now in fight or flight mode. When she does eventually hit the surf, she tries a small wave and her rigid body causes her to crash out instantly. She heads back to the beach where she mentally confirms the idea that she can't surf. Surfing is not for her; she isn't good enough. She just doesn't have the physical build or coordination to do it.

She gives up.

With passionate curiosity, the same leader looks out over the ocean with excitement (and a maybe a little fear). She is curious about the waves that are rolling in and where the rips are. She chats with a local surfer and confesses her inexperience. The surfer gives her some great tips on where and how to enter the ocean and which waves to try first. She enters the ocean knowing she's going to fall. It's inevitable but she is curious about how and why. She's curious about what it feels like to ride even a small wave and she understands that becoming a great surfer is a process that takes many repetitions.

She enters the ocean and laughs as she gets knocked around. She catches a little wave for a few seconds and topples ungracefully into the water. She quickly processes the experience and tries again, and again, and again. Sometimes she rides a lot further, other times she falls instantly. But all the time her curiosity keeps her eyes scanning the ocean for waves, watching the other surfers ride gracefully, she adapts something in her style with each wave she rides.

She ends the day, tired, cold, and still curious! She's still not a confident surfer, but she can surf better than she could two hours earlier. As one of the pro-surfers comes into the beach, she asks him more questions and manages to get a couple of great tips to try next time.

Two years later, she's the surfer out at the back catching the big waves (almost) every time.

The difference between the two scenarios is dramatic. One leader lasted five minutes and gave up focusing on improving her leadership ability and likely continued to get slammed by each new wave of disruption. The second Unnatural Leader became a great surfer, creating new waves of change that were bigger and bigger each year—all with an intention of being passionately curious and holding a growth mindset.

Being passionately curious allows us to seek help from others, and allows us to ask questions of ourselves that improve our performance. It acknowledges that it's okay to not have the answers or be competent at everything. Curiosity helps us achieve what's important to us by enabling our growth and evolution.

What goals would you be setting for yourself if you knew you could not fail?

—Robert H. Schuller[2]

Intention 2: From Performance Management to Growth

During my interviews with digital leaders, one of the biggest leadership challenges raised was performance management. Managing the performance of the people who directly report to us can be a challenge. Performance management all too often means we have identified low performance in someone and we need to intervene and restructure or terminate that person's employment. Now, as anyone with any leadership experience will know, unless gross misconduct is involved, we can't just fire someone—we have to "performance manage" them.

Gross misconduct aside, there are times when a person should not be in an organization, either because they are behaving in a toxic and disruptive manner or because they have little to no interest in the organization's products and vision. Either way, they have already mentally left the organization and there is no obvious way to bring them back effectively. However, these people and the ones who perform gross misconduct are a very small minority.

The majority of performance management scenarios involve the leader either poorly clarifying expectations and/or not giving the appropriate feedback early enough. By the time the employee's performance becomes an issue, it has usually become so severe that the conversation becomes difficult for the

---

[2]*You Can Become the Person You Want to Be* (NY: Hawthorn Books, 1973)

leader to have, and for the employee to receive. Worse still, in some situations the leader uses the performance management process to work toward firing an individual, having already predetermined their fate.

The irony is that the leaders who do this are actually under-performing at performance management. It is our job as leaders to be clear about expectations, to reiterate those expectations early and often, and provide feedback when it looks like the employee is failing to meet those expectations. It is almost always down to us, as leaders, if the conversation has reached a difficult stage.

So how can we fix this? To start, we need to flip this process on its head and focus on the growth of our people first (see Figure 13-3). This means caring for, growing, and supporting every team member from the day they join our organization. It involves understanding their goals and motivators, setting them exciting and challenging development plans, supporting them with timely and constructive feedback, and providing coaching and training when required.

TEAM SUCCESS

Intention

MOVE FROM PERFORMANCE MANAGEMENT TO GROWTH

Figure 13-3. Intention: move from performance management to growth

Leaders who genuinely care for a person's development and put the time and effort into growing their people are the leaders who succeed. They succeed both professionally and personally. As humans, we are wired for connecting with others to give and receive love and support. Immense (intrinsic) satisfaction comes from the positive relationships we have with people and this is amplified further when we nurture them and help them to grow.

It expands beyond just redefining our personal success to be that of our team's commercial or productive success. It's about the people in our teams rising to challenges, overcoming them, and doing something great together. Great leaders provide direction, challenge, *and* support: support to grow, to master, to evolve.

For Unnatural Leaders, professional success comes, in part, from building a sustained high-performance capability (where a significant part centers around attracting and retaining the best talent). The best people work for the best leaders in the best organizations. The best organizations become the best because they have leaders that genuinely care for and grow their people. Period!

The war for talent will intensify greatly (see Figure 13-4) as we move to a more advanced digital society and the demand for digital talent peaks. This peak demand is likely to be the last we will see at this level due to the ever-increasing capability of AI and robotics taking over even the most advanced digital development functions when AI learns to code.

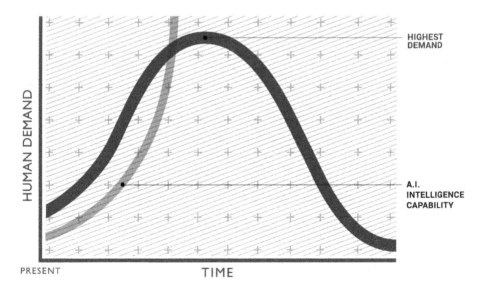

Figure 13-4. The intensifying talent war

Caring for People Doesn't Mean We Are Doormats!

Growing and caring for people does not mean we roll over and meet their demands, putting their needs before our own, or becoming a "doormat" for people to walk over on a daily basis. It's not about being a counselor or friend either. It is about challenging people to be the best they can; pushing them out of their comfort zones to try new and different things; to support and hold a space for them when they fail, because they will (and should because that's how they will learn!).

So, if you're going to do this, you need to be ready to let some of your people fail so they can grow. Are you okay with that? Are you okay with failure for them, and potentially for your team and your own outcomes?

We Can't Fake It Well!

I've said it before, but I'll say it again: Tech people are smart, very smart. However, no leader, including tech leaders, can sustainably fake genuine care for their teams. At some point, (probably sooner than you would like), your teams will know by your verbal or nonverbal communications that your care for their growth and development isn't genuine.

If you have any resistance to the concept of caring for people and focusing on their growth, can you give yourself permission to try it on for a few weeks? An easy place to start (if you aren't doing this already) is to get to know your people with real one-on-ones. I don't mean conversations where you communicate the latest strategy, changes, and priorities and then get a progress update from them—that's not a real one-on-one. I mean can you have a one-on-one and talk about none of that? Can you ask how they are, where they would like to go in their career, how their family is, and sit and listen? (Stop talking and listen; really listen!) Listening is a good discipline to practice at every level of leadership.

Intention 3: Build Long Lasting, Mutually Beneficial Relationships

Imagine a world where we had great relationships with all our stakeholders. Wouldn't that be awesome? As digital leaders, we have to engage and balance a wide variety of stakeholders from technical product teams, non-technical product functions, marketing departments, finance departments, and the senior executives of the organization. All too often we engage with stakeholders when we have to, in order to (hopefully) get what we need to enable us to deliver. This tactic is sub-optimal at best, giving us results with only those that we naturally connect with or that coincidentally have similar objectives. Instead,

Unnatural Leaders address this by setting the intention to build long-lasting, mutually beneficial relationships (see Figure 13-5).

STAKEHOLDER SUCCESS

Intention

**BUILD LONG-LASTING,
MUTUALLY BENEFICIAL
RELATIONSHIPS**

Figure 13-5. Build long lasting, mutually beneficial relationships

A mutually beneficial relationship is a relationship where both parties benefit from collaborating on the same outcome (such as delivering a project or cross-organizational initiative) or, over the duration of the relationship, both parties achieve their own individual outcomes that would have been difficult or impossible to achieve otherwise. In the latter case, person A might assist person B's activity with no immediate return on that investment. Both parties acknowledge the value of collaboration, and working toward higher priority, organizational objectives together and that when their initiative is a priority, others will assist them.

Over time, the interactions between two parties build trust. Each party develops their understanding of the other as commitments are made and delivered against. Even when commitments cannot be met—the relationship allows for honest and transparent communication early enough for appropriate action to be taken. This forms a foundation of trust, and a pattern for how to work together.

"Mutually beneficial" usually involves some give and take. Sometimes the other party assists us with our initiatives, other times we assist them with theirs. The ultimate outcome however is to drive alignment in both initiatives and find a common ground to build from. Every initiative in an organization should be connected to a goal, strategy, or mission to which both parties can align. If there is indeed no common ground, it's likely that one of the initiatives should not be progressed.

We Like People Like Us

One of the biggest challenges to creating *all* the relationships required for success is that we tend to avoid the people we don't like. We might avoid them completely or push through our initiatives hoping for the best or even try to railroad the other person into submission. When we don't like someone it clouds our ability to create professional and productive relationships that are required for ultimate success.

Have you noticed that the people you dislike seem to do everything wrong? They do things differently to the way we prefer; they don't understand where we are coming from and they communicate in a confusing or frustrating manner. On the other hand, the people you like seem to do most things right, and if they don't, we understand why and give them the benefit of the doubt.

Have you ever stopped and thought about the meaning of the word "like"? In everyday parlance, we use it to positively describe something we prefer and are happy to engage more in, be that food, music, sports, etc. When it comes to people, our use of like implies a positive relationship that we are happy to engage in. Another use for the word "like" is to identify similarities in two or more things. That car is just like my car, that dog is like the one next door, etc. What's interesting is that generally when we refer to liking someone (preference), we actually mean we are like them and they are like us—two parties that have similar worldviews, values, interests, goals, and ways of communicating. We like them and we *are* like them.

At the early stages of leadership, our focus tends to be on getting things done: delivering a product or project within a shorter-term focus. This, combined with our natural tendency toward detail and technology, can often see us avoiding stakeholders and only engaging with them when we have to. Often we engage with them when they get in the way, or when we need something from them. Our communications usually revolve around what we want or need, and potentially, why they "need" to help us. Equally, our conversations can be laden with technical jargon that alienates non-technical stakeholders.

As we grow, we become more aware of the relationship impact of "how things get done around here". We focus more on stakeholders and start to maintain relationships that transcend delivery projects. We still have a strong delivery and outcome focus, but appreciate the value of maintaining relationships more.

In later stages of development, we find a balance between delivery (action focused on outcomes) and the appropriate engagement of stakeholders. Not only do we actively engage stakeholders, we co-create solutions and delivery in partnership with them. We maintain the relationships over the long-term, giving and taking for the greater benefit of the organization.

Frames of Mind

Frames of mind are critical to stakeholder engagement and relationship building. If we conceptualize a stakeholder relationship as a battle, each interaction is either won or lost and usually at some cost. It's a negative and stressful way to exist. Even when we think we're winning the battle, we can often end up losing the war!

"Politics" or game playing is another negative frame commonly used by digital leaders. Politics usually involve hidden agendas, power plays, and abrasive or subversive behaviors. While we may encounter this with some stakeholders, and often can't be avoided, it's not an empowering frame to use for stakeholder engagement on the whole.

I've coached a number of senior leaders who have held negative frames about stakeholder engagement. In one scenario, the leader was having difficulty gaining traction and buy-in to drive the required changes in her organization. In our coaching conversations, it became apparent that she refused to engage with certain stakeholders, preferring to focus on more productive tasks. When I asked why this was, she told me that she didn't play politics and anyone she considered "political" she avoided.

Her lack of engagement with the required stakeholders meant her initiatives were getting stuck and facing resistance (sometimes silently). If she was to stand any chance of success, she had to either engage with her stakeholders or continue her struggle to gain traction. To enable her to do not just engage but build healthy relationships with her stakeholders, we reframed her actions of engaging them from "playing politics" to that of a game of chess. Like most digital leaders, she loved solving problems, and she also loved the strategy required to play and win chess. When she reframed stakeholder engagement as a game of chess, it became an enjoyable problem to be solved and a game to be played. From that point on, she actively engaged her stakeholders and had a significant impact on the organization.

In summary, Unnatural Leaders set three key intentions: to be passionately curious, to move from performance management to growth, and to build long lasting, mutually beneficial relationships with their stakeholders (see Figure 13-6).

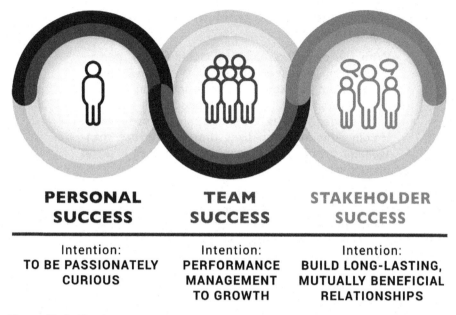

PERSONAL SUCCESS	TEAM SUCCESS	STAKEHOLDER SUCCESS
Intention: TO BE PASSIONATELY CURIOUS	Intention: PERFORMANCE MANAGEMENT TO GROWTH	Intention: BUILD LONG-LASTING, MUTUALLY BENEFICIAL RELATIONSHIPS

Figure 13-6. The three intentions

Define Your Own Intentions

Now we have defined three intentions that bring to life the things that are important to Unnatural Leaders—Personal Success, Team Success, and Stakeholder Success—it is time to define any intentions you need in order to realize any other important items on the list you created in Chapter 12.

When setting intentions for the items on your list, it can help to think about the following questions in order to develop and state a suitable intention:

- **What principle would help me focus on what's important?**

    We can think about intentions as if they were principles. For example, Unnatural Leaders hold a principle to always be passionately curious. These types of intentions are useful when we have a long-term vision that impacts how we want to be.

- **How might I flip the problem I want to fix to see it another way?**

  With the team intention, we identified that performance management was a problem. When we flipped the problem and started with an intention to grow our teams and give them constant support and feedback, suddenly the task became much more inviting. Holding this intention fixes the performance management problem at its core and reframes it as an opportunity.

Use these techniques to experiment with developing intentions that feel appropriate to you. Remember, there are no right or wrong answers, and our intentions evolve over time. The trick (like being tactical and strategic) is to balance defining intentions and evolving them without under-committing and frequently changing them.

Setting Intentions

We have now defined the intentions that we wish to use to guide our attention and energy. Step 4 of the Clarity Process (see Figure 13-7) guides us through the process of setting these intentions. Setting an intention is about making a personal commitment with ourselves, because new intentions mean change, they mean breaking old habits and doing things differently. This takes energy, effort, and conscious focus.

Figure 13-7. Set, Step 4 of the Clarity Process

The effort we exert to change involves thinking about people, scenarios, and problems in new ways, questioning our prior assumptions and being curious about alternatives. Our emotions and habits often pull us back into old behaviours and away from our intentions. We have to start the intentionality process with a commitment to ourselves. Can you commit yourself to be intentional? If your answer is yes, great! If not, can you give yourself permission to try being intentional for four weeks (or more)? If not, what's stopping you? Consider what is more important than doing this work—the work of evolving yourself and becoming more successful?

Success, as I pointed out earlier, is an inside job. We feel success as a positive emotional state. What's interesting is that we are able to create a positive emotional state right now by visualizing success in our minds and feeling it in our bodies. When we imagine what it would look, feel, sound, and smell like to be successful (utilizing all of our senses), we experience the positive emotional state we are hoping for in the future. When done correctly, the intensity of this (artificially created) state gets stored in our bodies as a real experience that we can utilize.

The power of creating success in our minds and feeling the positive emotions is the fuel for us to change. It creates positive energy in our system, which we can use to focus our attention to create the changes we desire for success.

Follow this six-step process to set your intentions:

1. Select the intention that you want to set (e.g., be passionately curious).

2. Recall any times in your past where you have been passionately curious and what you saw, felt, heard, and experienced as part of that experience. There will be a time in your past when you were passionately curious—maybe it was learning a new technology, skill, sport, or meeting a new person. You were probably excited and eager to learn more.

3. Allow yourself to feel into the emotional state and the thinking that came with this passionate curiosity. Amplify that feeling to bring more color, sound, and feeling to the state.

4. Now imagine bringing that to your daily leadership activities. How might it look to hold that sense of passionate curiosity?

5. You may want to choose a symbol (such as a letter or shape) that you attach to passionate curiosity. You may be comfortable with its name, or it may be powerful for you to choose a sound or movement that represents passionate curiosity to you.

6. Spend a few minutes imagining being passionately curious and associating it with your symbol.

7. Repeat the process for all the intentions that you have.

Holding an intention is a continuous process, and you can make this process easier when your intentions are based on what is truly important to you. However, our world is full of distractions. So we have to consciously practice holding our intentions front of mind in our day-to-day lives and support them with processes to enable us to focus and achieve what we desire. We discuss the process of holding our intentions in Part IV: Attention.

Summary

Success means different things to different people and so it should. In the context of digital leadership, Unnatural Leaders set the three intentions: to be passionately curious, to move from performance management to growth of our people, and to build long-lasting, mutually beneficial relationships. All of these are designed to bring about success in a professional context.

Over time, the intentions of Unnatural Leaders adapt to address the evolving landscape they operate in. For the foreseeable future, the three Unnatural Selection intentions are essential to successful digital leadership.

How we frame a situation determines the meaning we make and therefore whether we are drawn toward or away from it. Frames of mind are critical to achieving success as is being aware of the people we like and dislike. Our interactions with people change dramatically based on how much we like them, and negative frames can subconsciously impede our chance of success.

With a new awareness of these issues, we are better positioned to choose how we operate and what we do. We can better focus our energy and attention as set by our intentions.

Self-Reflection Questions

1. On average, how would you rate your level of curiosity in your role? Are there instances where you are more curious than others? What is present (or not) when you are most curious?

2. How would your team describe your attention to their personal growth? Do you have growth or development plans for each person? How did you last manage the poor performance of a direct report?

3. What frames do you hold about engaging stakeholders? Are there stakeholders where you know you have not put in enough time and energy? How might you revise these frames into something more empowering to enable you to engage with these stakeholders?

4. What intentions do you have for your personal growth? Is there something in Part II: Awareness that you learned about yourself that could fuel an intention?

Summary of Part III: Intention

Defining intentions helps guide our energy and attention to what is important. They shape how we approach our daily activities. Without intentionality, we run the risk of getting caught up in our busy days. We run the risk of being distracted away from the things that are really important to us and sometimes, we find ourselves behaving in a manner that brings about exactly the opposite of what we are trying to achieve.

James Cameron used intentionality to become one the most successful Hollywood movie directors of all time. He could have become caught up in the manic demands of movie creation or produced a movie that was on a par with the movies of the day. He didn't. He held an intention to push the boundaries of what was possible. His highest frame was to create new and innovative cinematic techniques. He starts each movie project with this intention and he executes on it.

Understanding what is important to us as leaders and humans is critical to our success and leading a quality life. Spending time understanding what we enjoy, love and value is time extremely well spent. All too often, leaders get pulled along with the social and professional tides, trying to keep their heads above water, and realizing too late that what they were striving for really wasn't important to us at all.

What's important to us changes over the years. When we have a true growth mindset, we realize that what is important today may not be next month or next year. As we grow, our awareness grows and often what's important to us changes. It is therefore essential to use the Clarity Process and set intentions for each major iteration of the evolution helix.

Attention

To give your positive or negative attention to something is a way of giving energy. The most damaging form of behavior is withholding your attention

—Masaru Emoto, *The Hidden Messages in Water*[1]

Step 3 of the evolution helix is Attention (Figure 1). It's what we do and where we expend our energy each day. Our intentions (discussed in Part III) focus our attention on doing the things that make us Unnatural Leaders.

[1]NY: Atria Books, 2011.

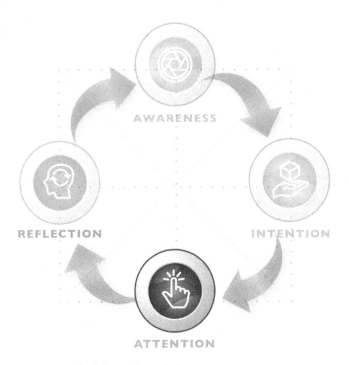

Figure 1. Attention, step 3 of the evolution helix

One of the biggest challenges we face is being distracted from our intentions. Leadership is messy; it's full of interruptions, context switching, and ball juggling. It's the difference between manager and maker time[2]. Often, it's all too easy to arrive at the end of the day only to find that we never got chance to work on the important stuff.

You may have heard of the invisible gorilla experiment[3]. In the experiment, you are asked to watch six people pass a basketball, wearing either a black or white t-shirt. During the video, your task is to count the passes made by the players wearing black shirts. (If you haven't watched the video and tried the experiment, have a go at it now and come back.)

At the end of the experiment, you confirm if you managed to accurately count the number of passes. This, however, is not the objective of the experiment.

While focusing all of our attention on counting the passes, the majority of us completely miss someone wearing a gorilla suit walking through the scene.

---

[2]https://unnatural.io/link/bp41
[3]https://unnatural.io/link/bp42

When we are very focused on an activity, we screen out much of the world in order to achieve our task. As leaders, this is extremely dangerous. It's all too easy for us to focus on the urgent demands and the valuable day-to-day execution and completely miss an opportunity or a critical threat—even when we have compelling intentions.

In Chapter 14 we will look at tools that help us focus our attention *and* keep an awareness of potential opportunities and threats.

Having intent helps us cut through the distractions of our busy lives and focus on what we want to achieve. Intention works at both the conscious and subconscious levels of the brain, activating areas that affect what is filtered in and out of our awareness.

In this, Part IV, we look at tools and techniques that allow us to perform as Unnatural Leaders. These tools build on the intentions of Part III and focus on our personal evolution, (Chapter 14), the growth of our teams (Chapter 15), and building long-lasting, mutually beneficial stakeholder relationships (Chapter 16).

We are measured by the things that we do, how and what we deliver, the cultures we build, and our strategic operation.

Let's take a look at how we can *execute for success!*

Attention: Self

The moment one gives close attention to anything, even a blade of grass, it becomes a mysterious, awesome, indescribably magnificent world in itself.

—Henry Miller[1]

Unnatural Leaders are proactive, not reactive. They take ownership of their time and attention and they use intention to devise systems that keep them working on the right things, in the right ways, to achieve success. These systems help them overcome the key challenges of choosing what to work on, holding the right frames and perspectives on the task at hand, and focusing on execution and delivery results.

Unnatural Leaders follow a process of *Choose, Frame, Focus* (see Figure 14-1).

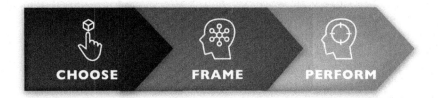

Figure 14-1. The Choose, Frame, Perform process

---

[1]*Henry Miller on Writing* (New Directions, 1964).

J. Brett, *Evolving Digital Leadership*, https://doi.org/10.1007/978-1-4842-3606-2_14

Choose

In order to achieve sustained success, we must consciously choose each and every day where we place our attention and what activities we will do and won't do. To choose well, we need to be clear about our priorities. Our intentions help shape where we focus our attention and what's important. We must then prioritize the day-to-day tasks in line with those intentions. It sounds simple, but so many leaders get caught up in urgent, unimportant activities[2] that they simply run out of hours in the day to get to what's really important. As we progress to more senior leadership roles, choosing what we work on becomes more and more critical as the number of things we could work on grows with the scale of our role. Equally, our role may stay the same in a startup organization that achieves tremendous growth—if we don't grow and keep pace with the organization we will be replaced by a new leader who can operate strategically at scale.

Choosing to Own Our Time

The single most important element of ensuring that we work on the right things is to take ownership of our time—more explicitly taking control of our calendars. Reactive managers let their calendars control them; they let other people control their time and how they spend it. Depending on your organization's culture, you may find that meetings magically appear in your calendar and before you realize it a majority of that nice clear week you had disappears into a black hole of back-to-back meetings.

Take the time to block out portions of your weekly calendar to refresh intentions, prioritize your workload, and create space for strategic thinking. The times you choose for these activities depend on your own natural cadence and are best aligned to the parts of the day when you have the most energy to be creative, make key decisions, and complete tasks. If you have more clarity of thought in the mornings (as I do), your daily performance profile may look something like mine, shown in Figure 14-2.

---

[2]https://unnatural.io/link/b144

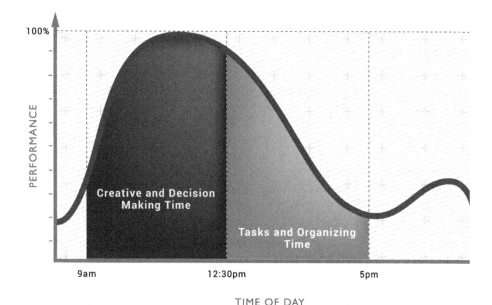

Figure 14-2. A typical daily performance profile

I am more creative and tend to make better decisions in the morning when my mental capacity is at its peak, and I move to more operational activity in the afternoon as my energy levels get lower. I often have a renewal of energy later in the evening, where I process tasks and plan for the next day.

Understanding your own personal energy levels is key to planning your day and week. Take some time to reflect on what your profile may look like and how that will help you shape your daily routine.

Similarly, we have patterns and cycles of energy through the week that impact our energy levels. Trying to make serious decisions and think creatively on a Friday afternoon is usually a bad idea for most of us, so try to avoid that when possible. Equally, to get the most out of a week we need to plan what we will work on—either at the start of the week or end of the previous week (weekly plan), followed by some time to assess the week's progress as the week closes out (weekly wrap).

It's essential to start each day by reiterating your intentions. It doesn't matter when or where you do this, as long as you spend time before the working day begins. You may have the ability to do this early in the morning at home, or during your commute to work. If you are a leader who gets into the office before a majority of the organization, then you could carve out space then. During this intentional time, review your intentions and your vision, bring them to mind and refresh their clarity. With this renewed spotlight on what is important and where you want to go, overlay your role context, the activities of the day and week and, get clear on any specific areas that you may need to prioritize, adjust, or focus on.

At the end of your day—usually at home or before leaving the office—take time to reflect on how the day went, what you did, the outcomes your actions generated, and how aligned they were to your vision of success. (We dive deeper into Reflection, which is Step 4, in Part V of the book.) Also reflect on any points of the day where you felt emotions rising for you. Were there any times that you felt defensive, anxious, frustrated, or excited? What was happening when those emotions surfaced? By simply noting these experiences, we can start to see patterns in our actions and responses to others that help us to take back control of four powers (as discussed in Chapter 11).

In addition to regular planning and reflecting, dedicating space to focus on strategic activities is essential. This strategic time allows us to gain a better perspective on ourselves, our role, our teams, and the industry. It's the catalyst for creating proactive, disruptive waves of change. I consistently found, during my interviews with digital leaders, that those leaders who used a calendar system and allocated time for strategic thinking did not struggle with the stress of trying to balance being tactical and strategic. Conversely, for those who had no system, this balance was usually one of their top three challenges. Carve out strategy time and make it sacred. Decline meetings if you have to—if you can't decline a meeting, move your strategy time somewhere else in the day or week, *but don't lose it!*

Unnatural Leaders organize their time to ensure they plan their weeks, act with intention, and lead strategically. Figure 14-3 is an example of an Unnatural Leader's week.

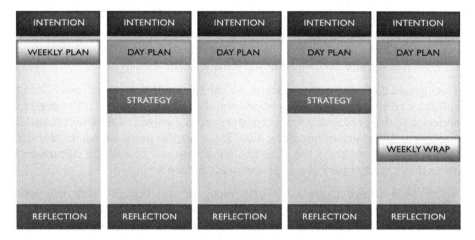

Figure 14-3. An example of a Unnatural Leader's weekly structure

Not everyone finds the same system effective. That's why there are so many productivity applications around. The important thing is that you use a system, and it's a system that works for you. One of the systems that has gained popularity recently (and is used in the Holacracy[3] movement) is Getting Things Done[4] (GTD) by David Allen.

Without a system in place, we can get stuck into the execution of our working week. Here, our attention will be pulled (and focused) in different directions as we move from meetings, conversations, research, presentations, etc. As we switch activities, it's important to be aware of the larger context of the activity that has our attention, to allow us to execute at a high level of performance.

Frame

All too often the initiatives that we work on are not framed effectively by their originator. Sometimes they prescribe a solution, other times they pose a problem without any context. Rarely are we provided with enough information to allow accurate decision making and delivery excellence.

Unnatural Leaders start by understanding the details of the initiative and the desired outcomes. They then take a step back and frame the activity in the larger context of the organization, seeking to understand: how it impacts other initiatives, any opportunity costs incurred, its impact on revenue or growth, it's alignment with organizational strategy, its impact on product and engineering roadmaps, and how it might impact culture.

---

[3]https://unnatural.io/link/b141
[4]https://unnatural.io/link/b142

Finally, once we fully understand the organizational context we take a second step back and consider the impact on the market and industry verticals. We ask the question, "How might this initiative drive the organization's ability to lead the market and stay ahead of movement in the industry?"

Throughout both of these two steps, we use our understanding of the Human Full Stack to test our own assumptions and those made by others. We seek to understand the personality drivers of the parties involved so that we can make intelligent and effective decisions. Our focus on the human element doesn't stop there. We calibrate the potential impact on our teams and culture and make that a critical part of our assessments before acting.

Figure 14-4 shows these steps—beginning at the bottom with the task specifics and growing outward and upward as we obtain broader context and perspective of the what and why of the task, which allows us to make better decisions on how (or why) to deliver.

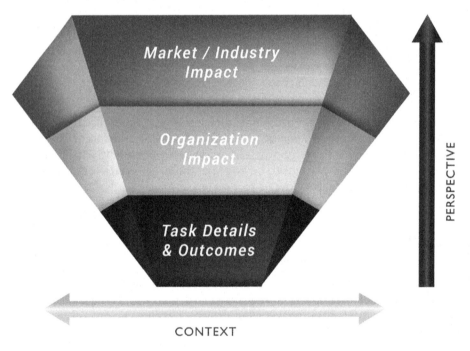

Figure 14-4. Framing activities

For these initiatives and the many more granular tasks that they complete throughout the day, Unnatural Leaders ensure that they are situationally aware and use the three frames to identify the most appropriate Digital Situational Leadership mode(s) (see Figure 14-5) (presented in Chapter 3).

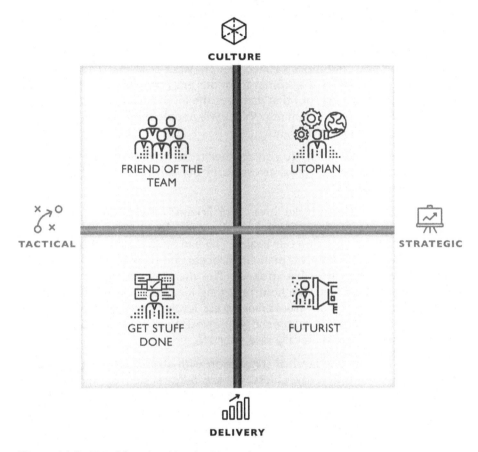

Figure 14-5. Digital Situational Leadership mode

All sounds too easy, right? Well, it is easy when our stress levels and physical-emotional state are optimal. But, with the exception of the extremely small minority of truly enlightening beings, I don't know many leaders who are able to remain calm and present consistently over time. Without consciously framing tasks, leaders can fall into the trap of blindly executing the requests (demands!) of others, or making sub-optimal decisions that limit their chances of success.

Perform

One of the major contributors to our underperformance is a negative emotional state. When we feel frustrated, anxious, or stressed, it impacts our ability to make decisions and it saps the energy needed to perform at a high level. Worse still, when we feel stressed, it often creates a cycle of negativity where we get stressed about being stressed!

Stress is a *big* challenge. Managing stress is critical to having better experiences and living a longer and more fulfilled life. So, what is stress? There are two types of stress: the stress that comes from our environment, such as the death of a relative, or a leaking roof that damages the interior of our house, and the stress that we create in our minds. What will people think of me? Am I being too directive? Did I get that right?

Although we have the ability to control the stress we create in our minds, we cannot control all the external stressors in our environment. The result— stress is unavoidable!

In her TED Talk, "How to Make Stress Your Friend,[5] " Kelly McGonigal (health psychologist and lecturer at Stanford University) shares her research on the negative impacts of stress on our health. The bad news is that stress kills. The good news is that it's how we mentally process and think about the stressful situations we experience that matters. The meaning that we make of the stress (the frame of mind we hold regarding it) influences our stress levels, sometimes amplifying and maintaining stress levels weeks, months, or years after the event. I highly recommend you invest 15 minutes of your time to watch her talk—it could literally save your life.

Often, we associate any level of stimulation with stress. This can lead us to experience stress every day, unless we are fully relaxed on vacation! The stress curve shown in Figure 14-6 is based on Yerkes-Dodson Law, which is an empirical relationship between arousal and performance.

---

[5] https://unnatural.io/link/b143

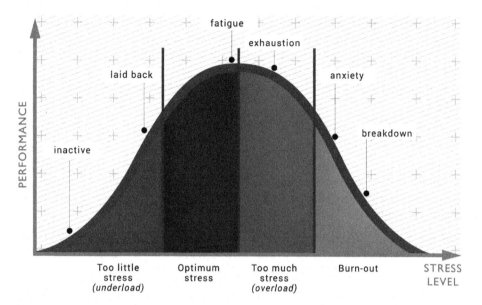

Figure 14-6. The stress curve

Understanding that not all arousal is stressful and that the right levels of arousal can increase performance is extremely beneficial to leaders. It brings a new meaning and frame of mind to how we feel and helps us manage our perception of stress. Too little stress and we become bored or inactive, while too much stress causes fatigue and exhaustion kick in. There is a level of stress that activates us, making us rise to the challenge and perform at our best. Understanding how that feels and mentally labeling this state as "activated" helps us re-frame our experience and maintain high performance.

The magic is in being aware of where we are on the curve at any moment. Knowing your personal stress and activation levels are the first steps to managing stress appropriately.

State Management

Have you ever been really excited to learn something new, by reading a book, attending a training course, or pairing with a more experienced developer on new technology? The passion and engagement we feel creates an ideal state to learn. This positive state brings curiosity, openness, and arousal (at the right level) and puts us into what Michael Hall calls a genius state.[6] Here our capacity to learn and retain information is enhanced.

---

[6]L. Michael Hall, *Accessing Personal Genius* (2013)

Now, can you recall a time when you didn't want to attend a training session or workshop—maybe it was on a subject you had no interest in, or late on a Friday afternoon, or maybe it even pulled you away from getting "real" work done. My guess is that your engagement and participation in the session were low and your retention of information was probably close to your lowest levels.

Our mind, body, and emotional state affect our performance, in some instances very dramatically.

Negative states are often accompanied by negative emotions (such as shame or guilt) and thoughts that are pessimistic, dark, or morbid. Our physical body's energetic state is usually contracted, heavy, tired, melancholic, or, in the worst case, all of the above.

Energized states, on the other hand, have emotions such as joy, happiness, and elation. Our thoughts are usually optimistic, confident, and bright, and accompanied by a bodily state that is full of energy and ready to perform.

So, if our state dramatically influences our performance and experiences, what can we do to manage our state and access the states that are most appropriate for success and life satisfaction?

The TEA Model

The TEA coaching model (see Figure 14-7), created by Hala Fayad,[7] defines the three components that create our state—our thoughts (internal processing), our emotions (internal states), and our actions (external behaviors). These three components interact with and influence each other to amplify, create, and change our state.

---

[7]Family and Life Coach, KUWAIT

Figure 14-7. The TEA model

The cycle of the TEA model begins with any of the three components. It may be that we think a particular thought (remembering a positive childhood experience) that triggers an emotion (joy), the emotion then triggers an action (smile). The cycle then continues as the action of smiling triggers further positive thoughts. This process continues until one of the three elements triggers a new state. For example, we might feel a sharp pain in our back (action), which triggers a negative thought that resists the pain, creating anxiety and frustration (emotions), followed by slouched shoulders and a frown (action).

In another scenario, we might smell the delightful aroma of coffee brewing in the morning. The smell triggers positive memories (thoughts) of comfort, warmth, and stimulation, which creates the emotions of joy, satisfaction, and anticipation, which gets us out of bed (action) and heading to the kitchen for a cup. Drinking the coffee (action) then reinforces the positive state and the cycle continues.

This happens continuously inside us, although not always as dramatically as just described. As we interact with others, we trigger different states in them, as they do in us. I'm sure you will recognize the state of frustration (emotion) when you come into contact with certain stakeholders. Without the stakeholder saying a word, they trigger a thought inside us, which triggers an emotion, which triggers a pensive or defensive state, which may manifest itself physically (such as crossing your arms across your chest, a self-protection mechanism). Consciously or subconsciously, the stakeholder detects this physical change and it triggers a similar, negative internal response in them.

The environment, including the people around us, are constantly triggering and influencing our state.

The good news is that now that we understand how this system works, and we have full control over our four powers (see Chapter 11) (our thoughts, feelings, communications, and actions), we can own and manage our state.

The more we are able to do this, the higher our performance and satisfaction levels will be.

■ **Note**   In Chapter 12, I outlined my purpose as "To positively influence the direction of society so that our children and future generations are able to have a high quality of life." I would argue that a high-quality life is a consistent (not necessarily permanent) series of positive states. Therefore, being able to manage our state directly impacts our quality of life.

To break a negative state or create a positive one, we need to change our thoughts, emotions, or actions. If we can change two elements at once, we often get a faster, greater state change. When choosing to change state, we usually focus on either changing our actions and or our thoughts—these then impact our emotional state. Let's take a look at two techniques for changing state. The first method starts with thoughts, the second with actions.

Method 1: Changing State by Changing Our Thoughts

Reading a good fiction book is a classic (and usually fairly easy) example of changing our state by changing our thoughts. We may sit down to read a book in a negative state, but as we begin to read, our mind is distracted by the content of the book. The book creates new thoughts as it immerses us in an imaginary world. As we lose ourselves in a "good book," we experience a fictional reality where our state is shifted by the author telling the story.

In a professional environment, we usually don't have the time or capacity to take a break to read a book. What we can do, however, is acknowledge our negative state, where we are placing our attention and the thoughts that we are having that contribute to this state. We can then choose to re-frame how we are thinking about a scenario. I gave a coaching example earlier where I reframed "politics" to a game of chess, which caused an immediate state shift for the leader to one that was energized and enjoyable. We didn't change the external environment, just our response to it.

The other mechanism that I employ with leaders is to transition their thoughts to be curious. Often, our negative thoughts are based on assumptions and judgments of others that cause frustration, anxiety, and anger. When we decide to interrupt these thoughts with a curious mindset that seeks more information and throws away judgment, we can see immediate breakthroughs in our state. Examples of curious questions include: Is it true that…? What if the other person didn't mean…? Even if I am wrong, what can I learn? Could I have shown up differently to create a different outcome? What context could I be missing that might explain their behavior?

Method 2: Changing State by Changing Our Actions

Have you ever felt refreshed by going for a walk, run, cycle, or swim? Ever have those "light bulb ideas" moments in the shower? I'm sure you have. Physical movement creates energy in the body and dramatically changes our state—either relaxing the stress levels or energizing us with endorphins. Interrupting our state by changing our physical environment and our actions is one of the easiest ways to change state. What's fascinating about this mechanism is that it doesn't have to be a 20-minute run to change our state. Adjusting our posture can have a similar effect. Most of us are aware of the concept of body language and how it impacts the way we are perceived by others. However, fewer are aware that our body language affects our own emotional state. If you're in a great mood (positive state), try frowning hard, looking down, slouching your shoulders forward, and generally contracting your body into a protective state. When we make these gestures, it feeds neurological information back into our brain that impacts our state in a negative way. Conversely, by reversing these— opening up our posture, stretching our shoulders back, looking upward, and smiling and moving more—we can elevate our state.

Most of us in digital spend a considerable amount of time working on our devices (laptops, desktops, mobiles, etc.). More often than not we lean forward toward the screens, our shoulders dropping down and forward, necks, and backs bent as we work. These positions not only put physical strain on our body, they also match the patterns of a negative, stress-inducing body language. Until technology does away with the keyboard and the need to type looking down at our hands, we need to actively manage our working posture to maintain a healthy state and healthy body.

▨ **Note** A simple exercise that you can do to combat this stress-induction is to spend five minutes reversing the posture and stretching out in the opposite direction: Tilt your head back and look up toward the sky, stretch your arms out wide to either side of you, and push your shoulders back. It may look a little awkward, but doing this helps to combat the negative impact caused by the considerable time spent hunched over our devices.

It takes time and effort to practice state management. Some of the negative states we need to work with have built up over the course of our lives and trigger the TEA (thoughts-emotions-actions) cycle so quickly that we never notice the thoughts that created them; we just feel the negative emotional state. Practice this process. It will be worth it, I promise you!

Summary

In this chapter we looked at the process of developing high-performance levels by consciously choosing what we work on, managing distractions, framing our work in the most effective way, and managing our state and stress levels.

Being able to successfully do any of these will make a dramatic difference in how you execute and what you achieve. Unnatural Leaders who manage their state have an understanding of the broader context and perspective. Unnatural Leaders who take control of their valuable time have a powerful advantage over their competition.

There are numerous articles and books on the subject of Agile and Agile leadership. Some of these identify the need for the leader to have an Agile mindset. For me, a critical component of the Agile mindset is the ability to be Agile in our emotional state; to have the ability to interrupt negative states and create powerful states throughout the day, driving our engagement, decision making, and curiosity to high levels of performance.

In the next chapter, we look at how we place specific attention on our teams. Leadership, after all, is about leading people!

Self-Reflection Questions

1. Take a piece of paper and draw what you think approximates to your own average Monday to Friday energy profile (as per Figure 14-2). How does it inform how you might restructure your day?

2. During your working week, what distracts your attention away from doing "important" work the most? Are these external distractions or something that you are doing internally (procrastinating)? What is it about this distraction that makes it so challenging to solve? (Is there something more important to you than the work?)

3. When considering Figure 14-4 and framing your task and initiatives, how would you rate your ability to step back (multiple times) to gain broader context and perspective? How is that impacting your effectiveness?

4. Watch McGonigal's TED Talk ("How to Make Stress Your Friend"). How do you think about stress? Are you aware if you are becoming over- (or under-) stressed?

5. What state do you need to create to have the biggest impact on your intentions? What strategy can you employ to manage this?

6. How do you think your Enneagram type and preferences impact your emotional states and distractions?

Attention: Team

Alone we can do so little. Together we can do so much.

—Helen Keller[1]

The development of ourselves is incredibly valuable if we are going to stay ahead of the fast pace of change *but*, as I presented in Chapter 4 (Recommendation #3, Redefine Personal Success), our own success also becomes the success of our teams and people. It's critical that they too evolve faster than the pace of change, and to do that we focus our attention on their growth.

Before we dive deep into how to do this, I want to take a step back and talk about building a great tech brand which helps attract and retain the best people.

Building a Great Tech Brand

There are numerous articles, books, and blog posts about what it takes to attract and retain the best technical talent. I've worked with a lot of organizations over my time in digital, in various roles from software engineer through to CTO, digital strategy consultant, and leadership development coach. During this time, I developed a list of seven elements that draw top talent to an organization, as demonstrated in Figure 15-1.

---

[1]Joseph P. Lash, *Helen and Teacher: The Story of Helen Keller and Anne Sullivan Macy* (New York: Delta/Seymour Lawrence, 1981), 489

© James Brett 2019
J. Brett, *Evolving Digital Leadership*, https://doi.org/10.1007/978-1-4842-3606-2_15

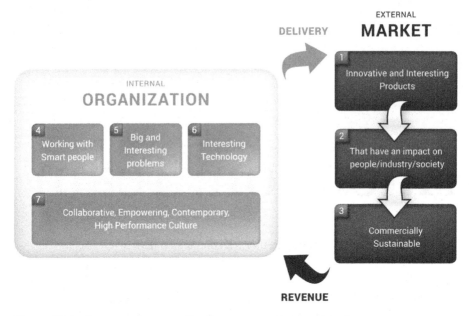

Figure 15-1. The seven elements of building a great technology brand

The seven elements are split into two distinct categories:

- The elements that are visible outside the organization, i.e., the company's products and services.

- The elements that are only visible inside the organization, i.e., the culture and people you work with

Let's take a look at the characteristics of the organization that are visible from outside.

Innovative and Interesting Products

As an external party, looking at the organization from the outside, our first exposure is to the products and services in market. If these are both interesting and innovative it draws talent in with a desire to work on them.

Impact on People, Industry, and /or Society

It's not enough for the products to be merely innovative and interesting, they have to be of use and have some level of impact on their users, industry or society. Without these latter elements, the products have novelty value only, which negatively impacts on the attractiveness of the organization.

Commercial Sustainability

Equally, if the products aren't commercially valuable and sustainable their longevity and that of the organization come into question.

With the first three elements in place, an interest in the organization develops. The best talent will likely investigate deeper into the internals of the organization in order to determine if it is somewhere they are passionate about and eager to join.

The subsequent four (internal) elements of a great tech brand are defined as follows.

Working with Smart People

When we work with smart people we learn, ideate, and create great products and it is one of the most enjoyable experiences we can have as technologists. Unfortunately, working with people at the other end of the spectrum can be extremely frustrating and demoralizing as we spend time trying to build capability and influence them.

Solving Big and Interesting Problems

Big problems are fun to solve. Technologists like a challenge and they like to work on big and interesting challenges. Google, for example, has an obvious advantage due to their vast amounts of data, market position, scale, and funding. The problems Google can choose to focus on are likely to be bigger and more interesting than those of a small startup that does not have the same depth of data to work with.

Using Interesting Technology

However, working with smart people and big problems can be really frustrating when the technology is old, unexciting, and generally not fit for purpose. We usually don't get to choose all the technology in our stacks (and development pipeline). However, the more interesting and effective the technology, the more appealing the organization will be to work with.

Collaborative, Empowering, Contemporary Culture

Great cultures are hard to define and take considerable time to explore in detail. I'm not going to do that here. What I will do is share what I see are the three main elements of an inspiring digital culture.

- A *collaborative culture,* where people work together and generally support each other, rather than contribute only as individuals striving for personal success

- An *empowering culture* respects the autonomy of individuals and teams to solve the interesting challenges with interesting technologies

- A *contemporary culture* is relaxed, friendly, and informal in nature. Contemporary cultures generally offer flexible hours, remote working, casual dress, and a pleasing working space and environment.

These seven elements act like multipliers to the attractiveness of an organization as follows:

$$\textbf{Attractiveness} = (1) \times (2) \times (3) \times (4) \times (5) \times (6) \times (7).$$

The attractiveness of an organization reduces to zero if any element is zero. The higher the value of each element, the more attractive the organization. Therefore, any organization that manages to achieve high scores in all seven of these elements will be in a world-class position and have the ability to pick and choose talent from the global stage.

Of course, what makes each element attractive or not is subjective and dictated by the candidate's desires and worldview. Each individual candidate will prioritize the seven elements in different ways depending on their current and desired status.

I've left the subject of financial reward out this conversation as I have made the assumption that you and your organization are offering competitive market rates. Financial incentives are less important to a candidate who is considering a role with a great technology brand. Offering great financial rewards does not compensate for a poor tech brand. You may be able to attract talent, but the likelihood of building a high-performance capability and sustaining it over time is exceedingly low.

As leaders, we must do our best to grow all seven elements to enable us to build a sustainable and enjoyable organization.

Where Should We Focus Our Attention When Growing Our Teams?

Now that we have a shared understanding of how a great technology brand attracts and retains the best talent, let's take a look at where we can focus our attention to grow the individuals in our organization. There are four distinct stages of an individual's employment that we can leverage in order to best grow an individual and our organization.

1. Hiring

The first stage is the interview and selection process. Here we begin our relationship with the candidate as both parties assess the role and cultural fit of the candidate. Upon acceptance of an offer of employment, the individual moves to Stage 2—Onboarding.

2. Onboarding

The candidate accepts our offer of employment and joins the organization. The onboarding process begins before the candidate's first day in the office and continues for a number of weeks. Onboarding is essential to setting the right impression with the candidate, establishing an effective working relationship, and ensuring that they have everything they need for success.

3. Growth and Execution

Once onboard, Stage 3 of the employee's time with the organization is fulfilling and executing their role. Here we focus a majority of our attention on the growth of the employee and support them in contributing toward the organization's objectives. At some point, an employee may proceed to Stage 4 and leave the organization

4. Exit

When an employee exits the organization, we have an opportunity to gain explicit and valuable feedback regarding their experience of the organization and their motivators to leave and, potentially, which of the seven elements of a great tech brand they think their new organization has, that our organization doesn't. How we deal with an employee's exit has a significant impact on the people remaining in the organization. A positive and constructive exit that ends on a high demonstrates our genuine care for our people. A negative exit often begins with the leader ignoring the employee immediately following their resignation and poor treatment of them during their notice period and after their exit. This poor treatment by the leader is witnessed by those who remain in the leader's teams and can cause them to question the leaders care for them.

The Two Phases of Team Attention

For us to excel at all four of these stages and truly grow our team members, it's critical that we leverage the Human as a Full Stack model in order to a get a deep understanding of the individual. This allows us to connect with and grow them to exceptional levels and drive the high performance of the organization.

The Human as a Full Stack model is applicable at all four stages. Rather than describe its application (and other tools) at each of the four stages, I prefer to group the stages together into two key phases (see Figure 15-2) of attention: obtaining a deep understanding of the individual (the primary focus of the hiring and onboarding touchpoints) and coaching and supporting them (through the growth and execution phase).

Figure 15-2. The two phases of team attention

Deep Understanding of the Individual

The understanding and care that Unnatural Leaders have for their people is holistic. We include and appreciate all aspects of an individual: their background, experiences, and the skills that they bring to the team and the organization. We include the whole person in our understanding, not just the "professional" person we see in the office. That is, we don't consider the individual solely for the contribution they make as part of their role—we acknowledge their life and the dynamic that exists outside the office, which allows us to also respect an individuals needs, such as caring for children or family members.

During the candidate's hiring process, most managers utilize the interviews to assess the candidate's skill and experience *but* Unnatural Leaders also determine how their Human Full Stack is configured. The Human Full Stack provides an invaluable tool to determine the suitability of the candidate—how they are motivated, how they communicate, and their team and cultural fit.

If you are hiring a leader for your organization, it is extremely valuable to assess their developmental stage (e.g., Early Expert through Late Achiever). Understanding the candidate's stage (see Chapter 8) gives us insight into how they may lead or manage their teams and whether their focus is primarily on competence (Expert) or outcomes (Achiever).

When Unnatural leaders transition from the hiring to the onboarding process, we switch from trying to predict the candidate's Full Stack configuration to one of co-developing this deep understanding with the employee. Sadly, this is often the first experience the employee has of a leader paying real care and attention to their growth. All too often, busy leaders pay lip service to the onboarding process, offering a tour of the office and maybe even a t-shirt!

Establish Effective Communication Patterns

Establishing effective communications with our new hire is critical to building a meaningful and productive relationship. The senior leaders I interviewed achieved this by explaining early on their preferred way to lead and communicate and establishing a level of interaction that works for both parties.

It is our responsibility, as leaders, to ensure that we communicate effectively with our people, and this doesn't mean that everyone must conform to our preferred channels and style. For really effective and clear communication, we have to modify our style to accommodate the preferences of those receiving our message.

In Chapter 9, we explored the frontend communication channel of the Human Full Stack, which identified the different representational systems of VAKAd. Communicating in the other person's preferred channel is essential for the message to be received as we intend. The Cognitive Scale meta-program (see Chapter 7) is another important element of communication. One of the biggest frustrations I witness from both leaders and their people is when the two parties are at opposite ends of this meta-program. That is, one party is at the global, big picture end of the spectrum and the other party is at the fine detail end. Discussing this meta-program and our preferred styles can dramatically improve the effectiveness of communication in both directions.

Note   If you are a leader with a preference for details, be warned. Your style can easily come across to your people as micro-management.

Co-Create Their Profile

Unnatural Leaders continuously develop their deep understanding of their team members by co-creating and maintaining a Human Full Stack profile of each employee. Together with the communication style preferences, leaders are able to broaden their understanding of the key meta-programs, values, beliefs, and Enneagram types of their team members in order to challenge, support, and grow their team members in the most effective ways.

Co-creation is a critical part of the leader and employee journey. Sharing and discovering the elements of both party's Human Full Stack is not only valuable for communication but will often be extremely engaging and enlightening for the employees, as they gain a deeper understanding of themselves and how they operate.

To give you an idea of how to do this, I'll outline the approach I use when co-creating a new employee's Full Stack. First, I start with a one-on-one session to introduce the concepts and share my own Full Stack. During this phase, I clarify my intentions (to grow and support them as an individual) and I explain the process and frameworks I use to develop a deeper understanding of them. We then take a break and I give the individual a questionnaire to complete, which they bring to our next session to discuss. The questionnaire is designed to make them think hard about what they want (and why they want it) and get them thinking about the frames they may hold about their role. We then use these insights to co-create their personal growth plan.

■ **Note**   If you would like to a copy of this questionnaire to use with your teams, download it from
https://unnatural.io/link/b156.

When it comes to the backend of the Human Full Stack, I utilize one of the Enneagram assessment tools mentioned in Chapter 10. I spend time walking through their report with them, which allows us to validate their type and identify key elements that they strongly resonate with.

At a later point in time, after the employee has settled into their team, I run the team through a group Enneagram session to allow the whole team to get a deeper understanding of each other, reducing inter-team member friction, and increasing engagement and productivity. Even if the team has done one or more Enneagram sessions before, sharing and reviewing our core drivers again is always valuable as it provides time to for the team to reflect on current events together. It is also often a refreshing and welcome break away from the detail of product delivery.

As an Unnatural Leader, we encourage the constant review and discussion of our experiences, motivators, and frustrations. We facilitate both individual and group sessions that expand our understanding of how each individual's Human Full Stack is configured. In order to create highly positive experiences and evolve both ourselves and the members of our team, we use the insights generated from these processes to connect with people on a deeper and more meaningful level and to support and challenge them in the most effective ways.

Co-Creating a Personal Growth Plan

The purpose of the growth plan is to create intentionality and concrete goals that develop the individual—faster than they would without guidance and support. It provides a clear and concise, shared understanding of what the individual wants to achieve, aligned with the objectives of the organization.

What goes into each plan varies dramatically by individual. Not only does it vary from person to person, their plan evolves over time (we are, after all, building future Unnatural Leaders!).

The T-shaped skills model has been a popular model (popularized by the likes of IDEO[2]) to represent a person's skillset. The crossbar of the "T" represents their shallow breadth across a range of skills and expertise and the vertical bar of the "T" represents their deep skills in a particular area. More recently, Kent Beck presented the Paint Drip[3] model which is, I believe, a more appropriate model of the type of individuals we need in our organizations. In the Paint Drip model, Beck argues that individuals acquire a wide variety of skills at various depths. The broad brush stroke across the page represents the individual's constant and curious exploration. Each paint drip that falls down the page represents a particular dive into a skill, some shallow and some deep, and changing over one's career.

Paint Drip people are curious people. The broad exploratory stroke and its associated drips are the mark of an individual that is able to grow, and therefore is in a better position to continue to evolve faster than the pace of change. T-shaped people, by the model's very definition are tied to a specific vertical development.

Unnatural Leaders are paint drip people and they grow paint drip people and teams.

---

[2]https://unnatural.io/link/b151
[3]https://unnatural.io/link/b152

Creating a growth plan should, therefore, represent this Paint Drip metaphor. It includes curiosity, concrete goals and objectives, and a deeper development of a variety of skills.

How you structure the specific growth plans is down to you to decide with your people. The plans need to respect the team and organizational context.

The time frame of the growth plan is also down to you. I find that focusing on a 1-2 year horizon to be useful for a majority of circumstances. I recommend setting phased intentions for new employees, as shown in Table 15-1.

Table 15-1. The Five Phases of a Growth Plan

Phase	Intention	Time Frame
Integrate	Support and integrate the individual into the organization, team and role	First 30 days
Productivity	Focus on getting them productive within their team	3 months
Stretch	Develop them further to stretch and engage them in their role	6 months
Impact	Helping them to have a wider impact on the organization	12 months
Next Role	Building them into their next role	18-24 months

■ **Note** If you are looking for a way to align objectives across an organization, I suggest you try Objective and Key Results[4] or (OKRs) and a tool such as Lattice[5] to facilitate their management.

Coaching and Support

I'm not going to go into details of how to set goals and manage performance—there are numerous books and articles that dive deep into those subjects. What I am going to discuss is how to become a (better) coach in service of the growth of your individuals and teams.

Coaching is mostly about listening and occasionally asking powerful questions that shift the coachee's awareness of a concept, situation, or worldview. These powerful questions assist the individual in their growth. One mark of a good coach is for the coachee to feel like it is them that has made the new realization and shift. When they make a realization and believe it, the shift is

---

[4]https://unnatural.io/link/b153
[5]https://unnatural.io/link/b154

transformational and long-term. Coaching this way can be quite challenging for leaders who feel the need to have and provide all of the answers. However, we are not the expert of our employee's mind, so we have to get out of their way and allow the individual to find the answers for themselves.

The two biggest challenges that I see most leaders face when attempting to coach and support their people are:

- *Have one-on-ones that are status updates and not coaching sessions*

  Most leaders tell me they are doing one-on-ones with their people. When I dig deeper, it's disappointing to find out that these one-on-ones are almost always transactional status updates, which involve the leader communicating priorities and the latest updates, while the employee gives status updates on the projects they are working on. The best leaders have one-on-ones that involve personal conversations around growth and learning. The purpose of the meetings is for you (their leader) to spend some (mental) time in their shoes, to empathize with them, understand how they are going, what they are motivated and frustrated by, and what other influences are impacting their state and their ability to be productive and grow. I recommend that you hold "real" one-on-ones every 2-3 weeks with each direct report (at a minimum).

- *Talk more than listen*

  Too many leaders like to talk and talk. When you are talking, you aren't listening. When you aren't listening you aren't learning. Don't get me wrong; there are times to talk and times when you must talk, but when it comes to one-on-one coaching conversations, the goal is to really listen, not simply wait for a moment to interject with your opinions. Instead, sit and listen to the other person, and receive all their verbal and non-verbal communications without interjecting. Don't be afraid of silence, it's a powerful tool. If you are a leader who likes to talk, spend some time reflecting on why you like to talk, and what it means to you to talk and share things?

Getting ourselves out of the way (and listening more) is one of the things that makes a great coach. It's all too easy to bring our own values, beliefs, preferences, and worldviews to coaching sessions and make assumptions as to what the other person means. A great coach listens, listens, and listens and, when appropriate, tests their own understanding with questions in the form of:

> ... *and so what meaning did you make from that?*
>
> ... *Can I just check in with you and confirm that...*
>
> ... *What was it about that (action) that frustrated you (the label they put on their emotion)?*
>
> ... *So, given all of this, where do you want to take this from here?*

Where possible we ask open-ended questions and avoid sentences that project our own assumptions and opinions such as:

> ... *that sounds like you are angry because they did...*
>
> ... *the other person was wrong to ....*
>
> ... *so what you're really trying to say is....*
>
> ... *oh that is so <judgment> they need to <X> ...*

One of the other tools I use, particularly when someone is having a challenging time, is to set a timer on my phone (for 5 or 10 minutes) and tell them that i'm going to say nothing and just listen for this period of time. During that time, I only nod or respond with "say more."

At the end of the time, I replay back to them what I've heard, using their words as much as possible, and sharing what I've seen from them as they shared - things like changes in posture, changes in expression, changes in pace or tone of their voice. These non-verbal clues are opportunities for inquiry, and in my experience, if you can uncover the topics where there are strong emotional responses, they are the opportunities for true growth for the employee. This playback sounds something like this:

> *"I noticed that when you talked about not being able to finish that feature on time, you voice quivered a bit—what was going on for you there?" or "Thanks for sharing that, I just want to check in, when you say you are struggling to implement this, I saw you slump down and let out a long sigh—what is it about this implementation that triggered this body reaction?"*

The purpose of this exercise is to let the other person share everything they are experiencing without interruption, and for us to hear them—really hear them—including all of the non-verbals (You will find it a lot easier to watch for non-verbal clues when you don't have to respond).

This exercise can be incredibly cathartic for the individual as it allows them to release all of their emotions attached to a situation. After which they are usually thinking much more clearly and are able to find their own solutions.

Like any skill, it takes practice to become a great coach. I've found that the best way to learn to be a great coach is to experience being coached by a great coach.

Note My coaching journey began in 2009 after attending an NLP and neuro-semantics training course held in Sydney. I made the decision to get a coach and dive deeper into understanding myself and others better. I have been enrolled in coaching ever since, and through my coaching, I experienced what it was like to be listened to, to be asked powerful questions, and to have my transformation facilitated by someone who just asked questions and showed me my own limiting behaviors. I learned what a great coach looked like, which has helped me become a better coach myself. I truly believe in the transformative powers of coaching and I will continue to invest in my growth through coaching.

As you will have no doubt guessed by now, our own Full Stack configuration impacts how we coach and which elements of coaching we struggle with and excel at as we begin the process of becoming a coach. Table 15-2 outlines the typical coaching strengths and challenges for each of the nine Enneagram types.

Table 15-2. Enneagram Types Coaching Strengths and Challenges

Enneagram Type	Coaching Strength	Coaching Challenge
1 - Reformer	Adherence to coaching process and high ethical standards	Can be overly perfectionist in their approach and demands on the coachee
2 – Helper	Genuine personal care and connection with coachees	Being over-responsible for the coachees state and performance
3 - Achiever	Outcome and growth focus	Avoidance of what can be seen as unproductive conversations or activities, such as coaching conversations

(continued)

Table 15-2. (*continued*)

Enneagram Type	Coaching Strength	Coaching Challenge
4 – Individualist	Passion and interest in understanding what makes people tick	Can dive too deep and become overly philosophical in a professional context
5 - Investigator	Systems thinking and strategic guidance	Can appear to ignore the emotional components of scenarios in favor of logic
6 - Loyalist	Strong awareness of cultural norms and group dynamics	Can be indecisive and influenced by strong opinions of others
7 - Enthusiast	Positive activation and energizing of others	Can avoid going too deep to avoid difficult topics
8 - Challenger	Direct and supportive	Lack of vulnerability and focus on power can prevent rapport
9 - Peacemaker	Non-judgmental approach	Can struggle to communicate clearly or take decisive action

As an example, the Challenger (Type 8) has the ability to be direct and supportive in their approach to coaching. They can challenge a person in a clear and concise manner by asking pointed questions with a supportive frame. However, they may struggle to show and experience vulnerability and as such fail to create rapport in coaching scenarios where power and vulnerability are the topics of conversation.

As we coach and develop our understanding of the coachee we use the Full Stack to listen for and determine the person's configuration. If we have followed the onboarding process, we will understand their Enneagram type and therefore the person's core motivators. In coaching sessions, we can then listen for highest frames (Chapter 12) of meaning, meta-programs, values, and beliefs.

Focus on Learning

It is common and, indeed, often desirable for coaching scenarios to dive into subjects that are challenging and difficult. Breaking through these big challenges is what creates big evolutionary transformations in people. This can make some sessions deep, intense, and uncomfortable for the coachee—especially if they have a fixed mindset and/or a global and pessimistic meta-program configuration. With this configuration employees who receive "constructive feedback" tend to take it personally and generalize the feedback across more elements of their life. They can become pessimistic about their chances of succeeding in the future. The best approach to take in these, and, indeed, all leadership coaching scenarios, is to focus on learning and how the individual can learn and grow from a situation.

Reframing failure is critical to the process of becoming an Unnatural Leader. (We will look more closely at failure and feedback in Part V.) Getting the coachee to a point where they embody the following quote from John Powell is what we aim to achieve.

> *The only real mistake is the one from which we learn nothing.*
>
> —John Joseph Powell[6]

In terms of tangible coaching skills you can use to guide conversations and facilitate the coachee's growth, I suggest using powerful questions that stimulate and clarify learning, such as:

- How might your actions have contributed to this scenario?

- What would you do differently next time?

- What have you learned about yourself, others, and the process?

- How have your grown in this scenario?

Keeping track of what has been learned is extremely powerful. When we get to the end of a week, month, quarter, or even year and reflect back on the progress we've made, it's all too easy to forget what we have learned and how much we have grown. We are wired to remember intense, emotional experiences (both positive and negative) such as a really successful product release or failing to get a promotion. However, more often than not, our evolution is a continual process of small steps, each of which can be easily forgotten. (Have you ever taken part in an Agile retrospective and struggled to recall the details of just the last one or two weeks?)

Writing down each lesson in a learning log or journal is an easy and extremely powerful process that reinforces our learning. For personal learning logs, I keep things simple and record the date, context, and what I learned. An example of a log entry is shown in Table 15-3.

---

[6]*The Secret of Staying in Love* (Argus Communications, 1974)

Table 15-3. A Typical Learning Log Entry

Date	Context	Learning
12-9-2011	General communications with my new boss	My boss has a strong preference for auditory communication and therefore doesn't usually respond well to the visuals I use.
		For important topics, I need to talk my boss through the details if I want to gain his buy-in.

The same principle applies to our engineering teams. As part of the iteration review (or sprint showcase), I encourage my teams to dedicate time in the session to talk about the lessons learned in that iteration. Jeff Patton has delivered a great presentation on Learning Velocity at Agile NZ 2016,[7] which I strongly recommend you watch.

Three of the four internal components of building a great tech brand (Working with Smart People, Big and Interesting Problems, and Interesting Technology) are all underpinned by the opportunity to learn. To help stimulate an individual's growth and learning, you can use these as categories to set learning goals or to assist in discovering lessons already learned. For example, you might ask the person what they have learned from a colleague about a problem space or regarding the technology being used.

Explicitly recognizing an individual or team's progress is a very powerful engagement tool.

The Challenge of Leading and Coaching

A true coach has no personal investment in the outcome of a coaching session and has no personal agenda. A coach engages his client in full service of the client and their needs. If you are a person's leader, it is impossible to engage in a true coaching relationship. As their leader, you have the authority to promote or fire that individual. Because of this, we can never expect to create a true coach-client relationship, which is a 100% safe place to share personal information.

However, we aren't trying to become that sort of coach. What we are looking to achieve is to develop coaching skills that allow us to develop a deeper understanding of (and care for) individuals so that we can better lead and grow them to their full potential.

---

[7]https://unnatural.io/link/b155

Summary

Building a great tech brand should be the goal of any senior digital leader because it facilitates the creation of a high-performance and high-engagement environment for us all to thrive in. Caring for our teams and our people is important to Unnatural Leaders, and we hold the intention to grow them constantly throughout their time in our organizations.

Developing a deep understanding of our people is a critical part of how we support and grow them. We utilize the Full Stack to develop our understanding of them and establish effective communication patterns. Our interactions are not basic transactional, status updates—instead they involve one-on-ones, where we challenge and support their learning and growth by coaching them to higher levels of thinking and evolution.

Coaching, guiding, and growing others is an incredible experience for both parties! I'm looking forward to a world where it's considered "normal" for leaders to coach and develop their people with this level of care and attention.

Self-Reflection Questions

1. Are you coaching your people right now? If not, what is stopping you? What is more important to you than their growth? (Be honest with yourself!)

2. How would you rate your organization's seven elements of a great tech brand? How would your teams rate it?

3. What meta-programs (discussed in Chapter 9) impact the effectiveness of communication between two people?

4. What do you think are your individual strengths and challenges in your role as a coach?

5. How might you create a real learning culture in your organization?

Attention: Stakeholders

> *You do not need a certain number of friends, just a number of friends you can be certain of.*
>
> —Itzik Amiel, *The Attention Switch*[1]

The third and final focus of our attention is to build long-lasting, mutually beneficial relationships. In this chapter we are going to look at the three steps: identifying the right stakeholders, understanding the stakeholders, and positively influencing them (see Figure 16-1).

Figure 16-1. The stakeholder process

---

[1]Croydon, UK: Filament Publishing, 2014

© James Brett 2019
J. Brett, *Evolving Digital Leadership*, https://doi.org/10.1007/978-1-4842-3606-2_16

Step 1: Identifying Stakeholders

Stakeholders come in all sorts of shapes and sizes. There are senior stakeholders we must "report" to, colleagues who are peers, various people across our organization we must work with, customer stakeholders whose expectations we must meet, and even stakeholders in our industry who have no direct involvement in our business.

In our digital world, we have the added challenge of dealing with stakeholders who are technical and those who are not (and even those that think they are, but, well… aren't). Often our stakeholder relationships are hinged around translating technical communications to business communications and vice versa as we coordinate delivery in our teams, across our business, and out to customers. This can be a frustrating experience for leaders who have to repeatedly explain technical and delivery concepts, to the same stakeholders who just don't understand the unpredictable and complex challenge that is digital product development. Equally, some leaders face the challenge of the "technical founder," who wrote the original codebase and now, some time later, still believes he knows the best technical solutions.

In Chapter 8, I discussed how our stage of developer (from Expert to Achiever to Catalyst) impacts how we view and approach stakeholder engagement. Statistically, 55% of leaders are at the Expert stage of development. This means they have a tendency to engage stakeholders only when needed and not focus on building long-term relationships. The critical stakeholder shifts that happen as we progress from Expert to Catalyst involve moving away from using our authority to influence, shifting from short-term interactions to long-term relationship-building, and from leaving behind either a passive or assertive style and growing toward one that is balanced and can flex appropriately to the scenario.

Let's begin by ensuring we are focusing on the right stakeholders.

Stakeholder Relationship Map

We simply don't have time to build and maintain deep relationships with all our stakeholders. We also don't have the luxury of not engaging stakeholders who impact our and the organization's success in a significant manner. More often than not, leaders don't focus their attention on the stakeholder landscape in order to understand who to engage and how. Unnatural leaders maintain a stakeholder relationship map that visualizes their stakeholders relationship requirements (see Figure 16-2).

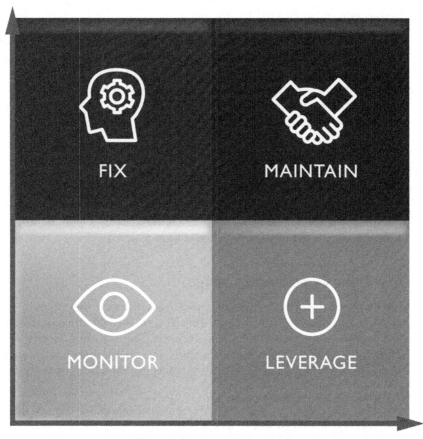

Figure 16-2. The stakeholder relationship map

The two axes of the stakeholder relationship map identify the current strength of our relationship with a particular stakeholder (X axis) and the impact that a stakeholder can have on the success of our role (Y axis). These two attributes create a quadrant model that describes how we should be approaching our relationships with the stakeholders in each quadrant.

Upper-Left Quadrant: Fix

In this quadrant, we have stakeholders who have the ability to impact our success and who we don't (currently) have a strong relationship with. It's advisable then, to engage new stakeholders in this quadrant and strengthen any relationships that already exist. If, for some reason, you aren't able to engage all stakeholders on your map, this quadrant is where you should focus your attention.

Upper-Right Quadrant: Maintain

This quadrant is where we want to move people to if they are in quadrant 1. These stakeholders have a great impact on our success *and* we have a strong relationship with them. We need to continue to put effort and attention into these relationships to ensure they remain strong and healthy. When we get busy and distracted, it's all too easy for stakeholders in this group to drift to the left quadrant, leaving the relationship requiring repair.

Lower-Left Quadrant: Monitor

The lower-left quadrant contains stakeholders who have less of an impact on us, and whom we don't (currently) have a strong relationship. The guidance I offer for this quadrant is to monitor these stakeholders as you identify them, and keep an eye on the impact they could have as it may change over time.

Lower-Right Quadrant: Leverage

The lower-right quadrant contains stakeholders who we have a strong relationship with, but the stakeholder doesn't have a significant impact on our success. Here we want to look at any potential opportunities where we can use a relationship to build other relationships (in other words, where can these stakeholders help us build or leverage relationships we don't currently have).

We need to be cautious how much time we spend with stakeholders in this quadrant, as the very nature of the strong relationship-low impact situation implies an enjoyable relationship that we will likely be drawn to.

To populate the stakeholder relationship map, I prefer to draw the four quadrants on a large piece of paper and populate it with each stakeholder's name written on a single sticky note. Using sticky notes allows stakeholders to be repositioned as we learn more about them or as circumstances change. I always make sure that I either socialize the map with others (and update it based on their feedback) or co-create it together with a select number of people.

Sharing your stakeholder map with stakeholders who sit in either the Fix or Monitor quadrants can actively enhance your relationship with them. It gives you an opportunity to discuss why you have placed them in a particular quadrant, and then to discuss your intent (to move them to the Leverage quadrant) and what it might take to build a mutually beneficial relationship together. I imagine that many of you reading this are thinking "No way would I ever do that with Bob (or stakeholder X)!" and so I challenge you to think about what co-creating a relationship with a stakeholder might look like, and how you both could grow through the process.

And so, maintenance of the map is essential as your role, stakeholders, and the environment evolve over time. The stakeholder map is living artifact that I suggest you revisit at least every month.

Once stakeholders have been categorized, you will need to determine who you are going to focus on and how. Once you have determined this, based on your specific context, it's time to look at ways of building relationships with these stakeholders.

Step 2: Understanding the Stakeholder

Communication preferences are critical for any person to person interaction we have, and stakeholders are no exception. Effective communication (described in Chapter 15) is equally applicable to stakeholders. However, with a majority of stakeholders, it's likely that we won't have the benefit of explicitly discussing their Human Full Stack. We have to determine their communication preferences primarily through observation. We observe their eye accessing cues (Chapter 9) and use of language such as "look, sounds, or feels" to determine their primary communication channel (VAKAd) and actively listen to the language they use to identify the key meta-programs they are running. A key technique used to develop a deeper and more explicit understanding of an individual is to focus your questions to get into the specifics of a topic. (In the psychology world, this is referred to as "searching for specificity.")

Getting Specific

Our language is laden with generalizations. Generalizations (described in Chapter 7) are labels that we use to process information in an efficient manner. However, these generalization can cause confusion and misunderstanding when we use them in our communication. Take this sentence as an example:

> *"No, I don't want to do that—I don't like cloud platforms."*

If a stakeholder made this comment, you might strongly disagree and be tempted to argue their statement—with an equally over-generalized response such as "Cloud platforms are the future; everyone is moving to them". The "debate" would then likely continue or escalate until either someone "wins" or a stalemate is reached. Usually, both parties walk away from these conversations feeling frustrated and the relationship weakened.

Conversely, Unnatural Leaders identify the generalized language and get curious about its specific meaning and how the stakeholder formed their opinion. There are two generalizations in the sentence and they are the words: "like" and "Cloud Platforms".

> *"I **don't** like **Cloud Platforms**."*

In order to get to the specifics of this communication, an Unnatural Leader might ask the following as a response:

> Q1: *"What Cloud Platforms are you referring to specifically?"*
>
> Q2: *"What is it that you don't like about them?"*

When these questions are posed with genuine curiosity, it is highly likely that the other party will respond positively and honestly like this:

> *"I don't like Source Control Platforms like GitHub because I am worried about security and hosting our IP online where it might get hacked."*

Can you see the difference? We now have three further pieces of information (which may or may not be what we had assumed in the first instance). They don't like *source control platforms* like *GitHub*, because of the potential *security risk*. This gives us a far more specific and useful understanding of their perspective and their concerns. Their communicated dislike of cloud platforms was a generalization of source control platforms and their perceived security risk. We might also surmise that this stakeholder is more oriented toward the global end of the Cognitive Scale meta-program (see Figure 7-2 in Chapter 7).

We now have more data to inform how we chose to respond and potentially address their concerns. In most situations there will be a level of validity in the stakeholders perspective that, if we acknowledge it, we are likely to foster a higher level of engagement, which in turn surfaces more information and context.

Asking for specific detail in the appropriate tone and acknowledging concerns often has the effect of diffusing tension and aggression in the other party. You may have noticed that the two example questions asked for specifics using "What?" rather than "Why?" This was not accidental—rather, there is a specific reason for exploring using questions that avoid "Why?"

Never Ask Why?

When someone shares their opinion (or even a judgment), I highly recommend that you do not respond with "Why?" For instance, if a stakeholder communicates the following opinion:

> *"Windows laptops are the best way to go; we need to buy them for our organization".*

It's tempting to search for specifics by asking "why?" or even "Why are they the best?" When we we use a "why" question, it triggers the other person to justify what they have said, which causes them to go on the defensive and take a stance ready to argue their position. If we don't have a strong, positive relationship, the conversation can easily degenerate into a professional "argument," as they feel compelled to justify and stand by their claim.

Unnatural Leaders understand that opinions stated as facts are merely the personal opinions and judgments made by the stakeholder. And Unnatural Leaders know that these are formed by the stakeholders' own perspectives of reality, values, beliefs, skill levels, and experiences.

To avoid alienating stakeholders *and* to uncover the specifics of their communication, we ask questions that follow the format of:

> *"What is it about X ...?"*

For instance:

> *"What is about Windows Laptops that make them the best way to go?"*

Avoiding asking "why" is a technique I recommend using in most conversations, both professional and personal. Imagine the reduction in household arguments if partners used this approach! Defensiveness and judgment dissipate, and conversations can focus on the meaningful topics that move both parties forward.

It does take time and practice to develop this habit. Most of us are socially programmed to ask "why?", we learn it early on as children. It takes cognitive effort to move from "why?" to a question that is structured to ask for specifics using "What is it about that...?"

Get Clear On What Success Means (To Them!)

Like us, every stakeholder is trying to achieve objectives in their role. Understanding what stakeholders are striving for and what success looks like for them is critical to building a mutually beneficial relationship.

Most stakeholders will happily outline objectives and targets they are delivering to, but we must dig deeper to understand their vision (assuming they have one) for what they want to achieve. We can do this by asking questions such as: "So, in two years when you have met those objectives—what's next?" or "What's your longer-term vision for you team/department?" and then based on their response, follow up with "What is it about ... that is important to you?"

Objectives, goals, roadmaps, and plans are specific to each stakeholder. What helps us excel at interactions with stakeholders is adding our understanding of how their Enneagram type impacts the way they deliver and operate. In Chapter 10, I presented the nine WIIFMs (What's In It For Me) for each Enneagram type (shown again here in Table 16-1).

Table 16-1. The Enneagram WIIFMs

Type	WIIFM
1 – Reformer	How can I do the right thing and change things for the better?
2 – Helper	How can I help someone or the group?
3 – Achiever	How can I be successful?
4 – Individualist	How can I express myself?
5 – Investigator	How can I demonstrate my competence?
6 – Loyalist	How can I support my group's needs?
7 – Enthusiast	How can have I have fun?
8 – Challenger	How can I do something that challenges?
9 – Peacemaker	How can I find harmony and calm?

These deeper motivators are not obvious to the average leader. However, they can dramatically affect what the stakeholder is drawn toward at a subconscious level (in most cases even they are unaware of these drivers). For example, a stakeholder who is a Helper (Type 2) may have a set of delivery objectives in which they take a people centric approach and focus on connecting and helping others to succeed. Therefore, to connect strongly with this stakeholder, we must ensure that our communication includes people, and highlights potential opportunities for them to assist us.

Success to them really is all about helping people and delivering their objectives.

Step 3: Positively Influencing Stakeholders

The third and final step of the stakeholder process (see Figure 16-1) is Influence. Once we have identified our stakeholders and gained and understanding of their preferences and what success means to them, we can positively influence them for mutual benefit.

How we approach our communication with stakeholders impacts our ability to Influence and gain support. Too many tech leaders approach stakeholder communication with a strong technical bias—often only including a request for investment in new technology (say backend software stack) and a high-level outline of the features and functionality that will be gained. This is an example of such a request:

> *We propose to move data to AWS, a cloud provider for our data lake and need an investment of $100,000 for the licensing and team to perform the transition. We need to do this because it makes our development process easier.*

It's a basic request (which may have been presented with pretty pictures in Microsoft PowerPoint). It outlines the required investment and a loose explanation of the requirement. Nowhere in the request does it explicitly identify any business benefits, its alignment to organizational strategy, or the business risks associated with not doing it.

An organization's budget is always constrained! When it comes to making decisions on where and how to invest, leaders are always making trade offs between what gets funded and what doesn't. They want to know that the available funds are being utilized in the most effective manner to grow and sustain the business. Non-technical stakeholders are often not interested in the technical details of a proposal, the question they are often asking (internally) is: "Are you (the technical leader) thinking about the business context and helping to drive the business appropriately with technology". Unless the stakeholder involved *is* technical *and* has a sufficient understanding of the domain and problem space, pitching with a technology first request is almost always a recipe for disaster.

Unlike our enquiry process earlier where we avoided the use of "why," when Unnatural Leaders are advocating and pitching strategies we utilize Simon Sinek's framework, called Start With Why.[2] Sinek recommends that we format our communications such that the order is Why, How, and What. Why do we want or need something?, How do we satisfy that need? And with what?

---

[2]Simon Sinek, "How Great Leaders Inspire Action," TED, recorded September 2009, 17:58, https://unnatural.io/link/b161

In this example, the leader communicated their request in the reverse direction: What technology we want: AWS and the investment: $100,000, How we will do it: With a team, and the why is a poorly articulated technology why: Easier development process.

Let's look at an example of how to increase the effectiveness of your digital pitches.

▦ **Note** For the purposes of conveying understanding in this book, I've written the pitch in plain text. Successful pitches include all three of the main communication channels (Visual, Auditory, and Kinesthetic) usually in the form of a presentation style workshop.

Why the Business Needs to Support the Initiative

Start the pitch by describing why the business needs to support the initiative by outlining the current business strategy and objectives, any business challenges being faced and your strategy to support the business. Doing so demonstrates a solid understanding and focus on the business and what it is trying to achieve. An example of this part of the pitch might be:

> *Our business is targeting real growth (10x) this year which, when achieved will be mean an increase in customer orders to over 1M per year. Our strategy is to scale efficiently by automating and simplifying our back-end systems to reduce costs by 10% and ensure they can service the higher demand.*

Notice that there is no mention of specific technologies or a request at this point. This part of the pitch reiterates a key goal (10x growth) and an identified challenge (capacity of back-end systems). It then outlines how we plan to attack the problem: efficiency through automation and simplification.

How We Plan to Address the Business Need

This is where we communicate further details of how our strategy will solve the challenge. Our pitch might continue as follows:

> *Server costs and capacity are critical to growth and efficiency. Our current systems will struggle to cope with the volume and would require significant server upgrades to support this. However, if we move to a cloud-based provider with automated monitoring and deployment, we can scale to meet these demands and increase our operational efficiencies.*

At this point, we have demonstrated our business focus and outlined clearly how we are going to approach the challenge while achieving the organizational objectives.

Where possible, we do our best to align the initiative (and pitch) with the stakeholder objectives and communicate how our proposal benefits them. If we have done a good job at the first two parts of the pitching processes, it's common at this point for the stakeholder to have already decided to back our initiative. The final step is to outline what we need, and any specific asks we have of them.

What We Require to Execute and Enable the Business

It's now time to get specific and provide clarity about the support we require, ensuring that our communication is still business focused:

> There are a number of cloud providers available of which Amazon Web Services (AWS) meets our required functionality, performance, and security requirements. (See comparison matrix.)

> The transition requires an initial investment of $200,000 for provisioning and first year hosting fees, a six-person Agile team for three months to complete the migration and an estimated ongoing annual cost of $50,000 (based on our strategic scaling objectives).

The final part of our pitch gets to the specifics that most leaders start with. However, unlike most requests, this request demonstrates that we have modeled the ongoing cost in alignment with the strategic scale required and the attributes we compared to make our decision—the Comparison Matrix.

A well thought through and articulated pitch like this demonstrates clear business alignment and is much more likely to gain approval than one that only states the required investment for a specific technology. So the next time you make pitch, remember to start with the business why, then how the request enables those outcomes, before specifying what you will do and the support required.

Gaining Buy-in to Reduce Technical Debt

As a digital leader, one of the most commons problems we face is managing technical debt. Product development is a delicate balance of building new features and repaying technical debt incurred over time. There are times when it's sensible to take on an amount of technical debt in favor of validating a business model or customer demand for a product or feature. The trade-off we make at this stage is to favor development speed (allowing for faster and more efficient in market testing) against scalability. (There are some instances where our organization's size and brand might mean that scalability is in issue from day one.)

Digital leaders make and communicate these decisions with their teams and stakeholders. In my experience stakeholders usually respond with comments similar to "well, if we get to that scale, it's a nice problem to have". Of course, those nice problems, become mere problems when we achieve scale and they result in technical migrations that involve significant development time and cost.

Asking for the ability to carve out large blocks of time from the product delivery roadmap to pay down technical debt incurred is usually a challenging conversation (even for those that approach with a business focused why first). The root cause of this is embedded in the articulation of the request. When pitching for capacity to pay down technical debt (to non-technical stakeholders) digital leaders often make the mistake of asking stakeholders to choose whether they would like the team to deliver new features or stop and fix things (that the stakeholder doesn't understand). When viewed like this, most stakeholders will push for feature delivery until something dramatic happens in production (system outage, financial transaction errors) that causes sufficient pain for technical debt to become the highest priority.

To counter this, rather than asking stakeholders to choose between new feature delivery or stopping to fix debt, a far more effective question is to ask:

> *"Would you like a new feature delivered or to be able to deliver features faster?"*

When presented with this question, both options sound appealing to a stakeholder. It subtly changes the rather negative frame of technical debt to focus on the business value (the why) of addressing it. I find that explaining the chart in Figure 16-3 to be really effective in getting non-technical stakeholders on-board with the value of addressing technical debt.

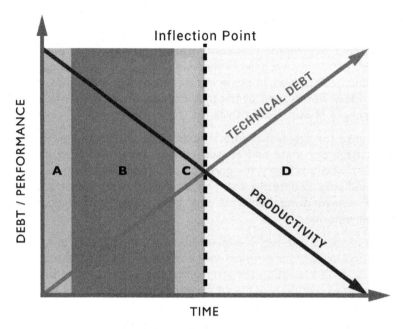

Figure 16-3. Technical debt and productivity

This chart depicts the decrease in productivity as technical debt increases. To the right side of the inflection point (Zone D), technical debt is at a level where the teams are spending more time fixing issues than they are creating new features—until finally technical debt is so bad that the team spends most of their time fixing bugs and errors and there is no more capacity to develop anything new.

We want to manage technical debt so that it stays to the left-hand side of the inflection point—ideally in Zone B. Too far to the left hand-side and we enter a warning zone (Zone A), where it's possible that we are over-engineering features and delivering too slowly for the business to capitalize the commercial value. Too far to the right side and we enter another warning zone (Zone C), which has a gravitational pull toward the inflection point and beyond. Technical debt in Zone C can quickly escalate if left unaddressed and pull productivity levels down past the inflection and into Zone D.

The chart helps stakeholders understand the relationship between performance and debt. It's also a tool teams can use to agree and communicate the current state of technical debt in a product. Plotting the current debt level on this chart and talking with stakeholders and teams about the desired technical debt level goes a long way to gaining buy-in and raising the transparency of a challenge that we all face.

When It All Goes Wrong

Digital product development is complicated and unpredictable. Things go wrong more often than we'd like! When big things go wrong, stakeholders are impacted and get involved. In some instances they can become angry and/or aggressive. How we respond significantly impacts the severity of the situation and the strength of our relationships.

Diffusing tense (or aggressive) interactions takes skill on our part. We must actively manage our state and remain calm and logical. When dealing with stakeholders who are angry, it's good practice to allow them to vent their anger. Immediately countering their negative comments can exacerbate the situation. Acknowledging their frustration goes a long way to helping them to diffuse their emotions.

Once the emotional intensity has lowered we can then engage in real dialogue with them and explain our position and propose a solution. Where possible we always try to have a solution (or strategy to find a solution) to the challenge at hand. Great executives want ways forward and not denial or shifting of the blame onto others.

Managing our emotional state is critical in these situations. It's all too easy for us to trigger a negative state in ourselves. It's key to remember that we have full control over our emotional state (our four powers) and so we can choose the most appropriate state for dealing with the interaction.

You may be thinking that it's not my responsibility to manage their emotional state and help them to diffuse their anger. That's true, it isn't! However, we aren't taking responsibility for them and their emotions, we are using our own state management and skills to move to a solution that gets the best outcome for the business and (where desirable) maintains the long-term relationship with the stakeholders.

Summary

A critical part of successful stakeholder engagement is identifying all the stakeholders we need to engage and focusing the right amount of energy on each relationship. Finding the time to maintain strong relationships with stakeholders can be challenging. However, when we use tools such as the stakeholder relationship map, we can visualize and keep key stakeholder relationships in our attention.

Building and maintaining strong relationships involves gaining a deep understanding of how a stakeholder likes to communicate, and using questions to gain a more specific understanding of their opinions, values, and beliefs. We use the same techniques to ensure that we understand what professional success means to them and how their Enneagram type influences the type of goals they set and how the execute toward their goals. This deep understanding allows us to align and, where needed, influence stakeholders to maximize our chance of success.

When we pitch strategies to influence stakeholders, we start with the business context and drivers first. This demonstrates the commercial alignment of our proposed solution. We then work backward toward our specific "What" request. We use language that is familiar to non-technical stakeholders and makes explicit the alignment to their (or their organization's) objectives.

Self-Reflection Questions

1. Populate your stakeholder relationship map. Are there any stakeholders who you are consciously not engaging? What do you believe about those stakeholders that is preventing you from do so?

2. Are there any stakeholders who you had not realized are key stakeholders you need to engage? Was there anything specific that caused you not to be aware of them initially?

3. How would you rate your ability to balance advocacy and inquiry when dealing with stakeholders? Does it change based on their authority level?

4. What do you need to learn about your organization's industry, commercial model, strategy, structure, or people, to put you in a better position to influence stakeholders?

5. Consider your current technical debt level: Are you and your team in agreement on the level of technical debt? What, if anything, do you need to do about it?

Summary of Part IV: Attention

Our attention is an extremely valuable commodity. How we use it and what we focus it on determines both our reality and the level of success we experience. Our intentions help us to focus our attention. However, using a personal system (as suggested In Chapter 14) allows us to take better control of our time and prioritize what we do.

Framing a problem or scenario and managing our state allows us to respond in the most effective manner with the most appropriate solutions. State management is a challenging skill to develop and those leaders (and indeed, all human beings) that are able to manage their state will experience a higher quality of life and realize more of their innate potential.

When it comes to attending to our teams, we develop relationships with our people by gaining a deep understanding of them from the first day they join the company. We then use this understanding to coach and support them in a way that challenges them to achieve their goals and positively contribute toward the performance and culture of the organization.

Attention, Step 3 of the evolution helix, is how we execute our leadership role. Some of the things we do will be highly successful, some of them won't. In some instances we will know why what we did worked and, in others, we will be utterly confused.

In Part V, we explore Step 4: Reflection. We look at how to better understand our performance and develop insights that raise our awareness and continue our evolution.

Reflection

Your perception of me is a reflection of you; my reaction to you is an awareness of me.

—Bobbi Chegwyn, Self-Empowerment Coach

Step 4 of the evolution helix is Reflection (Figure 1), and this is where the magic happens! Through open and curious reflection, we can gain new insights into ourselves, our teams, our organization, the industry—even the future. These insights shift our awareness and are our evolution.

Figure 1. Reflection, step 4 of the evolution helix

Taking time out of our week to reflect can be a challenge. For some of us, it can feel unproductive to "stop working" and reflect on our performance and gain perspectives on the future.

The chapters in Part V explore the different reflection mechanisms and approaches we can use to overcome the challenges faced when doing deep reflection work. A key challenge most of us face is that of judgment—the judgment of ourselves and the judgment from others as we reflect on their feedback.

Judgment allows us to understand the world by categorizing our experiences. We use it to label experiences as "good" or "bad," "successful" or "unsuccessful," and we do so without much conscious thought at all. While this works in some situations (such as identifying danger), judgment can create unnecessarily painful states that limit our growth.

I'd like to frame the reflection process by retelling an old Chinese folk story that has been told many times (and in many different ways) about a father and son who experienced some "good" and "bad" luck.

A Blessing in Disguise

A long time ago, a wise old man and his son lived on the plains of China. They enjoyed many a day indulging in their passion for horses and riding. Over the years they had acquired a collection of rare breed horses that included a magnificent, prized stallion. The old man and his son would ride their horses across the plains to trade goods, meet new people, and celebrate their good fortune.

Then, one day, a stable hand accidentally left the stable door open and the stallion bolted, galloping off into the distance and out of sight. After days of searching, the old man and his son declared the stallion lost. All of their neighbors came to console them. As the old man's friends expressed sympathy and shared how sorry they were that he'd had such "bad" luck, the old man replied "Is this bad luck? How do you know?"

The wise old man knew that judging the situation as "bad" would create more pain for himself, and he knew from experience that there was no way of knowing if losing the stallion was bad luck or not. The reality of the situation was that the horse had escaped.

A few weeks later, the old man was tending to his horses when the stallion returned home, bringing with him a mare. It wasn't just any mare; it was a rare and valuable white mare. When his neighbors heard the news, they rushed over to congratulate him on his good fortune, to which the old man replied, "Is this good luck? How do you know?" Yet again, the old man made no judgment of his situation, and merely accepted the return of his stallion (and the new mare). As he explained that there was no reason to be excited, his neighbors became even more confused than before.

Weeks later, his son was enjoying riding the beautiful white mare when she slipped and fell onto the son's leg, breaking it badly. The neighbors rushed to help take the son to the hospital, where the doctors managed to save his leg. Unfortunately, though, he would walk with a limp for the rest of his life. Angry at the horse, the neighbors insisted the old man either sell or shoot the horse and be rid of the bad luck that it had brought. The old man refused, again responding with, "Is this bad luck? How do you know?" He explained that they should not feel anger for the mare or sadness for his son—it was an accident that could not have been predicted and there was nothing that anyone could do to change what had happened. Finally, the frustrated neighbors gave up on the old man, assuming that he was crazy.

A few years later, the country was invaded and all of the old man's neighbors were drafted to fight and defend their land. It was a bloody war and most of them were killed in battle. Because of his lame leg, the old man's son was unable to fight and was not drafted. Instead, he stayed home safe with his father—saved from war by the accident with the mare that had happened two years earlier.

All too often, we judge scenarios in order to make sense of them—it's a programmed response that keeps us safe from danger. Most scenarios that we encounter in our life aren't life-threatening, and so sometimes when we jump to judge a person or a situation, we create pain and suffering for ourselves. The wise old man had achieved a level of awareness that allowed him to hold a perspective of time that was significantly longer than most of us can see. He was able to view each scenario in the broader context of life, without judgment.

Our responses (positive, negative, or neutral) are driven by the meaning we make of the situation, our beliefs of what reality "should" be (our expectations), and our internal emotional state. Reality happens; it's how we respond to reality that is important.

Reflection

There are three methods to gaining wisdom. The first is reflection, which is the highest. The second is limitation, which is the easiest. The third is experience, which is the bitterest.

—Confucius

Reflection, as Confucius points out, is a powerful tool for gaining wisdom, which is why it is the fourth and final step in the evolution helix. So, what is reflection and how do we do it? The Cambridge Dictionary describes the verb Reflect as:

Reflect: To think carefully, especially about possibilities and opinions.

—Cambridge Dictionary

Reflecting is commonly misunderstood to mean only looking backward into the past and "thinking carefully" about what happened, how we and others behaved, and the outcome of the situation. While this is true, reflecting is also the act of deep and focused thought about the future and possibilities.

As we reflect into the past, we take time to think carefully about our performance, the intentions we set, the actions we took, the actions of others, the outcomes achieved, and how well those outcomes aligned with what we desired. The objective of reflecting backward is to learn from our experiences in order to evolve and increase our performance the next time we face a similar situation.

© James Brett 2019
J. Brett, *Evolving Digital Leadership*, https://doi.org/10.1007/978-1-4842-3606-2_17

We reflect into the future to envision where we want to go and what we want to achieve, and to plan and predict the best course of action to get there. In doing so, we assess the trends that might influence the future and identify where we can be a disruptive catalyst, creating new waves of change.

In essence, we utilize reflection as a tool to evolve to higher levels of awareness and performance and to create and predict future disruptions (see Figure 17-1).

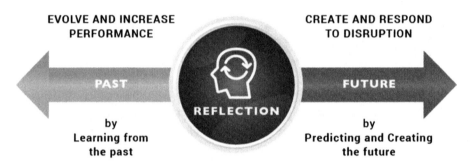

Figure 17-1. Two axes of reflection

Gaining Perspective

An essential outcome of reflection is the gaining of new perspectives. In Chapter 8, I presented the concept of stages of development (Expert, Achiever, Catalyst), where at each stage, a leader gains a new and wider perspective. We also performed an exercise to demonstrate the increase in perspective by framing your view with your hands (see Figure 17-2) and adjusting them to take in more (or less) elements of your field of view.

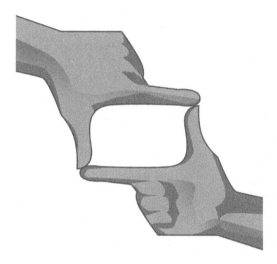

Figure 17-2. Framing your view with your hands

For digital leaders, there are a number of perspectives that we need to consider and reflect upon as we assess our past performance and look at future possibilities. As we develop our perspective on reality, we factor in more and more of the ecosystem in which we exist. We gain a broader context that spans an increasing time span, both back into the past and into the future. A micro-perspective involves a finite focus on, say, a task, and is only held for a few hours or minutes. A macro-perspective incorporates numerous systems that span (in some cases) centuries into the past and future. This broad perspective addresses the impact of what we have done and where we want to go with respect to society and the human race itself.

Levels of Perspective

I define 10 levels of perspective (see Figure 17-3) that you can use as a framework to reflect upon and develop your awareness. Let's take a brief look at each level.

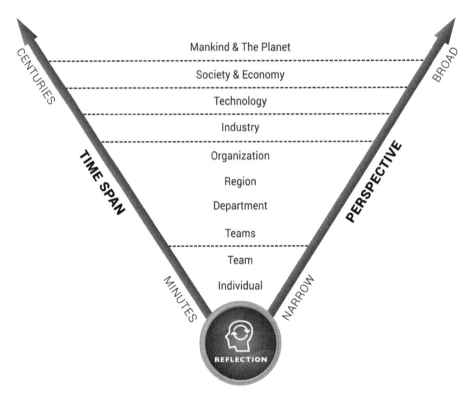

Figure 17-3. Levels of perspective

Individual and Team

These perspectives are easy to grasp and understand, as they are the perspectives that we have all been accustomed to using. Here, our focus is on the day-to-day interactions and delivery of tasks within our team and the individuals within our team. Our perspective is limited to the work at hand and the people we interact with every day. Holding only this perspective can cause challenges as the individuals and the team "can't see the wood for the trees."

Teams

As we take a step back and upward, we incorporate the perspective of the other teams that we interact with. We consider the impact that one team has on the other and we understand that, to have a big impact, we need to combine perspectives and share understanding across teams.

Department, Region, Organization

Department, region and organization are even broader perspectives that are intra-organizational. As we increase our understanding of how the various departments and regions function together as an entity, we broaden our awareness of the impact and contribution that each has on our outcomes. Our perspective includes the skills and styles that functional silos bring, which acknowledge the very different types of people in, say, a sales department compared to accounting. These perspectives allow us to build more effective relationships across the organization and to predict potential future activities. Here we hold perspectives of people and functions that we may not come into contact with for considerable periods of time, yet we consider how our decisions and actions may impact them and the organization's objectives.

Industry

Considering the industry perspective allows us to view our organization's market verticals and identify competitors and opportunities that exist outside of our organization. The industry perspective is the first level that allows us, as leaders, to predict and respond to disruption.

Our longer-term view looking back into the past helps us to understand the key shifts that have happened within our industry, allowing us to facilitate effective decision making in order to solve present day and potential future challenges. We may even go as far as to understand other verticals that may impact our industry as the world evolves.

Technology

The digital world has arrived. Technology is driving *every* industry. Therefore if we want to be successful in our industry and capture new markets, we must hold a perspective on the technical landscape and how the new digital world is transforming, killing, and creating new verticals.

Leaders who do not take time to reflect on the technology perspective will be disrupted by the ubiquitous nature of technologies (discussed in Chapter 5), such as AI, connected devices, the next new thing, etc.

Society and Economy

Taking an even broader perspective allows us to view technology and industries in the context of local and global economies and reflect on the events and trends in society over decades. The accelerating pace of change is having a dramatic impact on society and economies. As borders are lowered, diversity appreciated, and the way we live and work changes, it has an existential impact on industry verticals. Economic factors are now a global concern, with no country being immune to significant "market corrections" such as those in the United States that triggered the global financial crisis of 2008.

Society's values, beliefs, laws, and lifestyles are evolving faster than ever and the realization of the end of the office block (Chapter 5) will have a dramatic impact on a multitude of industries, including real estate, transport services, infrastructure, energy, insurance, maintenance, hospitality, tourism, and more. The list is almost endless.

Mankind and the Planet

Our final step brings into perspective the history and plight of the environment and of mankind itself. Elon Musk's purpose (Chapter 12)—to make the human race a multi-planetary species—is clearly a broad perspective held on mankind. One might argue that reflection at this level is more akin to philosophy than reality. However, it is true leadership to envision change at this level and execute a strategy that incorporates all of the lower levels of perspectives.

The Reflection Framework

When we combine the levels of perspective with the two axes of reflection, we have a complete framework that we are able to utilize for our evolution (see Figure 17-4).

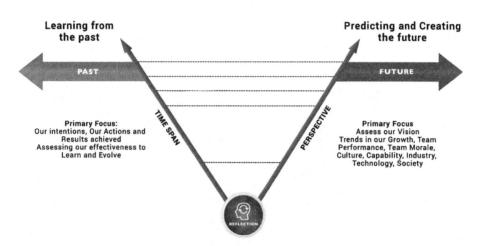

Figure 17-4. The Reflection framework

As we reflect on the past, we utilize the various perspective levels to assess our performance. We analyze our intentions, our actions, and the results obtained to generate new insights and lessons that raise our awareness.

When we look forward into the future, we revisit our vision with our new awareness to ensure that the direction we are heading is still correct and that our values and beliefs are appropriate for success. Equally, we reflect on key trends at each perspective level, such as our organization's capability and culture, and shifts in industry, technology, and society.

Embracing Change

Evolution is change. Disruption is change. Change is easy to talk about and less easy to achieve, especially when it comes to our own personal change. It's common in leadership circles to talk about change (and indeed the pace of change). But, all too often, when people and, in particular, leaders, talk about change, they are referring to the need for others to change (as depicted in Figure 17-5). Anyone that has been through an Agile transformation will be fully aware that to create a truly Agile organization, the leadership team must drive change AND act as role models of change.

Figure 17-5. Who wants (to) change?

Having a growth mindset (introduced in Chapter 6) is critical to the whole evolutionary process. Evolution is the growth and transformation of us as individuals. Change often gets harder the deeper we go down the Human Full Stack. Our Enneagram type motivators are prevalent in all areas of our life and have been with us since we were young. Changing core aspects of our personality takes considerable time if we are to sustain lasting change.

What prevents us from even attempting change most is fear—namely fear of failing. This fear is not actually a fear of failure itself, but a fear of how we will be judged by others. What we fear is looking stupid, clumsy, or incompetent. Fear is a natural part of being human and it has kept the human race alive since the early caveman days. Fear is designed to keep us safe and protect us from danger. It has a place. It has a purpose. However, in a professional growth context, it can paralyze us which, as leaders, can jeopardize not only us, but also our teams and our organizations.

What we believe (the frames that we hold) about a situation defines our thoughts. We know from the TEA model (presented in Chapter 14) that these thoughts impact our emotions and actions in a circular fashion. Fear is an emotion created by what we think and believe about a scenario. If, for example, we are preparing to deliver a presentation to a large audience and we believe that we aren't a good presenter (fixed mindset) and because of our fixed mindset, we cannot change, then it is likely that we will create a negative state and perform poorly. If, however, we have a growth mindset, we recognize that we haven't had a lot of experience presenting and that each presentation is an opportunity to grow and develop our skills. We also understand that even if we are judged poorly by the audience that their judgment is a reflection of their own limitations not ours. With a growth mindset, we create space for positive emotions such as anticipation and excitement. The reality hasn't changed—it's the same presentation, same audience, and same presenter—however, what has changed is what we choose to believe about our ability to present and our ability to change!

Evolutionary Belief System

In order to ensure their evolution, Unnatural Leaders have what I call an *evolutionary belief system* that empowers their growth and helps them overcome their natural fears. They reflect on these beliefs as they look back into their past and assess their performance, and as they look forward into their future to plan where they will go and what they will do. The five empowering beliefs of the evolutionary belief system are:

- **I am constantly growing, changing, and evolving.**

  The process of evolving is an enjoyable and natural state for human beings. This belief is at the core of the growth mindset. Knowing we are constantly changing means we can change for the better. It means we aren't doomed by our genetics or past failures. We know that we aren't the same person we were last year or even last week. Nor will we be the same next month or next year.

- **I have full control over my four powers and physical-emotional state.**

  We always have choice (see Chapter 11); the choice of whether or not to reflect; the choice of whether to take feedback as criticism or lessons; the choice to see and engage in empowering, positive emotional states or negative ones.

- **Curiosity and experimentation are fundamental to my personal evolution.**

  Getting curious about new things and giving them a try is essential to accelerate our growth. We are always changing; however, if we don't experiment and try new things (by getting curious about why, how, and what), then our growth rate will be substantially slower.

- **Feeling strong emotions (such as fear, anger or frustration) is part of our development. Emotions show us our opportunities for growth.**

   This belief helps our brain rewire itself to embrace the strong feelings that we label as fear (or anger, sadness, frustration, etc.) and not be controlled by them. Believing that these emotions arise when we are growing and that they are a natural part of our evolution helps us to break the negative cycle of feelings, thoughts, and actions.

- **The only person I can change is myself.**

   It's easy to blame other people for the challenges we face. Sometimes, it's even easier to try to change others than to face our own shortcomings. And when things don't go as planned, some of us have a tendency to fall into a "victim" mindset, where we believe we are powerless to deal with our negative states until an external person or environment changes for us. However, with this belief, we acknowledge that the only person we can actually change is ourselves, and we take ownership of our own growth through active awareness, intention, attention, and reflection.

At the earlier stages of development (or for those with a more fixed mindset), the evolutionary belief system can seem like idealized principles that may not be very realistic. Let's face it, failure isn't pleasant; it can be embarrassing, expensive, hurtful, and, in some instances, can have a severe impact on careers and lives. Fortunately, a majority of the failure scenarios we experience are more short-term and not catastrophic in nature. These short-term failures pass and, with honest and open reflection, offer us the opportunity for growth.

While taking time to reflect on the past and into the future, it is beneficial to revisit the evolutionary belief system in order to remind ourselves that we do have control of our state and four powers, and that we are always evolving and growing.

Reflection Methods

There are a variety of methods that we can use for daily and weekly reflection. I suggest that you experiment with each of these methods and establish a process and combination that work for you. Leadership (and life) is complex and chaotic. There are times when we struggle to keep our head above water and times when everything goes smoothly to plan. I suggest that you choose and adjust your reflection methods accordingly to suit your current physical-emotional state and context.

The following sections discuss the six key methods you can use to facilitate your reflection.

Method 1: Journaling

Journaling is the process of recording notes about our experiences in order to develop insights that we may have otherwise missed during our busy week. The process of journaling creates space for deep reflection as we record our experience (thoughts, emotions, actions) and how effecitvely we performed. Journaling often provides a more objective (less emotional) view of reality as we reflect back, after the experience. Where possible, we journal at the end of each day, and then review our journal notes at the end of each week. This helps us gain a wider perspective of the week and identify any patterns that are valuable for our evolution and performance.

Method 2: Feedback

Feedback is critical to our evolution and performance as a leader, as it provides us with the subjective perspectives of those we work with. This subjectivity is vitally important to understand because, more often than not, our effectiveness is based on other peoples' perceptions of us over time (rather than how we believe we performed).

Feedback can be solicited in a variety of ways, from informal, impromptu conversations, to organization-wide, structured feedback initiatives.

Method 3: Coaching

I have espoused the benefit of coaching and the impact it has on accelerating growth throughout this book. Coaching sessions help us reflect to understand why we did what we did, and then focus on the future to create empowering states that are aligned with our true intentions.

Method 4: Mentoring

Like coaching, mentoring allows us to reflect on the past and plan for the future. However, unlike coaching, mentoring is usually offered by mentors who have experience, knowledge, and perspectives about our domain that we don't. Mentors can help us to see our blind spots, to think about our domain and leadership differently, and accelerate our learning through the sharing of their insights.

Method 5: Meditating

Meditation is extremely valuable for "knowledge workers" such as ourselves, who are constantly connected and juggling technical and leadership priorities. Our roles require us to use our gray matter intensely, all day, every day. Meditation calms the mind (and body), reduces stress, and increases clarity, creativity, and overall performance. The space created for our minds by meditation often presents innovative solutions to challenges that have been ruminating in our heads for a while.

Method 6: Levels of Perspective

In order to identify trends and create and respond to disruption, we must be aware of the trends and patterns that are driving change. We must continuously gather information at conferences and meet-ups, from online content, from fellow peers, and from thought leaders. This solid foundation of information allows us to utilize the levels of perspective from Figure 17-3 as a framework to reflect on the future, paying particular attention to the technology perspective.

Reducing the Learning Delay

We use reflection to look back on our performance and (hopefully) gain new insights that allow us to improve our effectiveness. If we consider a scenario where we trigger a negative state while interacting with a specific colleague, the gap between our interactions and the realization of our negative pattern may occur days, weeks, or months later. This gap between the real-world event and our realization is what I call the *learning delay*. In some scenarios, we are able to identify the pattern (through journalling) the very same day. In other scenarios, the learning delay may be weeks as we take time to become aware of the patterns we have deeply habituated.

The more we focus on and watch for a pattern in ourselves, the faster we tend to see it each subsequent time it occurs. Our initial insight may have been weeks after an event. The next few instances we observe the pattern just a few days later, then a few hours, and ultimately in the moment. This in-the-moment awareness allows us to adapt and modify our approach, pulling away from older habits and utilizing new methods of communicating, behaving, thinking, and feeling.

Repeated application of the new approach integrates it deeply into our mode of operation until it becomes our normal way of operating. This is our evolution.

We must, therefore, dedicate time and practice to the assessment of our performance and understanding our thoughts and emotions in order to evolve them to more effective, less stressful, and more satisfying experience of life itself.

Reflection Is a Lot like Software Testing

Reflection is a lot like testing in software development. Everyone knows it needs to be done well to efficiently build great products, but not all of us do it well. Skipping testing is often a shortcut we take when we're rushing to meet delivery deadlines. The only way to sustainably increase delivery speed is to increase quality through testing and test automation. It's a false economy in software development to ignore quality and it's a false economy in your evolution to ignore the practice of reflection.

Summary

Reflection is key to accelerating our evolution. It is the process that we consciously use to assess our past performance and prepare for and create the future. When we embrace change and practice reflection on a regular basis, we accelerate our development.

Gaining new levels of perspective allows us to better assess our performance and look toward the future to create and respond to change. Spotting the trends in technology and society early is key to maintaining success in digital leadership. Ignoring key trends here could mean the demise of our organization as our commercial model and/or market share are disrupted.

Even with the broadest perspectives, we need to want to change and want to overcome the fear of trying something different. The five beliefs of the evolutionary belief system support our ability to overcome this fear and the failures we experienced in the past.

In the next chapter, we dive deeper into the methods we can use for reflection.

Self-Reflection Questions

1. Are you ready to commit weekly time and energy to reflection? If not, what is more important to you?

2. When considering the levels of perspectives in Figure 17-3, which levels would you consider are your weaker ones?

3. How often in a week are you frustrated with those around you? Think back to a recent situation where you felt this way. Was there anything you could have changed about yourself in this situation to cause a different outcome?

4. Which of the five beliefs do you resonate with most? Is there one that, if you adopted it in your life, could positively change the way you show up each day?

5. Spend time reflecting on your answers to Questions 1-4. Are there any insights you gained?

Reflection Methods

I think it's very important to have a feedback loop, where you're constantly thinking about what you've done and how you could be doing it better. I think that's the single best piece of advice: constantly think about how you could be doing things better and questioning yourself.

—Elon Musk[1]

In this chapter we are going to take a look at how to reflect using journaling and feedback and explore how to use the levels of perspective for future reflection.

▓ **Note** The reflection methods of Coaching, Mentoring, and Meditation (introduced in Chapters 4 and 17) are extremely powerful methods that facilitate our reflection and evolution. I highly recommend that you engage (at least as an experiment) in all three in order to experience the impact that they have. I have espoused their benefits throughout this book and so I won't be discussing them further in this chapter.

---

[1]Lance Ulanoff, "Elon Musk: Secrets of a Highly Effective Entrepreneur, Mashable, April 13, 2012, https://unnatural.io/link/b1813

© James Brett 2019
J. Brett, *Evolving Digital Leadership*, https://doi.org/10.1007/978-1-4842-3606-2_18

Journaling

How we perform our reflection is less important than ensuring that we actually do reflection and dedicate adequate time and attention to make it effective. Getting into a habit of doing reflection is key to our evolution, and Unnatural Leaders journal their reflections on a regular basis.

The journaling process causes us to slow down and think about what is important. As we reflect on our day (or week) to take notes, we are forced to think about the key elements that we wish to record. Notes can be recorded either electronically or hand-written in a notebook. Hand-written notes offer the benefit of increasing the activity levels in the brain's motor cortex, causing an effect that is similar to meditation.

For accelerated growth, I recommend journaling your reflection at the end of each day and then performing a weekly review of the journal either at the end of the week, or the beginning of the next.

Your journal entries will vary in nature, depending on your communication style and the intensity of your experiences that day. Experiment with recording your reflections in your own way and at the level of detail that feels most appropriate. If you haven't journalled before you may find the process rather awkward; keep at it and develop a style that works for you. Remember, what we are looking to achieve in our journaling is to develop our awareness and performance over time.

Most of us have the ability to make an instinctive judgment about our own performance. We might reflect on a one-on-one meeting with a stakeholder and determine "that went pretty well, [they] agree with my comments". This assessment is often more tactical in nature (did I get what I wanted) and doesn't bring the added benefit of deep reflection. To help drive deeper reflection, I recommend the structure in Table 18-1 for a majority of scenarios.

Table 18-1. Basic Reflection Structure

Field	Notes
Date/time	
Summary of the interaction	
How well did the *outcome* align to my *intention*(s)?	
Personal insights	
What I am going to do differently next time?	

▓ **Note**   You can download an electronic copy of this document at `https://unnatural.io/link/b181`.

This structure captures the context of the scenario (date, time, and summary of the interaction) and then prompts us to consider how well the outcome aligned with our intentions.

What's powerful about this format is that it puts a focus on outcomes and forces us to assess what we achieved, and how well the outcomes aligned with our intentions. As you reflect, record any insights that enable you to adapt and evolve (it may be that at the end of the next meeting, you decide to explicitly confirm expectations with the other party).

Reflecting and Journaling on Critical Events

Journaling using this simple framework works for a majority of circumstances. There are, however, times when you may want to dive deeper and understand key, critical interactions, and your performance. You can explicitly leverage the Unnatural Selection tools to facilitate your reflection process by considering the following questions:

- *What other perspective levels (Chapter 17) can I consider during the Reflection process?*

  It's easy to become limited in perspective when we get busy and are juggling multiple activities. You can use the 10 Levels of Perspective (presented in Chapter 17) to check for any views that you may have missed, and to help you consider the broader system that impacts the scenario you are reflecting on.

- *What external feedback can I solicit and integrate?*

  Gathering external feedback allows you to gain insights into how you are perceived by others. I will address feedback in more detail later in this chapter.

- *Which of the four modes of the Digital Situational Leadership model (Chapter 3) did I utilize (consciously and unconsciously) and how effective were they?*

  The four modes of the Digital Situational Leadership model are 1. Get Stuff Done, 2. Futurist, 3. Friend of the Team, and 4. Utopian. Reflecting on which of these modes you operated in (and how it impacted the outcome) can give you further insight into your preference for Tactical/Strategic and Delivery/Culture.

- *How might the communication preferences (Chapter 9) of the parties involved have impacted the outcome?*

  Consider how the communication channels of Visual, Auditory, Kinesthetic, and Auditory Digital for the parties involved may have impacted the effectiveness of your communications. Is there a way that you could modify your approach to achieve a better outcome?

- *How might the Enneagram types (Chapter 10) of the parties involved have impacted the situation?*

  Are you aware of what Enneagram type the others parties are (or might be)? How might the attributes of your Enneagram type and theirs have affected the interaction?

- *What assumptions did I make? How did these assumptions impact the outcome?*

  Are there any assumptions that you made before, during, or after interactions that were not true or have still not been validated? What can you do to avoid making these types of assumptions next time? What can you do to validate (or invalidate) any assumptions you are currently holding?

- *Who/how/what triggered any negative states I experienced (Chapter 13)?*

  Did you feel any negative emotional states such as anger, frustration, embarrassment, fear, anxiety, stress, or sadness? What triggered this state? What impact did the state have on your responses? Considering the TEA model of thoughts, emotions, and actions: How might you manage your state differently next time?

- *Were there any of the five evolutionary beliefs that would have assisted in my performance (Chapter 17)?*

  If you truly believed (110%) all five evolutionary beliefs, would you have responded differently? Which belief is a challenge for you? What would it mean to you to commit to this belief?

Note   You can download an electronic copy of this document at https://unnatural.io/link/b182.

These eight questions provide a deep and rigorous framework from which to reflect on significant events. It takes time to complete this reflection and in some instances it may be weeks or months before you realize the answers to the questions. Holding the questions in mind on a regular basis will help you to develop a perspective on yourself and others that is evolutionary in nature. This process forces you to constantly seek deeper awareness of what, how, and why events occur and what subconscious patterns you may be running. Sometimes, we need time and space from an event to process it from different perspectives. Going back over your past journal entries and reflecting on your old mindsets can show you patterns where a small tweak can amplify your awareness or performance.

Looking for Patterns

Once a week, take the time to review your journal entries and look for any patterns you can identify. An example of a pattern you might notice is the subtle, negative emotional state when interacting with one of your direct reports or a resistance to dealing with a certain type of task. This emotional response was probably so subtle that it wasn't immediately obvious to you during your initial reflection and journal entries. However, through review, it becomes clear that the tone of the journal entries related to a particular theme is not positive. As you reflect on the series of journal entries, the root cause of the challenge may become obvious or you may require more time to reflect on the triggers (using the eight questions to assist in your inquiry, if needed).

Equally, as we look for patterns in reflection, we may gain new insights into the behaviors of our teams, stakeholders, and other key individuals.

Feedback

Regular performance feedback (provided by others) is invaluable in developing a more rounded and true image of ourselves and how those we interact with perceive the type of leader we are.

At the earlier Expert stage of development, we tend to categorize feedback through our black and white worldview of "right" or "wrong" and "good" or "bad". When we judge feedback like this, we tend to judge ourselves in the same way—"bad" feedback means we failed and "good" feedback means we did well. When we receive "bad" feedback, it's easy to jump to judging the provider of the feedback in order to dismiss the validity of what we perceive as criticism.

The challenge is that "good" feedback feels good, so we want more of it. However, in making a judgment of whether the feedback provided is "good" or "bad," we subject ourselves to the torment of receiving "bad" feedback. Our interpretation of "bad" feedback usually results in a negative emotional state. This can trigger a harsh internal dialogue of self-blame or cause us to become outwardly aggressive and angry as we try and cope with the unwanted negative emotions we are experiencing. The net result is that we tend to avoid seeking out feedback to avoid the negative emotional cycle, and so miss out on the opportunity of accelerating our growth.

As our stage of development progresses (through Achiever), we realize the importance of feedback and begin to solicit it from people who we have strong relationships with. These safer relationships allow us to process the feedback and engage in a dialogue about our performance.

At the later developmental stages of Catalyst, we develop a real thirst for feedback from as many sources as possible (not all positive). We do this because we appreciate the very subjective nature of feedback. Feedback provided by another person is based on their Full Stack configuration and worldview, and on what they deem to be great and horrible leadership. The feedback provider's perspective is valid (at least for them), but we understand that it is their subjective view founded on a limited number of professional interactions that we have had with them. As such, we seek to understand their perspective and integrate it with others in order to determine what changes we want to adopt.

Practices

As we reflect (through our own journaling and from external feedback) we may gain a new awareness of ourselves and the world we live in. This new awareness may provide direct insight into what we could change to perform better, or it may generate yet more questions as we search to understand the world from this new perspective. In either case, for us to evolve, we need to practice a new mode of operation.

I usually meet with a leader who I am helping transform every two weeks for a coaching session. During these sessions, we use reflection together to develop an understanding of their performance and experience. As a coach, the main part of my role is to facilitate a new awareness that would have been difficult for the individual to see for themselves without considerable time and effort. At the end of these sessions, I provide the leader with a set of practices for the following two-week period (before we meet again). These practices are designed to assist them in developing a deeper understanding of themselves (by bringing their focus of attention to particular areas that they have highlighted as important).

If, during your reflection process you identify areas that you'd like to focus on, use the eight questions to facilitate a deeper understanding of (and to gain clarity on) on your intentions. Then, identify your topic and write it down. It might be "Become more aware of my preferred Digital Situational Leadership mode." As you explore this space, I recommend instigating a practice for two weeks to push you out of your comfort zone while you "try on" different ways of operating. Using the example, a practice might be to operate from a different Digital Situational Leadership mode each two-week cycle and journal daily on the outcomes. Over time, your new awareness of the four modes in this framework will drive you to know what your preferred or default operating mode is. The next practice may then involve understanding (through your new awareness) why that particular mode is your preference. Each two-week cycle evolves and develops both our self-awareness and the awareness of those we interact with.

Future Reflection

As we journal and process feedback, we do so while thinking about what we want and where we want to go in the future. We ask questions (not always consciously), such as "Is this feedback helping my career? What should I focus my attention on next? What is important to me this week, this month, or this year?" As we assess our past performance and experiences, we do so in order to improve them for the future. That something inside of you that made you read this book is more than likely focused on the future—it's looking for answers to improve your performance.

As a digital leader, you are no doubt familiar with the constant evolution of technology and the risk of not keeping pace with (and leveraging) these advances. Are you a leader that's been playing catch-up? Have you managed to keep up with the pace of change? Or are you a digital leader at the forefront of disruption? Unfortunately, most leaders are doing their best to barely keep pace, sometimes lagging behind and sometimes leveraging new technology to their advantage. Of course, it's not just a matter of identifying new disruptions; we have to deliver the disruption (or our response to it). For some leaders, that involves creating a new startup that directly targets the disruption, but for a majority of us, it's getting our teams and organizations mobilized to create (or adapt to) the waves of change.

We can use the levels of perspective (presented again in Figure 18-1) as a guide to help us reflect on the future, and to improve ourselves and our organization.

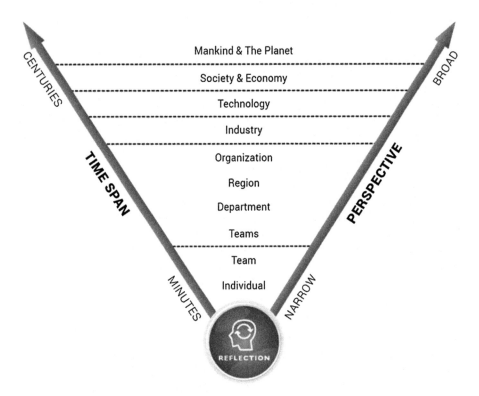

Figure 18-1. The levels of perspective

We often have a better sense of where we are going at the lower perspective levels of individual and team. To gain similar clarity in the higher perspectives, it can help to think about the larger organization and how the teams, departments, and regions interact, and what trends are occurring within the organization.

Reflecting on the Future of Technology

As a digital leader, we are in the technology business. We've been around technology for most of our lives, with many of us learning technical skills before we landed our first professional job. We've already learned multiple technologies, utilized the big trends of our time, and for some of us, we've been at the forefront of ground-breaking innovations. Because of this, the technology perspective is usually the most significant and influential perspective digital leaders use, and so this is where we will begin our process of future reflection.

Some leaders rely on industry and analyst reports to inform them of the changing and developing trends in the technology world. These reports are used to confirm our insights or catch up on trends we have missed. However, by their very nature, they are usually a historical analysis of what has already happened in the industry, i.e., what disruptive leaders are already doing in the market. Thus, relying on industry reports as a key source for opportunities to create disruption is limited, but not entirely fruitless.

We maintain an effective awareness of technology trends by constantly absorbing new information about the technology landscape. We do this primarily through our daily conversations with digital natives (developers, leaders, thought leaders) of varying backgrounds and experience levels (graduate developers offer a view that is often a generation apart from senior developers). We interact with tech leaders in our organizations, at conferences and meet-ups, and in other social spheres to expand our knowledge while supplementing our learning with content from the multitude of sources online (Twitter, tech news sites, analysts reports, books, etc.).

Even when we engage in these interactions on a regular basis, it's not easy to distinguish the signal from the noise. Often, new innovations are espoused as the next big thing but fail because the founding team couldn't deliver a solid product, the product-market fit wasn't right, or because one or more of the hypotheses made wasn't valid.

Equally, some technologies can seem insignificant and yet they become mainstream, with overnight "hockey stick" growth and adoption. Often, this is because the teams involved have iterated (quietly) on a product and found the right market fit, and then made a significant investment in marketing, sighting early adopter success case studies and driving the belief that the innovation really is the next big thing.

Reflecting on 3D Printing Technology

There are technologies that take years to move from their initial innovation to mass adoption across multiple industries—3D printing is one such technology. The origins of 3D printing can be traced back to over 30 years ago in the early

1980s. However, the technology really developed during the first decade of this century to include the printing of human organs and prosthetic legs. The last decade has seen the proliferation of consumer-grade, DIY, and industrial use of 3D printing. Adidas now 3D prints shoes with their "Futurecraft 4D"[2] line of runners. Construction companies are using 3D printing to "print" houses in concrete in fewer than 24 hours.[3] Thingiverse[4] is one of the first web-based platforms to buy and sell 3D printed designs that allow anyone with a 3D printer to print a real object within minutes. As I write this, news has just been announced[5] that we are one step closer to a real world Star Trek Replicator—a device that creates anything we request in an instant.

Where am I going with all this? Well, as you can see—technology comes in waves. 3D printing eventuated decades ago. It went mainstream (consumerized) around 10 years ago, and more recently we are seeing the technology being developed to a level where it's applicable across a huge number of industries, from organ printing to footwear, furniture to houses. For some of these industries, it is likely to revolutionize the production of products by increasing quality, reducing cost of production, and facilitating individual customization of products that weren't previously possible.

The net result is that leaders in both digital and non-digital organizations need to reflect on the future of technology. The CIOs, CTOs, and CDOs in verticals such as construction (a non-digital industry) must leverage the technological developments in order to lead and survive in the markets of tomorrow. For those of us in digital verticals, 3D printing provides a new market for digital services (Thingiverse being a great example). Outside of the construction of buildings, 3D printing is likely to change society and the way we buy products. Imagine a world where anything can be 3D printed at home. The impact on current retail models, delivery infrastructure, international shipping, and even the environment would be significant (Catastrophic if we print, use, and dispose of objects or a dramatic improvement if we are able to recycle our goods back into our 3D printers.)

---

[2]https://unnatural.io/link/b183

[3]Rae Johnson, "This 3D Printed House Took Only 24 hours to Make," Gizmodo, March 20, 2017, https://unnatural.io/link/b184

[4]https://unnatural.io/link/b185

[5]Eric Mack, "A Real World 'Star Trek' Replicator Is Now Possible Thanks To New Breakthrough," Forbes, March 9, 2018, https://unnatural.io/link/b186

3D printing is just one of the current technological developments that has the potential to disrupt multiple industries, societies, and economies. Other developments to consider are:

- Artificial intelligence, including machine learning, Big Data, and analytics
- Driverless cars and autonomous drones
- Virtual and augmented reality
- Blockchain, including decentralized compute, cryptocurrencies, and decentralized ledgers
- Serverless and cloud compute, including Infrastructure as a Service (IaaS), Platform as a Service (PaaS), and Software as a Service (SaaS)
- IoT and connected devices
- Health and wellness tech, including wearables, implantables, bionics and exo-skeletons, and brain interfaces (see Neuralink[6])

The Importance of AI

You may decide not to pursue a technology—or monitor its use for a period of time before making a full assessment. Some of these advancements are more significant and wide-ranging and if you ignore them, you do so at your peril. The impact of AI (discussed in Chapter 5) will impact all industries and society in a significant way. Does that mean we should all pivot our organizations to building companion robots and human-like intelligence? Obviously not! What we *all* need to be doing is developing our organization's capabilities in these key areas.

Any intelligence (artificial or not) needs to learn. For machines to learn, they need data. Capturing and analyzing data, therefore, is a critical first step that you should have made already. Big Data is now an old term, as is Analytics—both are valuable and essential, just not as cool as AI. Machine learning, until recently, has been a big leap to make for the average organization. Machine learning requires different skillsets, tools, and systems to create value for a business and therefore requires a focused investment of resources to implement it well. The cost and complexity barrier for machine learning is reducing as the likes of Amazon and Google release their cloud-based machine learning platforms, which allow developers to create learning systems that were the sole domain of AI PhD post grads just five years ago. However, AI still requires

---

[6]https://unnatural.io/link/b187

a capability uplift in organizations and therefore you need to have a strategy in place to build this capability and leverage its competitive advantage. Do you have such a strategy? Do you have AI-specific roles such as Machine Learning Specialist and Data Scientist?

Here are some questions to help you and your leadership team reflect on the future of AI in your industry:

- How might your competitors utilize AI to disrupt your organization and industry?
- How might digital native organizations do the same?
- What are the risks and impacts of ignoring AI?
- How might you develop an AI capability that works for your organization?
- What efficiencies could you gain by using AI?
- How might you utilize AI to increase customer experience and engagement?

I suggest that you work through these questions with your senior leadership team *and* your own team(s). Here are some more questions to work through with just your teams to help reflect on how you might approach AI:

- What tools and platforms can we leverage to implement AI?
- What can we learn from organizations that are already heavily invested in building their AI capabilities? (Uber has an AI Residency[7] that is "A research fellowship dedicated to fostering the next generation of AI talent".)
- What capability do we need to build and how? (For instance, it might be that all engineers upskill with AI or new AI roles are introduced.)
- Where in our products and services can we leverage AI today?

Both 3D printing and AI will revolutionize industry. The dramatic impact of these technologies will shape the way our societies operate—much like the way the Internet and mobile devices have.

---

[7]Jason Yosinski, Zoubin Ghahramani, and Raquel Urtasun, "Introducing the Uber AI Residency," Uber Engineering, February 20, 2018, https://unnatural.io/link/b1810

Reflecting on the Future of Society

Society has radically changed in a relatively short period of time through the advancement of technology. It's not just digital advancements that change society; engineering developments (such as the mass affordability of jet travel) have shifted the very nature of what it means to be a sovereign country and citizen. An energizing debate can be easily instigated by asking a group what it means to be an American (or Australian or British or Chinese)—what does dual nationality mean or imply? The fluid and regular movement of people and products through the reduced cost of transportation has created a global society for those who can afford it. And yet, even with these developments in society there is still an unacceptable number of fellow humans living below the poverty line.

So, what are some of the trends and shifts that will have a significant impact on our future?

End of the Office Block

In Chapter 5, I outlined the end of the office block, an event that will dramatically and visibly alter society. Advancements in VR and ultra-fast Internet connections will mean that knowledge workers will be able to work from anywhere. When VR becomes sufficiently advanced, it will be close (and eventually indistinguishable) from working in our offices of today. No longer will we need to commute to cities and work in office towers. Transportation, real estate, restaurants, bars, and even tourism will be impacted. It will take a number of years, but a fundamental shift in how and where we live and work is coming.

Sharing Economy

Peer-to-peer services such as car sharing, bike rentals, Uber,[8] and Airbnb[9] have already leveraged technology to allow people to make better use of their existing assets. These companies improve customer experience (through convenience, quality of service, or reduced cost), generating marketplaces that benefit both the supplier and the consumer in a mutual manner. These companies have accelerated their growth to provide equivalent scale services to customers at a pace that is an order of magnitude faster than the incumbents in the same market.

---

[8]https://unnatural.io/link/b188
[9]https://unnatural.io/link/b189

Smart Homes, Smart (Driverless) Cars, and Smart Cities

The increase in capability and reduction in cost and size of IoT (or connected devices) will drive the technological advancement of almost every aspect of society—three significant ones being smart homes, cars, and cities. Like 3D printing, home automation has been around for decades (I should know—I ran a failed home automation startup back in 2002). Technology and society are now at the point of readiness where products such as Apple HomeKit, Google Home, Amazon Echo, and other intelligent sensors and devices are becoming commonplace in main street stores and in our homes. The importance of the smart home market to these big industry players is not to sell consumer grade tech products, but to capture more and more data about how we live our lives, what we like, don't like, when we are ready to buy, and how we are influenced.

As our homes become "smarter," so do our cities. Technology that makes cities more enjoyable (personalized, relevant delivery of information), environmentally friendly (energy-saving devices), and easy to commute around (parking information, live timetable information, and traffic guidance) improve the experience and the impact on the planet.

Driverless cars are likely to have an earlier and as significant impact on society as the end of the office block. In a future society where we are able to instantly summon an appropriate vehicle to take us to our destination, very few of us will own a car. The cost savings of not owning a car that spends 95%[10] of its time doing nothing (but depreciate), doesn't need a parking space (at home, or work, or at our destination) a garage, servicing, maintaining, fixing (after an accident), insuring, or a license to drive will mean the end of the car industry as we know it.

The transportation industry will be dominated by the likes of Google and Tesla (or even Uber), which are currently at the forefront of driverless cars where they manufacture huge global fleets of driverless, AI-driven vehicles. Incumbent car manufacturers who have (so far) failed to respond to this shift will go out of business, as will the service industries that rely on the car industry such as insurers, car dealerships and parking providers. Governments will need to realign revenue generation models to include the loss of on-street and government owning parking, car taxation, and even the loss of revenue generated from speeding fines. The visible landscape will be transformed by the reduction in the number of cars, parked cars, parking lots, houses with garages, and the loss of car dealerships, mechanics, and service centers.

---

[10]David Z. Morris, Today's Cars Are Parked 95% of the Time, Fortune, March 13, 2016, https://unnatural.io/link/b1811

Virtual Societies

As I complete this book (early 2018), Steven Spielberg is scheduled to release the movie *Ready Player One*[11] at the end of March. The movie, set in the future, features a society that lives more in a virtual world than the real one. This virtual world provides endless possibilities and realities where people go to explore and be anything they want. While being a typical sci-fi movie, it does offer a view of the future that I believe we are heading toward. More and more of what we call society will migrate to the virtual world. Organizations that take advantage of this will lead and disrupt economies and societies as geographical boundaries dissolve and reachable markets grow. These virtual world experiences will require seismic shifts in thinking much like the shift the Internet has caused. Is VR mainstream today? Can it sustainably support profitable commercial models today? No! But it will; it is something that digital leaders must consider over the coming years as it evolves what it means for human interaction and connection.

Facilitating Reflection

As Unnatural Leaders, we are no longer individual contributors. We redefined our personal success to be the success of our teams and the people around us (see Chapter 4). If we are to support their growth and evolution, we must facilitate and assist them in their reflection.

Agile teams hold retrospectives at the end of each iteration (or Sprint), in order to continuously improve their performance. Retrospectives are held by the team and are primarily focused on improving the product development and delivery process by asking questions such as: What do we need to stop doing? What do we need to start doing? What do we need to continue doing? What have we learned? Reflection, however, is a deeply personal and individual process and, as such, complements the team retrospective process.

The journaling questions can be adapted for use in a team context (and work well with both Agile delivery teams or leadership teams). The questions provide a deeper, more personal view of team experiences, the subtle, undefined roles each individual contributes, and any potential improvements that can be made. This personal nature requires a level of safety in the team to work well and not make the individuals feel overly vulnerable in their sharing. I recommend that each of the team members work through the reflection process individually to experience it before submerging a full team into a reflection session.

---

[11]https://unnatural.io/link/b1812

When facilitating an individual's reflection process, it's advisable to begin by describing what reflection is and the benefits of investing time and effort into it. Sharing our own personal experience with reflection is a great way to create a safe environment for the them to try reflection and for us to demonstrate leadership by example. As reflection is incorporated into the regular activities of their role, we can use our one-on-one sessions to discuss their reflections and any insights they discover. Some of the insights developed can then be integrated into the individual's personal development plan to power their evolution.

Summary

Journaling and feedback are two powerful methods that enable us to do deep reflection and raise our awareness levels. Journaling facilitates the thinking and analysis of our performance and experiences and captures the context and insights we develop on a daily basis. We are then able to review these daily journal entries in order to identify patterns in our operation that were previously hidden to us.

Feedback provided by others, either in person or through structured assessments (such as the LeadershipAgility 360), allows us to better understand how others experience our leadership. We all make assumptions and have personal blind spots; feedback helps us see these, and where appropriate, adjust our operation to achieve higher levels of performance and/or enjoy better experiences.

The accelerating advances in technology will continue to radically change economies, societies and industries. To lead this disruption we must maintain our awareness of these developments on a daily basis by absorbing content and information from as many sources as possible. This background context provides us with a solid foundation to Reflect on the future with the levels of perspective (see Figure 18-1), paying particular attention to the technology and society perspectives.

In the next chapter, the final chapter of the evolution helix, we are going to do some reflection together on the journey this book has taken us on.

Self-Reflection Questions

1. How do you feel about soliciting feedback from a wide variety of sources? Are there some sources that you don't feel comfortable asking for feedback? What do you believe about that source that makes receiving feedback from them difficult?

2. Who might you seek feedback from that would assist in your development at this stage in your journey?

3. What new practice could you try in order to raise your awareness of any patterns you may be running or blind spots that you have?

4. On average, do you consider yourself to be a leader that is a) struggling to keep pace with change, b) keeping pace with change, or c) leading change and disrupting? What do you need to do to lead change more often?

5. What strategy do you have (or need) in order to build your organization's AI capability?

6. What changes in society are happening right now that your organization might leverage?

7. How might you and your organization make a positive contribution to these changes in society?

8. How, and with whom, might you apply reflection techniques within your organization?

Reflecting Together

It is good to have an end to journey toward; but it is the journey that matters, in the end.

—Ursula K. Le Guin, *The Left Hand of Darkness*[1]

I want to thank you for taking this journey with me and making it to this, the last chapter on the evolution helix. Thank you.

What is a more appropriate way to wrap up this exploration together than to reflect on the book journey itself? With this in mind, I split this chapter into three sections. In the first section, I share with you my reflections as a digital leader, writing my first book, and holding an intention to make a positive impact on the world. The second section summarizes the reflection process and the third and final section is designed to facilitate your reflections on the reading experience—insights gained, any resistance that you might have felt, and the positive shifts you experienced as you read each chapter and completed the self-reflection questions.

I hope that *Evolving Digital Leadership* has, and will continue to, fuel your personal evolution and that of your people.

---

[1] Ace Books, 1987.

© James Brett 2019
J. Brett, *Evolving Digital Leadership*, https://doi.org/10.1007/978-1-4842-3606-2_19

My Reflections on Writing Evolving Digital Leadership

As I reflected on the book-writing process, the main insight that struck me was:

Everyone should write a book!

Writing a book is an intense journey of personal evolution. It's impossible to write a book and not have to face your demons. No matter what your personality type, values, and beliefs, writing a book forces us to overcome something inside us in order to complete and publish it. It might be that you need to overcome your desire for perfection in order to get something to market. It might be that your pattern of procrastination causes you to put off doing the work required, or the big challenge that many of us face (including myself)—the fear of failure. This fear of failure manifested itself early in my journey because I found myself overly concerned with trying to write a great book that smart, critical thinkers would enjoy, rather than engaging in a more empowering state and enjoying the creation process. What helped me overcome this challenge was my desire to provide something of value to the world and the support and encouragement of my friends and family.

My objective was to produce a book of great value to both you (our digital leaders tribe) and your people. I made a conscious decision to buck the trend toward slim volumes and to write a book that would contain a lot of powerful content, to give you value in each and every chapter. I realize that it may take you some time to truly digest, understand, and integrate into your way of being and so I hope you come back to this book (with new levels of awareness) and get value from it time and time again.

■ **Note** I'd love to hear any thoughts or feedback you have on the book, either "good" or "bad". If you have a few minutes to spare and would like to help me in my own personal evolution, you can submit your perspectives at https://unnatural.io/link/b193. Thank you.

Here are some more reflections I have on my book writing experience.

Focusing Considerable Time and Energy on One Thing Has an Incredible Amplifying Effect

This book is a collection of my experiences, knowledge, ideas, and concepts— most of which were present inside of me long before writing the book. Putting them all into one place in a coherent and accessible manner creates something that is way more than the sum of the individual parts and is incredibly rewarding!

State Management Is Critical to Completing a Book

Managing physical-emotional state is essential to overcoming challenges and completing the project. There were numerous times when I didn't want to write, couldn't write, or got feedback (that I wasn't ready to hear) that triggered a state that wasn't empowering. I repeatedly made a conscious effort to sit with an awareness of these feelings and acknowledge them, and continue to work on the book.

Equally, I found that mornings are when I'm most creative, and so I would develop new concepts or write new content early in the day. The evenings, when my energy was lower, I completed tasks that were more mundane in nature—yet needed to be done. This kept the wheels of progress moving and the mornings free for essential creative work.

Early Feedback Has Been Exciting!

I've shared initial draft chapters of the book and presented some of the concepts at conferences, and the early feedback has been very positive. I'm excited as I reflect on the future and imagine the impact that we might all have as we grow together.

Taking a Lean-Startup Approach and Interviewing 40 Digital Leaders Was Invaluable

Research for this book involved interviewing 40 digital leaders in order to gather and understand as many perspectives as possible on the journey to successful digital leadership. It took me three full months to complete the interviews, analyze the results, and develop my insights. I would do it again in a heartbeat. Each leader offered something valuable to the process—a perspective, idea, strategy, or even a book reference. There were some dramatic differences in perspective, particularity around what each wanted from this book! This led to the innovation that is TL;DR (Chapter 2) and "It's Not Cheating" (Chapter 21). I am really grateful to each and everyone who contributed. Thank you.

Not Enough People Are Thinking Far Enough Into the Future

Throughout the writing process, I've discussed the book's topics with over 100 people. Upon reflection, I realized that most are not considering how the future will unfold and the true impact of technologies such as AI and VR. People who aren't thinking about and planning for these trends are likely the ones who will get disrupted. I hope this book stimulates more of us to consider, prepare for, and shape the future in a positive way.

Build, Measure, Learn: Getting Feedback Is Essential

As I wrote drafts of chapters, I circulated them with peers for review. What amazed me early on was that the same paragraph would be identified as the best in the chapter by one person and the worst by another. I learned to factor in their subjectivity (experience and personality), then I got specific on what they liked and didn't like so I could decide on a path forward. In some instances, I changed nothing (it never ends well when we try to please all the people all of the time), and in other instances, I went with one perspective. In a majority of situations, I found a way to adjust the paragraph so it had a positive impact on both individuals.

The Book Writing Process Is Way More Than "Just" Writing

I had set out expecting writing to be a challenge for me. I hadn't predicted that the writing component would only be about 50% of the total effort. The other 50% was spent on deciding what goes into the book and what doesn't, how to structure the book so that it flows both at the chapter level and across the breadth of the book, and how and when to use visuals to minimize learning effort and provide clarity. Book creation is a heady cocktail of logical thinking, creative ideation, and attention to the details. It requires tenacity, the support of others, and incredible patience.

Summary of Reflection

If you change only one thing by reading this book, I hope it is that you start doing regular reflection. Reflecting and developing an increased awareness of both yourself and others is your evolution. Reflecting on the future raises your awareness to the potential disruptions of society and the human race. Facilitating reflection for your people and teams and creating the positive habits of reflection is an incredible gift to give a fellow human being.

This is what it means to be an Unnatural Leader—welcome to the club!

Facilitating Your Reflection on Evolving Digital Leadership

You may choose how to approach these questions. They are not structured in a particular sequence. You may find some questions truly enlightening and some may not resonate at all—that's okay! As you work through them, remember that there are no right or wrong answers, just as there are no right or wrong paths to growth. You will find that if you revisit these questions over time (perhaps coming back after a few years), your answers will change. This is a reflection of your shift in awareness.

I hope that these questions provide sustained value to you and highlight your own unfolding each time you revisit them.

Note   If you want to complete these electronically, you can download a copy from https:// unnatural.io/link/b191 (I expect this question set will evolve over time, and I will keep this link as a living document so you can access the latest thinking for you and your team).

I hope that we will build a community of like-minded Unnatural Leaders and, so, if you would like to share your answers anonymously with the purpose of shared learning, head over to the home of the online community at https://unnatural.io/link/b192.

Evolving Digital Leadership Self-Reflection Questions

1. What are the top three things that you have taken away from reading this book?

2. Did you do the self-reflection questions in the book? If not, why not?

3. What ideas or changes have you implemented already? How is that going? Would you recommend these changes to others?

4. What parts of the book have you (consciously or not) dismissed or avoided? What is it about these parts that you don't align with? Could they be pointing to a growth opportunity for you?

5. What did you enjoy most? What was it that made it enjoyable?

6. At which stage of development would you consider yourself to be: Expert, Achiever, Catalyst (or above)? Has reading this book shifted your development perspective?

7. Can you recall a time (from earlier in your career) when you operated from an earlier stage of development? How has your thought process and style evolved since then? What triggers or events caused major shifts for you?

8. How has your awareness developed through reading and using the concepts in this book?

9. Have you ever mentored someone? Are you willing to be someone's mentor? What steps might you take to start that process?

10. How might you apply concepts from this book to develop and grow your people?

11. Are any of your people currently struggling to make a digital leadership career choice? How might you help support them?

12. How has your view of what it means to be a digital leader changed after reading this book?

13. How does having an awareness of the Career Success Pyramid change your approach to your leadership career? How does it change how you support your future leaders?

14. Which of the four steps of the evolution helix do you think is the most important for you to focus on first? What is it about this step that makes it the most important?

15. How does having an awareness of the Human Full Stack (and its key components of frontend communications, meta-programs, enneagram personality types, and stages of development) change your perspective on yourself and others? How might it increase your effectiveness and experience as a digital leader?

16. Consider a time when you allowed your attention to distracted enough to cause a problem. What will you now do differently in order to keep your attention focused on what's important?

17. As you complete this book and reflect into the future, what choices have you made or need to make for success? Are you owning your choices and Four Powers as you move forward?

Ignite

"Curiosity is a strong fire, and once ignited, it is not easily put out."

—Susan Dennard, *Something Strange and Deadly*[1]

In Chapter 1, I began our journey together by expressing my desire to build a relationship with you that continues past the life of this book. It's my vision that together we form a community of like-minded digital leaders who create the best possible future for our fellow humans, future generations, and our planet.

I believe that together we can create better experiences for digital leaders (us) that are less stressful, more empowering, achieve higher success, and have a more significant impact on the world. Because Unnatural Leaders value their teams, we will create the same improvements for them too. At a basic level, an organization is a collection of people organized in a particular manner. Therefore, if we can impact the people in the teams, we can impact organizations. With better organizations, we can positively impact society and the human race.

Ignite

Nothing changes unless we change, do something different, or start something new. We must ignite this change! My call to action to you is to become a fire-starter and ignite change: ignite your own evolution, ignite your team's evolution, and ignite our community.

---

[1]HarperTeen: 2012.

© James Brett 2019
J. Brett, *Evolving Digital Leadership*, https://doi.org/10.1007/978-1-4842-3606-2_20

Ignite Yourself

Leaders lead by example. When we ignite our evolution, our people will see and experience our change. They will see us approach our roles in new and different ways. We are modeling the evolution that we want to help facilitate for them. As importantly, by living and breathing the steps of Awareness, Intention, Attention, Reflection we experience evolution ourselves. What better way to connect with and assist others than to talk from personal experience, model new behaviors, and share our evolution.

So what do you need to do to ignite yourself right now? What action are you going to take to decide what is important to you? What intentions do you need to set in order to accelerate your own personal evolution? Where are you going to place your attention? And finally, how are you going to develop a deeper understanding of your own Human Full Stack?

Ignite Your Teams

Chapter 21 provides details of how to download the complete set of visuals used throughout this book. Use these for your own personal reference and to ignite your teams. The following is a list of activities that I recommend you run to spark your team's (and your organization's) evolution:

- **Future Technology Reflection Session**

  Use the Levels of Perspective model to facilitate team and organizational conversations that reflect on the future of technology and how it might impact your organization and society.

- **Leadership Team Digital Situational Leadership Workshop**

  If you are a senior leader with direct reports who are also leaders themselves, discuss the four modes of the Digital Situational Leadership model. Then have each individual share their preferred mode and discuss the impact that it may have on their effectiveness.

- **Facilitate a Technical Career Path Workshop**

  Hold a workshop with members of your teams that haven't yet made (or are struggling to make) leadership career path decisions. Leverage the visuals in Chapter 3 (Figures 3-3, 3-5, and 3-6) to discuss the shifts and choices that technologist choose when making career choices.

- **Human Full Stack Exploration**

  Using a visual (download from the website), take the three main elements of the Human Full Stack: The frontend communication channel, the meta-programs (or API) layer, and the personality types (or backend) and explore the different components as a team. Share insights and take notes as to how each team member believes they are configured.

  For a deeper dive, you may also complete Enneagram assessments and/or Leadership Agility 360 assessments prior to the workshop to share and better understand how you operate together.

- **Intentions for Success Workshop**

  Use the material in Part III to discuss intentionality, the three core intentions of Unnatural Leaders, what they mean for your team and as individuals. Set personal intentions and run a follow-up workshop for each team member to share their intentions and discuss why they are important.

- **Regular Reflection Workshop**

  After the team has been journaling and performing reflection for a while, run a group session for individuals to (voluntarily) share their reflections and insights.

Note Further ideas and supporting material for team-based activities can be found online at https://unnatural.io/link/b207. If you develop a new approach or have great results with a new approach, I'd love to hear about it.

Ignite Our Community

Let's build a community of Unnatural Leaders and start a movement of change. Let's accelerate the transformation and creation of amazing places to work and change people's lives for the better. Let's create a world where everyone works with purpose!

By reading this book, you are already part of the community. However, I would *love* for you to share your journey, passion, challenges, and questions and evolve alongside the rest of us in the community. By joining the community, you will be connecting with like-minded people going through similar scenarios and facing similar challenges. You might find a coach or mentor to support your growth and development. Maybe you are the person who can mentor a leader who needs help. Unnatural Leaders don't stand alone. They don't struggle alone and they don't let others struggle alone.

Come and join us now at http://evolvingdigitalleadership.com.

What If?

All fired up? Great! Before you run off to change the world, I'd like to leave you with a few questions to ignite your thinking. These questions are focused on potential future scenarios and take the form of "What If?". I hope they challenge you (in a supportive way) to think about the future and ignite you to shape it positively.

What If Artificial Intelligence Takes Over?

In my opinion, this isn't really a what-if scenario, it's a when, and a "then what?" question.

Artificial intelligence is going to change the world in the most significant way we have ever seen; it will be a transformative shift for the human race, much like the end of the dinosaurs.

If we look far enough into the future, robots will become ubiquitous and automate almost everything we do. The majority of jobs performed by humans will disappear. At a sufficient intelligence and capability level, I can't currently see any job that would survive. I'm not even sure that I can comprehend the incredible levels of intelligence that AI could reach and what it will mean for us.

Think about it for a moment... Take the most intelligent person who has ever walked our planet and increase their intelligence by an order of magnitude. Now put that intelligence into a robot! Its capability would be immense. Every single thing we humans could think of, "it" would have thought about already and with a greater ability.

It's possible that this incredible capacity might solve the meaning of life or how the universe was created. Maybe robots will destroy us and the universe—if indeed it can be destroyed. (If you've ever studied physics, energy at a universal level is never destroyed, it is merely converted.)

Maybe they will discover dimensions of reality that we don't know exist. Much like the story of the fictional, 2D man who exists and perceives reality in only two dimensions. When he views an object, all he is able to perceive is its width, height, and boundaries. When presented with a 3D cube, he has no ability to perceive its third dimension. So, as the cube moves closer to him (through the third dimension), he perceives a 2D shape increasing in size. As the cube moves away, he perceives it as getting smaller. All he perceives are the X and Y dimensions and therefore the shape and size of objects. He has no awareness or concept of the third dimension.

What if humans are just like the 2D man, only we can see one more dimension? Will these new hyper-intelligent robots be able to perceive other dimensions and, if so, how many more might there be?

These advances in "intelligence" cause me to wonder what it is to be human and what consciousness is. At the later stages of human development, a non-dual, unity awareness is achieved (often called enlightenment). With it comes the realization that all of reality is constructed, not just our beliefs and assumptions, but our physical bodies too. The illusion that we are merely an individual human mind and body falls away as we become aware of our full connection to the universe, the source, or the "divine". What does that mean for robots—they came from the same matter we did—we are all made of the same atoms, molecules, and elements that came from the universe? If robots become "conscious," are they our equals? How should we recognize robots both legally and ethically?

In the not-so-distant future, a majority of jobs that humans perform will disappear as robots take over and complete them more efficiently, more safely, and more reliably. I predict that the same powerful humans who control the wheels of commerce, industry, and political systems today, will continue to get richer and more powerful as they expand their control over the organizations that build the robots that run our world.

What I'm unsure of is, what will happen to everyone else? Will we all become part of a poor, underground race that eats rat burgers to survive (as in the 1993 movie *Demolition Man*), or will we all live a utopian life of bliss as robots perform our tasks and chores for us? If we do move to this seemingly utopian existence, what will we do? Will we search for purpose or merely enjoy the pleasures of life? How will we pay for these pleasures? Aside from robotics, will pleasure providers be the only businesses left?

I'm sure that virtual reality will play a big part in how we experience pleasure. Consider, if you will, the advancements made in technology over the last 40-50 years. Computers have evolved from blocky, green screen displays with kilobytes of memory to 8K ultra-high definition, real-time, photorealistic rendering, multi-channel spatial audio and force feedback systems.

Now factor in the exponential rate of change and what VR will be capable of in the next 40 years. I believe that future VR systems will generate these new experiences through a direct connection to our nervous system (a neuralink). This connection will trigger all of our senses electrically, allowing us not only to see and hear new realities in ultra-high definition, but also taste, feel, and smell them! At some point, the "virtual realities" that we have will become indistinguishable from actual reality!

This situation then poses another question: If virtual realities can be created that are indistinguishable from actual reality, did someone or something already beat us to it? Are we the ones living in the matrix? Maybe the robots (or an alien race) conquered the planet centuries ago and everything we experience, including ourselves, is not real? If this were true, it would mean that TEA model that describes how our thoughts, emotions, and actions inter-operate could merely be a function in a much larger, complex artificial universe.

What If We Prepare Our Children for the Digital Future?

We've spent this book looking at how digital leaders can deal with disruption today and how we prepare for the future, but what about our children? How do we prepare them for a future where jobs might be extremely limited? What skills and capacities should we teach our children to give them the best chance of a good life?

Some think that the creative side of humans will survive the artificial intelligence wave. They believe that art, music, and innovative thinking are what we need to focus on. I think that is a reasonable answer, but only for a short period of time. Creativity (with enough knowledge and intelligence) can be modeled. After all, most creative, innovative pursuits are not divine acts of inspiration. They are products of an individual's experiences, skills, knowledge, and, more often than not, their ability to connect different ideas and concepts in a new "creative" way. Therefore, with enough intelligence and knowledge, robots will at some point be "creative". Even now, in this present day, you probably can't tell can't tell the difference between Bach and music written by AI in his style.[2]

So how do we prepare our children for the future? For me, the gifts I plan to give my children are the skills and knowledge to live a self-sufficient life and the ability to deeply understand themselves (and who they are) in order to live a satisfying life.

To be able to live self-sufficiently, I have already started to give my children the skills to live off the grid by harnessing renewable energy and performing basic construction. I plan to teach them how to farm their own organic food and source clean water. These skills will enable them to survive in a future where there may be no jobs for them or the safest places are far from city blocks.

The required investment in time and energy to develop these skills is minimal. So if the future is utopian, very little is lost and we have all had the enjoyment of creating and learning together. And, they will have learned what it takes to live self-sufficiently.

---

[2]Dave Gershgorn, "You Probably Can't Tell the Difference Between Bach and Music Written by AI in His Style," *Quartz*, December 15, 2016, https://unnatural.io/link/b211.

These skills must be accompanied by developing a mindset and awareness that brings them contentment and satisfaction from their experiences.

Understanding ourselves is the journey of life. Universally, the journey of life begins with programming and beliefs that cause us considerable challenges as we age. It may be that the purpose of life is to overcome these challenges. I don't know. What I do know is that we need to change the basic way we program our children. We need to remove the judgments of "good" and "bad" from our language. We need to become conscious of the limiting beliefs that we pass on, either explicitly with comments like "You're not a very musical child" or "It's okay, why don't you try sport instead" or implicitly, by not modeling positive behaviors such as healthy eating and exercise. The evolution of the human race is fueled by the evolution of parenting and education. As we evolve as adults and parents, we need to evolve our parenting and the systems of education.

I'd like to see high schools consistently teaching basic psychology, including self-awareness, resilience, non-judgment, and emotional regulation.

What If We Genuinely Believed Every Challenge (or Failure) We Faced Was a Gift?

My understanding of what it means to be "enlightened" is to realize that reality as we perceive it is a construct in our minds and is not true reality. I believe that it is possible that we are given challenges and failures to experience for a reason—to show us where we need to focus our attention in order to grow. For example, when we experience frustration, it's usually because the world isn't how we want or expect it to be. We become frustrated because people aren't behaving how we want them to or because we don't feel or look the way we want to, or even because we didn't get that promotion we know we deserve. We resist actual reality because it doesn't conform to the reality we constructed in our minds. Put simply, most of our struggles in life occur when our expectations are not met.

Our development is to understand these challenges and learn not to resist and judge reality in a way that creates pain for ourselves. Being enlightened is the appreciation and acceptance of what actual reality presents to us, without resistance to it.

There are times when I directly experience this state of acceptance and appreciation, and then there are times when I resist reality and have a negative response to how others behave.

Writing a book can be a challenging experience for first-time authors. It's uncomfortable, amazing, enjoyable, disheartening, and insightful—and sometimes all those things at once. I realized early on as I struggled through the self-doubt, self-judgment, and fear of failure that writing a book (for me at least) isn't actually about the act of creating a book. It is a deep journey of personal development. I'm not sure any new author could publish a book without having to face at least one personal challenge (e.g., perfectionism, judgment, or a belief that you just aren't good enough or don't know enough) and conquer it. Writing a book has been one of the biggest opportunities for growth that I have been given and I genuinely appreciate it.

Another such "gift" was that of my (extremely messy) divorce, which lasted over three years and involved my 8-year-old son. For a few dark weeks, I lost my way and, to be honest, I almost didn't find my way back. Diagnosed with deep clinical depression, my doctor prescribed antidepressants. I don't know why, but I couldn't take them; it just didn't feel right. I wanted out of the dark days but something inside me would not allow me to take the medication, so I struggled on.

My divorce and my depression led me to the coaching world of NLP—neuro-semantics, integral theory, and the Enneagram—to find a way out of the darkness. Learning how humans construct perspectives on reality, how we create beliefs, and how personalities are constructed changed my life; the coaches changed my life; I changed my life.

This book wouldn't be in your hands today if it weren't for my divorce. Don't get me wrong, it was not a pleasant experience at all. And for years after I hated and resented it. But now, after considerable reflection, I accept and appreciate the gift it gave me.

So if you are struggling right now, I offer you this: in your darkest moments, know that it's going to be okay. Know that the experience will pass and that there is support out there even if you can't see it or believe it.

> *Remember to look up at the stars and not down at your feet. Try to make sense of what you see and wonder about what makes the universe exist. Be curious. And however difficult life may seem, there is always something you can do and succeed at. It matters that you don't just give up.*
>
> —Stephen Hawking[3]

How would your life be different if you knew every challenge, every failure, was a gift?

Think about it for a moment…

If every challenge was a gift, there would no more challenges!

---

[3]Recorded speech given at a symposium at Cambridge University for his 70th birthday in 2012.

It's Not Cheating

You don't get any points in life for doing things the hard way.

—Tim Fargo, entrepreneur, author and investor[1]

It's not cheating to have a set of quick reference materials that you can use—either electronically on your devices or printed versions that can be displayed as big visual charts around your space. For most of us, visuals are a really powerful tool to assist our understanding and recall of information. Having visuals displayed prominently in our environment keeps the content front of mind and helps us break old habits and drive our evolution. I highly recommend you find at least one visual that resonates with you and display it where you will see it regularly throughout your day.

Online Companion Website and Community

A book for digital leaders would not be complete without a companion website. A community of digital leaders would not be possible without an online home. You can find both of these at evolvingdigitalleadership. com. The companion and community site will evolve over time (as all good digital products do). So, be sure you visit and register in order to keep up with developments and to engage with the community.

---

[1] http://alphabetsuccess.blogspot.com/2013/07/you-dont-get-any-points-in-life-doing.html

© James Brett 2019
J. Brett, *Evolving Digital Leadership*, https://doi.org/10.1007/978-1-4842-3606-2_21

The links in the remainder of this chapter point to various parts of the evolvingdigitalleadership.com website. You can use each one to directly access your required content, or you can head to the main home page and navigate through the pages manually.

■ **Note** The links presented here (and in each chapter of the book) have been shortened for your convenience and to allow them to be dynamically redirected should the content or location change post publishing.

The main companion website: https://unnatural.io/link/b201

The online community: https://unnatural.io/link/b202

Visuals

To browse the book's visuals and download high-resolution versions, head over to:

https://unnatural.io/link/b203

Self-Reflection Questions

If you want access to new and updated questions, head over to:

https://unnatural.io/link/b204

Quotes

Did you enjoy the quotes from the book? If you did and would like to browse them online, head over to:

https://unnatural.io/link/b205

Feedback

Finally, I'd love to hear from you. If you have any observations, feedback, questions, insights—whatever—either head over to:

https://unnatural.io/link/b206

Or send an email to feedback@evolvingdigitalleadership.com.

I look forward to interacting with you in the community,

James

I

Index

A, B

Accelerating Pace of Change, 67–69, 278

Agile
lean, 37–38

Anxiety, 12, 49–50, 130, 169, 173, 174, 201, 229, 231, 290

Artificial Intelligence (AI), 4, 13, 27, 67, 70, 71, 73, 90, 193, 204, 277, 297–298, 300, 307, 314–316

Attention, 21–25, 215–268

Awareness, 16–17, 91–160

C

Career path
people leadership, 43–44
thought leadership, 41–43

Career success pyramid
recommendations, 61

Caring for people
We aren't doormats, 205
We can't fake it, 205

Choice, 170–171

Choose, Frame, Perform
Process, 220, 223–227

Clarity process, 18, 20, 81, 167–168, 179, 180, 199, 210, 213
define, 160, 199
own our career and choices
Time Zone Meta-program, 169
set, 168, 169, 210, 211
understand, 168

Coach and Support, 54–55, 183, 190, 191, 244–248

Commoditization of development, 70

Communication channel
auditory, 123–124
auditory digital, 124
kinesthetic, 125
visual, 123

Companion Website, 320

Customer centric, 37, 64, 111

D

Daily performance profile, 21, 220

Deep understanding
development profile, 242–243
effective communication, 241
growth plan, 243–244

Digital Leader
career success pyramid, 12–13
Digital Situational Leadership, 10–12
evolution of leadership, 13–14
unnatural selection, 14–16

Digital Situational Leadership, 10–12, 36, 89, 225

Digital Situational Leadership Model
four modes
friend of the team, 35
futurist, 35
get stuff done, 34–35
utopian, 35–36

Digital society, 13, 69, 70, 204

Disruption and change, 3–4

© James Brett 2019
J. Brett, *Evolving Digital Leadership*, https://doi.org/10.1007/978-1-4842-3606-2

Printed by Printforce, the Netherlands